CONTENTS

To Be a Boy, To Be a Reader

2nd EDITION

Engaging Teen and Preteen Boys in Active Literacy

WILLIAM G. BROZO

INTERNATIONAL
Reading Association
800 BARKSDALE ROAD, PO BOX 8139
NEWARK, DE 19714-8139, USA
www.reading.org

The International Reading Association attempts, through its publications, to provide a
forum for a wide spectrum of opinions on reading. This policy permits divergent viewpoints
without implying the endorsement of the Association.

Executive Editor, Books   Corinne M. Mooney
Developmental Editor   Charlene M. Nichols
Developmental Editor   Tori Mello Bachman
Developmental Editor   Stacey L. Reid
Editorial Production Manager   Shannon T. Fortner
Design and Composition Manager   Anette Schuetz

Project Editors   Tori Mello Bachman and Rebecca A. Stewart

Cover Design   Linda Steere

The publisher would appreciate notification where errors occur so that they may be
corrected in subsequent printings and/or editions.

Library of Congress Cataloging-in-Publication Data
Brozo, William G.
 To be a boy, to be a reader : engaging teen and preteen boys in active literacy / William G.
Brozo. -- 2nd ed.
     p. cm.
 Includes bibliographical references and index.
 ISBN 978-0-87207-508-5
 1. Boys--Education--United States. 2. Reading--United States. 3. Boys--Books and
reading. I. Title.
 LC1396.5.B76 2010
 428.4071'2--dc22

                                                                    2010005719

I dedicate this book to the first man I saw reading—my father.

William G. Brozo is a Professor of Literacy in the Graduate School of Education at George Mason University in Fairfax, Virginia. He earned his bachelor's degree from the University of North Carolina in Chapel Hill and his master's and doctorate from the University of South Carolina in Columbia. He has taught reading and language arts in the Carolinas. He is the author of numerous books and articles on literacy development for children and young adults. He is also a contributing author to Prentice-Hall Literature, a program for adolescent readers. He serves on the editorial review board of the *Journal of Adolescent & Adult Literacy.* He was the "Strategic Moves" columnist for the journal *Thinking Classroom* and currently coauthors the "Content Literacy" column for *The Reading Teacher.* He is also a past member of the International Reading Association's (IRA) Commission on Adolescent Literacy, the Adolescent Literacy Committee, and the PISA/PIRLS Task Force. He was a coinvestigator on a Carnegie Grant team that compiled an important report on best practice in adolescent literacy.

As an IRA-USAID consultant, he has traveled frequently to the Balkan countries, where he provided technical support to secondary teachers. He regularly speaks at professional meetings around the United States and consults with states and districts on ways of building capacity among teacher leaders, enriching the literate culture of schools, enhancing the literate lives of boys, and making teaching more responsive to the needs of all students.

Bill can be reached by e-mail at wbrozo@gmu.edu.

FOREWORD

Much has changed in the discussion of gender and education in the last 30 years.

For most of that time, our concerns revolved around girls; as a society we rightly saw the need to provide them with equal access to education. In our schools, in our families, in communities, and at state and national levels, we applied concerted pressure to help girls do better. We gave girls better role models and heralded the benefits of higher education and the financial independence it brings. We surrounded our girls with support and mentoring. In an effort to improve their outcomes in math and science, we rewrote curriculum to become more girl-friendly and demystified the sometimes laborious process of gaining mastery in those subjects. Using the force of public opinion and the might of the courts, we waged a battle of hearts and minds over the individuals and institutions that would limit the dreams of our young females.

The result was nothing short of revolutionary. Girls now make up nearly 60% of the undergraduates in the United States. And in the wake of their successes, another conversation about gender and education has begun. And this one focuses squarely on boys. From preschool to college, there are signs that boys are not thriving. They are expelled from preschool at five times the rates of girls, left back in kindergarten and first grade at twice the rates of girls, and they do less homework and get more C's and D's. With the exception of sports, they have withdrawn from extracurricular activities; they take fewer college preparatory classes, and they are more likely to drop out of high school and less likely to attend college. The implications of boys' failure to keep up with the progress of girls will have far-reaching implications in their lives and the lives of their children.

In order to write *The Trouble With Boys: A Surprising Report Card on Our Sons, Their Problems at School and What Parents & Educators Must Do* (Crown, 2008), I spent years researching the genesis of the boy problem. My conclusion: Many of the struggles boys face in school originate from their failure to become fluent readers. Boys come into school speaking fewer words and having fewer preliteracy experiences (they are read to less often and attend story hours less frequently). From the very earliest assessments, their average scores are lower than the average scores for girls in reading. They are less flexible in how they are taught to read: They tend to struggle more when they are not given a solid phonics-based instructional program. When children are required to make the all-important transition from learning to read to reading to learn, it is boys overwhelmingly who experience the dreaded "fourth-grade slump." By high school, our national reading scores tell the story: The average sophomore girl reads about as well as the average senior boy.

Who is to blame? It is easy to blame the boys themselves. And plenty of teachers do. They are harder to instruct, teachers say. They are resistant—often refusing to engage with the classroom material. Teachers describe a world in which their adolescent boys dwell—one that is untouched by words, and poorer for it. The research is clear that failing to become a fluent reader leads to school failure. The more one reads, the better one reads. And tragically, the inverse is also true. Unenthusiastic readers become poor readers. Boys are being left behind.

Boys, however, tell a different story. They will tell you that they like to read—just not the books that English teachers are assigning them. They reject "relational" type books that describe, in microscopic precision, the nuances of a friendship. They reject tales of brave young girls who endure misfortunes inflicted by evil-doers and, by sheer cleverness or connection to others, triumph. They don't like to read about suffering. They like to read nonfiction and biographies (particularly of heroic men or sports figures). They like books that have pictures, books that are funny, with plots and characters that are irreverent. They like to read books that involve action, swashbuckling, arrows flying, and yes, some decapitation. Blood is good. They just don't get the opportunity to bring that energy and excitement for reading into the classroom.

Teachers often respond to the enthusiasm of boys for this kind of reading with bewilderment and not a little frustration. Why can't boys transfer some of that appreciation to the books on the reading list? Perhaps these teachers should start with a popular book on middle school reading lists (and one of the books most universally loathed by boys), *The House on Mango Street* by Sandra Cisneros.

The chasm between what teachers think boys should be reading and what boys want to read seems very wide. And our boys are losers for it. Into this breach steps Bill Brozo with his book *To Be a Boy, To Be a Reader*. His approach is fresh but his basic notion about education is evergreen: Begin to teach literature by teaching children where they are—and that includes the place where boys are. And then think about where we want them to be. But Brozo's book offers more: His Jungian framework and his discussion of archetypes like Warriors, Pilgrims, and Kings will give some teachers a tentative framework through which they can expand boys' view of literature.

If his book is used in the best possible way, it will allow teachers to perform a great academic good—helping boys become immersed in the life of the word. It may also help teachers perform an even greater social good—using literature to expand the ever-shrinking box of masculinity that constrains too many of our boys.

At best, reading can provide us with a road map to our sometimes shadowy inner lives. It ratifies our experiences. It makes us see how our variable actions and emotions, taken as a whole, form intention, wit, and character. It can encourage us to push against the psychological and human bonds that limit us. It can also lift us out of our own experiences and provide us with a way to connect with other people with whom we might seem, at first pass, to share little.

Brozo gives us the practical strategies to unleash the formidable power of reading for our boys—and they need it. Now, more than ever.

—Peg Tyre, author of
The Trouble With Boys: A Surprising
Report Card on Our Sons, Their Problems at School,
and *What Parents & Educators Must Do*

ACKNOWLEDGMENTS

I am once again extremely grateful to all the teachers and students who welcomed me into their classrooms and the parents and sons who invited me into their lives as I researched this new edition. I am equally grateful to the young men who gave their voices to the Boy Talk sections in each chapter and to all the others who left their marks in the real-life stories of boys interacting with books. Each of these people breathed life into this project and made it entirely worthwhile.

I want to extend a special thanks to the International Reading Association, particularly Corinne Mooney for her continued commitment to this project and Tori Bachman for her indispensable feedback and revision guidance.

Ultimately, I owe the most gratitude to my mother, Genevieve, who taught me the importance of being a reader, and my daughter, Hannah, whose playful spirit allows me to be a boy.

INTRODUCTION

I t has now been over 30 years since the start of my career as an educator. I began my first job teaching English at an all-black high school in rural South Carolina, USA. In that single-level school building with the leaky roof, undersized gymnasium, and no air conditioning system, I came face to face with adolescent boys who, in the words of Sven Birkerts (1994), "had never bathed in the energies of a book" (p. 84). These were boys who could not read at a level necessary to understand and enjoy the stories and plays from the required literature anthology. William, a 6'7" 17-year-old star basketball player, was in one of my 11th-grade sections. As I handed out textbooks on the first day of class, he leaned close to my ear and whispered, "I don't know how to read." I quickly came to the realization that to engage William and his classmates as readers, I would need to use every bit of my creative energy. Although it ran counter to my sensibilities as an English teacher, I made a fateful decision in those first weeks to dispense with my beloved *Silas Marner* and *Julius Caesar,* and all the other vaunted poets, playwrights, and novelists of the past and experiment with young adult literature.

I was looking for something that the students would find more accessible and meaningful. I found it in Alice Childress's (1973) *A Hero Ain't Nothin' But a Sandwich.* This story of an adolescent boy's maturation and alienation while growing up in Harlem transformed my class. Attendance and behavior problems decreased noticeably. Students were eager to read, or at least try to read. When we finished the book, they clamored for more of the same. Even William made modest progress that first year, although he dropped out the next. I would often spot his looming frame hanging out on the only street of commerce in our small, poor town. Unfortunately, he was eventually arrested and found guilty of dealing narcotics. It was the last I ever heard of him.

Of course my own literate history is very different from that of African American teens growing up in hot, dusty tobacco country, whose ancestors were slaves and sharecroppers. Nonetheless, when it comes to literacy, we all have something in common—where we begin our literate journeys may have little resemblance to where the journey takes us and, certainly, where the journey ends.

Since those days as an inchoate literacy teacher, I have spent untold hours in general and remedial classrooms in numerous secondary schools around the United States and across the globe, observing and learning from other teachers, conducting demonstration lessons, and gathering research data. The overwhelming impression I have been left with is that more must be done to reach the growing numbers of listless, detached, and struggling male readers. I have also found a clear and recurring pattern of concern among teachers: Too many preteen and teen boys do not like to read, are choosing not to read, and are suffering academically as a result.

I wrote this book based on an ongoing desire to share my experiences and ideas with the many teachers, parents, and others who are equally concerned about adolescent boys' literate futures. The guiding premise for this second edition remains the same as for the first one: Engaging adolescent boys in literacy should be the highest priority when developing reading curricula and seeking to foster independent reading habits. To achieve engaged reading, I propose the use of a great variety of texts along with a range of practices that are likely to improve boys' thinking about what they read and increase their motivation to read.

The Unique Nature of *To Be a Boy, To Be a Reader: Engaging Teen and Preteen Boys in Active Literacy*

In the years since publication of the first edition of *To Be a Boy, To Be a Reader* we have seen several new books about boys and their emotional, psychological, and academic development, such as Fashola's (2005) *Educating African American Males: Voices From the Field*; Sax's (2007) *Boys Adrift: The Five Factors Driving the Growing Epidemic of Unmotivated Boys and Underachieving Young Men*; Tyre's (2008) *The Trouble With Boys*; Weaver-Hightower's (2008) *The Politics of Policy in Boys' Education: Getting Boys "Right"*; Noguera's (2008) *The Trouble With Black Boys: And Other Reflections on Race, Equity, and the Future of Public Education*; McClure's (2008) *Making It Better for Boys in Schools, Families, and Communities*; and Keddie and Mills's (2008) *Teaching Boys: Developing Classroom Practices That Work*. These books remind us that concern for boys' educational and personal growth is as strong as ever.

Books that deal with both gender issues and literacy for boys, though still small in number, also have increased. Titles such as Newkirk's (2002) *Misreading Masculinity: Boys, Literacy, and Popular Culture*; Booth's (2002) *Even Hockey Players Read: Boys, Literacy, and Learning*; Sullivan's (2009) *Connecting Boys With Books 2: Closing the Reading Gap*; and Zambo and Brozo's (2009) *Bright Beginnings for Boys: Engaging Young Boys in Active Literacy* have made significant contributions to the practical literature. More rare, however, are books focused exclusively on the literacy needs of adolescent males. With the exception of Smith and Wilhelm's (2002) *"Reading Don't Fix No Chevys: Literacy in the Lives of Young Men"* and

Tatum's (2005) *Teaching Reading to Black Adolescent Males,* this book, *To Be a Boy, To Be a Reader,* is one of a very small group devoted to explaining gender-based research on learning and promoting promising practices of literacy for teen and preteen males. Indeed, this is the only book of its kind that provides teachers with practical strategies for using literature with positive male archetypes as well as a variety of other engaging texts and media to motivate adolescent boys to read, improve their reading abilities, and capture their unique male imaginations.

Why a Book Just About the Literacy Needs of Adolescent Boys?

Adolescent boys need special attention with respect to their literacy development and attitudes. Evidence from the United States, Australia, Canada, and the United Kingdom as well as over 40 other countries around the globe (Mullis, Martin, Gonzalez, & Kennedy, 2003, National Center for Educational Statistics, 2008; Organisation for Economic Co-operation and Development, 2001; Perie, Grigg, & Donahue, 2005), shows that boys have the lowest scores on standardized measures of reading and verbal ability. Boys dominate the rolls of remedial reading classes and those who have difficulty learning to read (Connell & Gunzelmann, 2004; Hunsader, 2002; Lietz, 2006). They also make up the largest group of dropouts and delinquents (Slade & Trent, 2000). These, however, are only school-related phenomena. When one considers that males (a) commit all but a small percentage of homicides, (b) are far more likely to be victims of violent crime than women, (c) take their own lives at alarming rates, and (d) make up most drug addicts and people who are homeless (Ferrell, 2001; Hallfors et al., 2002; Noguera, 2008; Office of Juvenile Justice and Delinquency Prevention, 2006), addressing adolescent boys' needs becomes all the more urgent.

It is well known that boys who drop out of school are likely to have weak or poorly developed literacy skills (Sokal et al., 2005b; Whitmire, 2006). These dropouts become vulnerable to a life of underemployment and unemployment and, far worse, are at a higher risk of becoming criminal offenders (Fashola, 2005). It is also known, however, that engaged readers have a much greater chance of staying in school, expanding career and life options, and maturing into self-actualized adults (Hofstetter, Sticht, & Hofstetter, 1999).

This book, then, is devoted to describing how teachers have used engaging texts and practices to help teen and preteen boys find entry points into literacy and stay the course as readers. Once entry points are found, boys may develop a sense of self through active literacy and increase their chances for an expansive intellectual journey throughout adolescence and beyond. This is critical because it has been shown that possession of highly developed literacy abilities can ultimately lead to better lives for themselves and those around them (Herbert, 2007; Hofstetter et al., 1999).

I have found that boys become more engaged readers and learners when motivated by exposure to texts that capture their imaginations. These engaging texts include books and novels as well as graphic novels, comic books, manuals, guides, and new youth media. This second edition provides numerous examples and descriptions of how these texts can be used to build capacity and enjoyment in reading for male youth. One important source given special attention in this book is text that speaks to traditional male archetypes. As in the first edition, this second edition presents multiple ways in which teachers, parents, and caregivers can use texts with positive male archetypes to entice adolescent boys to read, keep them reading, and improve their thinking about what they read.

Organization and Content

Each chapter begins with an excerpt that relates to boys' reading and ends with a "Boy Talk" section. The goal of this element is to give voice to real-life boys' thoughts about books they have read. Boy Talk demonstrates the depth of understanding and levels of personal engagement that are possible when young men are given and have the choice to select quality texts to read.

Chapter 1 introduces the primary issues of the book and raises concerns about adolescent boys' literacy behavior. I present evidence that supports the need to help boys discover or become reacquainted with the pleasure and value of reading. I also discuss the connection between reading ability and academic success, and explore reasons why reading sometimes disaffects male youths. I assert that reading engagement should be the highest priority to teachers of disinterested and struggling readers, because only as boys encounter texts that speak to their unique male imaginations are they likely to become regular and lifelong readers. I propose that creating opportunities for adolescent boys to read books with positive male archetypes is a promising way to capture boys' imaginations and help them practice active literacy.

Chapter 2 focuses on positive male archetypes. I define the archetypes and describe characteristics and examples of each. Based on Jungian theory, as well as the work of contemporary psychologists and sociologists, I explore in depth the origins and modern applications of 10 of these archetypes: Pilgrim, Patriarch, King, Warrior, Magician, Wildman, Healer, Prophet, Trickster, and Lover. Each description is accompanied by examples of characters from young adult literature that embody the archetype. Teachers can take advantage of these positive male archetypes to further adolescent boys' literary pilgrimage.

Chapter 3 depicts numerous scenes of English, reading, science, and history teachers using innovative strategies and activities that involve young adult books rife with positive male archetypes. These teaching vignettes are organized around the 10 archetypes.

Chapter 4 presents additional ideas and practices that teachers can use to engage boys and keep them reading. The approaches cut across particular archetypes and demonstrate how teachers can find appropriate texts for adolescent boys and structure their classrooms to make these texts accessible to young men.

Chapter 5 draws entirely on my personal experience working with two seventh-grade teachers on a unit devoted to exploring masculinity with a young adult novel. The teachers and I developed, implemented, and taught the unit with a junior high school language arts class of 14 boys and 2 girls. The school is situated in an economically depressed community of primarily Hispanic Americans and African Americans. Painting scenes of classroom life, I describe how the teachers and I designed the unit, selected an appropriate young adult novel, implemented instructional strategies, and documented students' responses.

Chapter 6 is a new chapter that focuses on alternative texts and the innovative ways these texts can be offered to boys. Expanding the definition of what counts as reading, I describe a variety of texts that are not necessarily archetypal in nature, but have been shown to interest adolescent boys. These include graphic novels, comic books, information books, hobby manuals, survival guides, and electronic media. Examples are provided of how teachers can employ these texts in ways that motivate male youth to make in- and out-of-school connections, bridge familiar texts to academic texts, and sustain their efforts in reading and writing. Also in this chapter is a section devoted to guiding teachers through the process of establishing and conducting boys' books clubs.

Chapter 7 describes how teachers can work with and learn from adults in the community to create conditions that give adolescent boys a chance to be readers. Every concerned adult can inspire teen and preteen boys to read, and almost anyone at home and in boys' communities can help boys continue to grow as readers and as learners. I present several vignettes, including one new interesting scenario, of parents, relatives, friends, neighbors, and others who have had profound influences on boys' attitudes about and behaviors toward literacy.

The last chapter reviews the book's critical themes and briefly reflects on new pertinent evidence that supports these themes. I call on teachers to use this book as a resource to help boys find entry points into active literacy.

The Appendix follows Chapter 8 and presents scores of titles of current young adult literature. This literature is organized around the 10 positive male archetypes and further classified into the following categories to aid in the selection of books for teen and preteen boys: Adolescent Novels, Informational Books, Easier Reading, and a new section of Graphic Novels.

Common Questions About Working With Books With Positive Male Archetypes

What follows are answers to some typical questions I often receive from teachers who are intrigued by the approach I advocate and interested in implementing it in their classrooms.

Is There Some Way to Diagnose a Boy's Archetypal Preference, So I Can Introduce Him to the Right Book?

This is probably unnecessary. My intention is not to create a prescriptive approach to active reading but to propose that literature with positive male archetypes can make adolescent boys more engaged readers. It is only through this engagement that boys can ever be expected to become competent critical readers and thinkers. The added benefit of working with the books I recommend is that they offer a variety of masculine images.

Nevertheless, I do know a middle school teacher who has created her own inventory that consists of statements meant to represent particular archetypes. She gives it to the boys in her class and asks them to indicate which statement most closely matches behaviors and characteristics that they aspire to. With this information, she claims to be able to find reading material that matches students' preferences more efficiently than she might otherwise be able to do.

Should Adolescent Boys Be Exposed to All Archetypes?

Boys often show a strong preference for certain archetypes, such as Warrior or Pilgrim. This does not mean, however, that they should not be exposed to books with characters that possess different archetypal qualities. Remember, the primary goal in using any of the books I recommend is to capture a young man's imagination and keep him reading. One significant benefit of *just* making these books accessible to young men is that these boys may come to appreciate the many expressions of masculine identity.

What About Boys Who Aren't Into Traditional "Masculine" Books?

This question always fascinates me because it presumes that books for boys must automatically deal with ultramasculine themes and plots, such as the suave male who can easily attract many girls but discards them just as quickly, the gun-toting maverick lawman who defeats criminals coldly, or the chiseled, muscular athlete who never loses. Nothing could be further from the truth. Many of the books I recommend attest to the unique and nonstereotypical dimensions of masculinity. For example, books that have characters that embody the Lover or Prophet archetypes often present a unique and surprising face of both boyhood and manhood, because positive expressions of masculinity can come in a variety of forms and from male characters that are decidedly not "masculine." Popular media has contributed to the stereotypical construction of males as one-dimensional, incapable of self-reflection, and physically or psychologically oppressive. Exposing adolescent boys to quality literature filled with a variety of positive male archetypes can only help to provide them with realistic, in-depth images of what it means to be a man.

Should These Books Be Used Therapeutically?

Those of us who are readers have no doubt heard other readers say, or perhaps have said ourselves, that "reading is my therapy." The use of the word *therapy* in this case is really a euphemism for an escape from the day-to-day toils that everyone experiences. In a more technical sense, therapy implies a condition or state of being that needs remedy. Boys do not need to be diagnosed with a dominant archetype, then provided with particular books as treatment.

Good books for boys should ideally capture boys' imaginations and get them hooked on reading while reaffirming their inherent goodness as males. If people expect much more from this literature, they may be disappointed; however, teachers and parents have shared stories with me about how their students or sons were rescued by certain books. Some of the scenarios described in Chapter 7 leave open the possibility of using literature with positive male archetypes, if not therapeutically, at least as an important source for personal and interpersonal transformation.

Don't Most Boys Behave in Ways That Reflect a Combination of Archetypes?

The answer to this question is an unequivocal "Yes!" Exposure to multiple archetypes is worthwhile because it increases the chances that a young man will find something that engages him and leaves him wanting more. I present the positive male archetypes in this book in their most basic forms. Few men or boys match only one model perfectly. For example, although a young man may exhibit dominant characteristics of the Patriarch, he may also demonstrate attitudes of the Trickster, as well as other archetypes. Although positive male archetypes have been investigated scientifically and described in ways that suggest exclusivity, it would be a mistake to expect behavior from boys that is consistent with only one archetype. Exposure to a variety of archetypes helps boys affirm their true and multidimensional masculine selves.

Do Male Characters in Young Adult Books Always Embody a Single Archetype, or Do They Behave in Ways That Are Consistent With Different Positive Male Archetypes?

Just as most boys exhibit qualities of more than one archetype, so do characters from books. Although similar to our male students or sons, they may be more representative of one archetype than another.

I Teach Both Adolescent Boys and Girls, so How Can I Use This Approach That Is Just for Boys?

Like most essential questions, this defies a pithy response. In answering it, I like to begin this way: As a literacy educator, former junior and senior high school teacher, spouse of an experienced teacher, and a school-based researcher, I believe I speak from experience when I assert that most teachers are desperately seeking strategies and materials to reach their male students. This desire alone can serve as the impetus for exploring the potential benefits of using books with positive male archetypes. My experiences have further shown that with some originality and risk taking, teachers of male and female adolescents can create learning environments that have include special support for boys' literacy efforts without excluding girls.

In Chapters 3, 4, 5, and 6, I share numerous examples of middle and secondary school teachers in mixed-gender classrooms who use creative approaches to make books for boys accessible and employ teaching strategies to make these books engaging. These strategies, as will be demonstrated, may also benefit girls. Young women are just as steeped in mass media's constructions of masculinity as boys are. Books that depict males as multidimensional individuals who break masculine stereotypes do as much to erode girls' rigid conceptions of boys as they do for boys. This situation is not substantially different from one in which a teacher uses literature with diverse ethnic and cultural themes to promote pluralism and demonstrate sensitivity to students of diverse ethnic and cultural backgrounds.

If Most of the Boys in My Classes Are Already Exhibiting Stereotypical Masculinity, Why Should I Give Them Just Masculine-Type Books to Read?

The answer depends on whether these adolescent boys are already regular and engaged readers. If not, and that is what I suspect, the assumptions inherent in this question oversimplify the issue. Books with positive male archetypes may be just what these boys need to help them see that being a reader is not incompatible with their rigid self-ascriptions of masculinity. Bo Brewster, Chris Crutcher's (1995) *Ironman*, shows that he is capable of restraining his anger and outbursts, training for a triathlon, and falling in love. Boys have found that this book and others by Crutcher give them familiar glimpses of male characters while forcing them to think more expansively about what it means to be masculine. Adolescent boys who swagger with stereotypical bravado have much to gain by exposure to books like *Ironman*, which depicts the Warrior archetype.

Are Male Archetypes the Only Criteria for Appropriate Book Selection for Adolescent Boys?

To this question, I must give a resounding "No." The top priority for all teachers and adults is to help boys find entry points into literacy; they should support any way that this can be accomplished. My ideas about archetypes are rooted in my concern that we not only engage boys as readers but also engage them with books that are identity affirming.

Shouldn't Boys Read Material With Both Good and Bad Male Archetypes, Because There Are Plenty of Men Who Are Bad in Real Life, Too?

Because there are so many real-life men who behave deplorably, I stress the need for boys to be exposed to as many positive models of masculinity as possible. Keep in mind that the male archetypes described in this book are not gods. They are endowed with the same human frailties that everyone possesses. When adolescent boys read the books that I have suggested, they are reading about males who do not always make the right decisions and are not blameless; therefore, these archetypes are a good deal like the boys themselves. What separates positive male archetypes from others is that they ultimately prevail in doing what is right for the people around them. Books with positive male archetypes, then, serve as a counterbalance for both boys and girls who are daily exposed to real, deplorable male behavior and injurious popular myths regarding masculinity.

What if I Believe a Book You Have Placed in a Particular Archetype Category in the Appendix Would Be Better Suited to Help Teach a Different Archetype?

There is nothing scientific about the way I have categorized the young adult books in the Appendix. As previously stated, most characters and individuals exhibit traits associated with more than one archetype. A book's placement in the Appendix is based on my best judgment about the dominant archetypal qualities of the fictional or real-life characters in the book. Other people, however, may disagree with these categorizations. By its very nature, creative writing engenders different interpretations. Whether or not there is complete agreement about these categorizations is far less important than whether quality young adult literature finds its way into the hands of teen and preteen boys. So if the books I categorize for one particular archetype are used to teach a different archetype, I support that practice without reservation.

Those of us who are active readers already know that the thrill of entering a book's unique world is the only reward we need to engage us in reading, although our love of books reaps other rewards as well. Active and engaged reading directly contributes to our sophisticated literacy and thinking, which has also made our professional accomplishments possible. The purpose of this book is to help boys obtain the same benefits and pleasures we enjoy. Young men cannot bypass the path we have all traveled to become who we are as literate adults. *We*, however, can make the beginning of this journey possible by providing boys with appropriate and enjoyable texts and activities.

In the following chapters, the practical ideas and strategies embedded in scenes of school- and home-based life show how engaging texts have been used to help make reading an integral part of boys' lives.

Boys and Reading: The Challenges and Possibilities

And then the whining schoolboy
With his satchel and shiny morning face
Creeping like a snail
Unwillingly to school.

—William Shakespeare, *As You Like It*

For as long as there have been schools, there have been boys who would rather be elsewhere. It is the rare young man who faithfully attends school without grousing and with high purpose. This idea calls to mind Burris Ewell's ineloquent though pithy pronouncement in Harper Lee's (1960) *To Kill a Mockingbird* as he walks out of the Maycomb schoolhouse on the very first day, saying flatly, "I done done my time for this year" (p. 27).

Teen and preteen boys who are only "doing time," who are mentally absent from school and who are academically detached, place themselves and all of society at risk. There is ample evidence to suggest that early and cumulative reading and learning failure are often precursors to unemployment (Bureau of Labor Statistics, 1999; Day & Newburger, 2002; Sum, Khatiwada, McLaughlin, & Tobar, 2007), crime (Davis, Byrd, Arnold, Auinger, & Bocchini, 1999; Vacca, 2008), drug addiction (Ellickson, Martino, & Collins, 2004; Register, Williams, & Grimes, 2001), homelessness (Cauthen & Fass, 2008), and prison (Public Safety Performance, 2007; White, 2002).

As adults, parents vest their futures in all children, not just their sons. And most certainly all children need adults to imbue them with hope and imagination of possibilities. This book, however, focuses on stressing the importance of engaging and keeping adolescent boys as readers to help ensure that they have successful academic futures and, consequently, richer and more meaningful lives. Mounting evidence suggests that the time has come to begin paying special attention to the literacy needs of adolescent boys. Consider these sobering facts:

- Boys are three to five times more likely than girls to have learning or reading disabilities placement in schools (Flynn & Rahbar, 1994; National Center for Education Statistics, 2000).

- Boys in elementary school through high school score significantly lower than girls on standardized measures of reading achievement (National Center for Education Statistics, 2007).

- Boys are 50% more likely to be retained a grade than girls (Kleinfeld, 1999; Neckerman, 2004).

- Fewer boys than girls study advanced algebra, geometry, or chemistry (Freeman, 2004; National Center for Education Statistics, 2008).

- Boys are less likely than girls to take advanced placement examinations and go to college (Francis, 2007; Freeman, 2004; Mortenson, 2008).

- The number of males earning academic degrees in traditional male professions, such as medicine and law, is decreasing, and the number of these degrees earned by females is rapidly increasing. In 1970, men earned over 90% of medical and law degrees; today, those percentages have declined to between 50–60% (Peter & Horn, 2005; Sommers, 2000).

- Of the estimated three to seven thousand students who drop out of U.S. high schools each day (Alliance for Excellent Education, 2007; Annie E. Casey Foundation, 2008), the majority are boys (Greene & Winters, 2006).

- Five out of six children and adolescents diagnosed with attention deficit disorder (ADD) and attention-deficit hyperactivity disorder (ADHD) are boys (Centers for Disease Control and Prevention, 2005).

Skillful and critical reading ability is an important tool that boys must have to become academically successful. This tool or its lack can contribute to either a virtuous cycle of successful living or a grinding cycle of difficulty and failure (Franzak, 2006; Herbert, 2007). Reading ability is highly related to overall academic success (Grigg, Daane, Ying, & Campbell, 2003; Grigg, Donahue, & Dion, 2007; Kirst, 2003). In other words, good readers are better students in every subject area. It is also known that high academic achievement increases career and life options for young adults. Superior students perform better on entrance examinations, making it easier for them to access postsecondary educational opportunities and, ultimately, find better jobs. For instance, research done by Hofstetter and colleagues (1999) found that, regardless of their cultural background, people who achieve and exercise power over their lives spend more time reading than those who have less power or feel powerless. Reading, the authors assert, leads to knowledge, which is associated with power regardless of other barriers that citizens face. People who practice active literacy acquire knowledge more readily than others, and knowledge is the great equalizer in terms of access to personal and professional power.

All too common in the United States (The Education Alliance, 2007; Tyre, 2008)—as well as in Canada (Canadian Council on Learning, 2009; Gambell & Hunter, 1999), England (Murphy & Elwood, 1998; Younger & Warrington, 2005), and Australia (Alloway, Freebody, Gilbert, & Muspratt, 2002; Collins, Kenway, & McLeod, 2000)—are teen and preteen boys who find themselves caught in cycles of reading failure. One possible explanation as to why boys are not the readers they can and should be is that reading often conflicts with boys' sense of masculinity (Strauss, 2005). Findings from recent research reports (Gunzelmann & Connell, 2006; Mead, 2006) strongly suggest that the steady decline in reading achievement experienced by boys between the ages of 7 and 16 is largely a consequence of peer pressures (McCarthey & Moje, 2002). Adolescent boys undergo tremendous pressure not to appear nerdy or brainy, so many of them turn against reading and learning because, in the words of Browne and Fletcher (1995), it's more "cool to be a fool" (p. 74).

When boys turn away from reading, they unfortunately miss out on unforgettable, identity-affirming experiences with books and other texts. People who have had these experiences as young men share similar stories. For instance, I had this experience when I discovered a new novel at age 10 in the Montieth Branch Library in Detroit, Michigan, USA, on a rainy summer morning. Stephen Meader's (1963) *The Muddy Road to Glory* held me spellbound for days. The character of Ben Everett, a young Civil War enlistee in the Union army, embodied everything that I wanted to be. I was already a Stephen Meader junkie, snatching up any of his books I could get my hands on, and thankfully Mrs. Oshob, the librarian, did her best to keep me supplied. Meader's writing was transcendent, taking me on one gripping adventure after another. How can I ever forget sitting atop my upper bunk in the attic of my family's small, clapboard house—one house within hundreds of blocks of blue-collar neighborhoods in a working class city—reading *Lumberjack* (Meader, 1934), *Whaler 'Round the Horn* (Meader, 1950), or *Boy With a Pack* (Meader, 1939)? Reading these books, I felt as if I were lost in the Appalachian wilderness, sore yet strengthening day by day as I worked one end of a saw felling giant virgin red pines, or that I was the one wiping salty sea foam from my eyes as I stood at the helm of a 19th-century schooner.

Sven Birkerts, author of the recent *Reading Life: Books for the Ages* (2007) and a muse to any of us who have made literacy an integral part of our lives, comments in *The Gutenberg Elegies* (1994) of his early experiences with books:

> [R]eading was once, in childhood, a momentous discovery. The first arrival was so stunning, so pleasant, that I wanted nothing more than a guarantee of return.... Here was the finding of a lens that would give me a different orientation to what was already, though only nascently, the project of my life. Through reading I could reposition the contents of that life along the coordinate axes of urgency and purpose. These two qualities not only determined, or informed, the actions of whatever characters I was reading about, but they exerted pressure on my own life so long as I was bathed in the energies of the book. (p. 84)

Today's adolescent boys have an equal chance of discovering or rediscovering the magic of books and the joy of flights of imagination inspired by the written word (Horton, 2005). Appealing to boys' creative imaginations by using texts that speak to their unique male interests could help them become engaged and regular readers (Brozo & Schmelzer, 1997). Helping adolescent boys find entry points into active literacy must be the highest priority for teachers, because it is from young men's early interests in books and other texts that a lifestyle of habitual reading can be nurtured (Young & Brozo, 2001).

Texts With Positive Male Archetypes: Entry Points Into Active Literacy

Teachers always are seeking new ways to reach adolescent students through innovative teaching strategies, by genuine displays of concern about students' day-to-day learning needs, and from inquiries about students' future academic and personal desires. What better way to demonstrate this concern for boys than by introducing them to the right texts—texts that they feel comfortable reading on their own, that sustain their attention, and that reaffirm their burgeoning sense of male identity while offering many visions of masculinity? Young adult literature with real-life and fictional characters who represent positive male archetypes can help teen and preteen boys identify with their own masculine identities, as well as other masculine identities.

An archetype is an inherited idea or mode of thought that is derived from the experience of the race and present in the unconscious of the individual (Jung, 1955). Fairy tales contain some of the most common male archetypes of Western civilization. The hero, for instance, shows up everywhere to thwart some untoward force or rescue someone who is weak (for example, a damsel, an ailing king, and so on). Carl Jung, a Swiss psychologist, was one of the first to scientifically investigate the uniqueness of the male psyche. Jung (1968) proposed and contemporary psychologists and sociologists have confirmed that within the psyche or collective unconscious of all men, there are archetypal or generalizable models of maleness (Arnold, 1995; Gilmore, 1990; Johnson, 1989; Moore & Gillette, 1992). What is most fascinating about Jung's theory is that the range of positive male archetypes that exist within our culture strongly supports the idea that boys exhibit *multiple* expressions of masculine identity (Katz & Sokal, 2003; Kehler, Davison, & Frank, 2005; Sokal et al., 2005a), which means that virtually all young men should find something familiar and reaffirming in books with positive male archetypes.

This book explores the origins and modern applications of 10 positive male archetypes derived from the work of Jung (1955) and others (see Arnold, 1995), describing each archetype and illustrating each with characters from young adult literature used by middle school and secondary school teachers to engage their male students. These archetypes are also the framework used in the Appendix for identifying and selecting appropriate books for teen and preteen boys. My intent in discussing positive male archetypes in association with young adult books is not to propose a new canon to be adhered to rigidly. As I have stated, my primary concern is to help boys find entry points into active literacy. My purpose in using the 10 positive male archetypes is to demonstrate one way (and there are potentially many other ways) in which good books for adolescent boys may be classified and how these books can be put to good use.

Developing a Love of Reading in Boys

It is one thing to say teen and preteen boys need to experience texts that are identity affirming, but it is quite another to motivate them to read such texts with enthusiasm. Teachers cannot transform boys who are unengaged readers or learners or who have poor reading skills into highly skillful and enthusiastic readers simply by handing them a young adult novel or other text with content and themes they should be expected to enjoy. This effect can happen for some, however. For example, many boys who did little or no free reading were instantly transformed by their infatuation with first the faddish Goosebumps and then the Harry Potter series. Although interest in them will inevitably wane, these books have reacquainted many nonreading boys with the joys of literacy and may compel boys to begin a lifelong search for exciting and personally meaningful texts (Weeks, 2001). In other words, Goosebumps and Harry Potter books have served as entry points into literacy for many adolescent boys. Everyone has their own entry points into literacy. What adults read may have little similarity to the texts that initially engaged them as children. However, adults' skillful reading abilities and their wide tastes and interests, which they often take for granted, are traced to their initial experiences with engaged reading—or their entry points into literacy.

My experience tells me that adolescent boys who view reading as unacceptable male behavior have not fallen under the spell of a well-told story or have not found male characters in fiction, biography, or history who speak to their unique and evolving needs. Robert Chaseling, a junior high student, offers the following advice for helping boys to see reading as cool:

> If you want your son to read
> Get him the sort of book
> Some parents don't seem to see.
> It's all about image and being cool
> And a lot depends on what you read at school.
> *Bugulugs Bum Thief*
> *Goosebumps*
> *Point Crime*
> *Paul Jennings*
> The list goes on...
> So take my advice
> And you'll feel quite proud
> Please don't make them read aloud.
> If you do
> They'll quit reading like a flash
> And your reading scheme
> Will fall down with a crash.
> So if you take my tips
> And do everything right
> Your son could be reading
> By tonight! (Sanderson, 1995, p. 153)

Robert's lighthearted, although incisive, poem makes two critical points. First, when it comes to motivating adolescent boys to read, story content and genre are extremely important elements. Second, the very ways in which teachers offer literacy to students either draws them into reading or instills indifference.

Many teachers and administrators I know who work with adolescents say that students' lack of motivation for learning is at the heart of many school-related problems. Regardless of the reasons, unmotivated students often find themselves in a downward spiral of declining academic achievement, diminishing self-esteem, further disinterest outside of school, and so on. Teachers know that creating positive academic experiences is critical to improving self-esteem, eliminating behavioral problems, and increasing learning involvement (Baumeister, Campbell, Krueger, & Vohs, 2003; Filozof et al., 1998; Hamre & Pianta, 2006). They also know that motivated students are more likely to learn at a deep, meaningful level and internalize their new learning whereas unmotivated students' learning is superficial, shallow, and easily forgotten (Guthrie, 2008). There is nearly universal consensus that one of the best ways to motivate student reading is through the use of interesting books (Brozo, 2007; Brozo & Gaskins, 2009; Guthrie, Alao, & Rinehart, 1997; Strommen & Mates, 2004). This motivation translates into significant improvement in reading achievement (Taylor, Frye, & Maruyama, 1990; Unrau & Schlackman, 2006). Unfortunately, recent U.S. surveys of the reading habits of adults (National Endowment for the Arts, 2007), as well as of adolescents (Mokhtari, Reichard, & Gardner, 2009; Nippold, Duthie, & Larsen, 2005), reveal an overall decline in the past 20 years of the reading of books and other nonassigned material.

In U.S. and global studies of reading habits among adolescents, a stark gender gap emerged (Brozo, Shiel, & Topping, 2007; Libsch & Breslow, 1996; Mok & Cheung, 2004; Mokhtari et al., 2009; Skaliotis, 2002). Although there has been a disturbing increase in the number of both females and males reading few if any books, far more females read at least one to five nonassigned books per year. Males are also reading fewer magazines and newspapers on a daily basis than females. The data also revealed that students, particularly boys, would rather watch television, interact with digital media, or engage in other leisure activities than read. Regardless of what boys substitute for leisure reading, today's adolescent males are at risk of failing to develop the necessary literacy skills for future academic and workplace success (Nagourney, 2007; U.S. Chamber of Commerce, Center for Workforce Preparation, 2004). This is true because to a large extent, reading achievement is a function of the amount of time and energy that students invest in reading activities both in and out of school (Brozo et al., 2007).

Clearly, a highly effective way of motivating young boys to read and keep them reading is to look carefully at their interests (Baker & Wigfield, 1999; Guthrie, Hoa, Wigfield, Tonks, & Perencevich, 2006). Boys have shown a consistent pattern of preferring texts with male protagonists (Blair, 2000;

Clark & Foster, 2005; Johnson, Peer, & Baldwin, 1984; Jones & Fiorelli, 2003; Knobloch, Callison, Chen, Fritzsche, & Zillmann, 2005; Langerman, 1990; Ollmann, 1993; Samuels, 1989). When preferences and interests are matched with texts, the depth of processing and learning are enhanced (Alexander, Kulikowich, & Hetton, 1994; Guthrie, 2008); this appears to be particularly true for boys (Cavazos-Kottke, 2005; Sullivan, 2009).

Adolescent boys are also known to be especially enthusiastic for nonfiction and informational books (Doiron, 2003; Herz & Gallo, 2005). For most boys, however, reading nonfiction in school consists almost exclusively of reading textbooks, which has been found to be a principal culprit in creating disaffection with reading for both boys and girls (Dreher, 2003; Sullivan, 2004; Taylor, 2004). I am always amazed at how turned-on junior and senior high students become when I pass around nonfiction and informational books. I watch adolescents shift their postures from complacency and disengagement to involvement and curiosity. These observations reinforce how rarely young adults are exposed to nonfiction books written specifically for them (McFall, 2004; Smith & Wilhelm, 2005). There are biographies that chronicle the life stories of great men (past and present) who are emblematic of admirable male archetypes. Fact-based accounts of Galileo, Pelé, and Nelson Mandela, for example, give teen and preteen boys detailed views of heroic and creative accomplishments of men. In addition to engaging adolescents as readers, biographies help adolescents discover goodness in real-life men and introduce them to archetypes on which to base their own lives.

Juliet Turner's extensive research on motivating students within classrooms yielded specific guidelines for motivation (1995; Turner & Paris, 1995). She discovered two critical ways for creating meaningful incentives for students to read and learn—*choices* of texts and tasks and *control* over learning. Choice is essentially self-determination or volitional engagement. Students' self-determined actions, as compared with students' actions driven by external pressure, have been found to be related to higher degrees of internal motivation, greater conceptual understanding of content, and better recall (Margolis & McCabe, 2004). In other words, students who *choose* to read have a better chance of success than students who are pressured to read. Giving students control over what they read and reading-related tasks is also essential in keeping them motivated. Control not only increases engagement in literacy and learning but also allows students to reflect on their own competence (Moje, 2006).

Choice and control are two ingredients commonly missing in instruction provided to adolescent boys who are not reading as would be expected for their grade level and who are disinterested and reluctant readers (Sanford, 2005; Tatum, 2006; Williams, 2004). Typical remedial reading schemes tend to strengthen a boy's self-perception as an incompetent reader because they leave little or no room for choice and control. Although basic reading achievement may show some improvement, the boy becomes increasingly bored. An alternative approach should focus on giving reluctant or bored male readers the opportunity to choose reading materials and control the kinds of responses and extensions, such as assignments and activities, associated with those materials.

My years of work in reading centers have verified much of the research and theoretical knowledge regarding adolescent boys and reading. Other than the obvious fact that males have always outnumbered females in remedial reading centers, I continue to see how boys need personally meaningful reading material to genuinely improve their literacy abilities (Hall & Coles, 1997). Otherwise, they politely go through the paces, but nothing sticks. For example, Carlos, a 14-year-old Mexican American, began making huge connections when we moved from simple skills-based activities to low-rider (a type of car) magazines and ultimately to novels such as Paulsen's (1990) *The Crossing*. With these materials, his eagerness to read, share, and respond expanded greatly. Furthermore, his response journal revealed a deep empathy and connection with Manny Bustos, the novel's main character from Ciudad Juarez, Mexico, who has many qualities of the Pilgrim archetype. As the reading clinician and Carlos worked through the book, Carlos came to see life through Manny's experiences, such as coping with the adversity of being an orphan, resolving interpersonal conflict with stronger street boys, and acting against stereotypes and racism with Sergeant Robert Locke. Before Carlos left the center, we made sure he had an armful of other books, which he and his tutor selected together from the half-price bookstore, to take home over the summer. These included novels by Rudolfo Anaya and Gary Soto. A $10 investment is a small price to pay for a young man who now enjoys reading, knows how to make personal connections to his reading, and, because he reads regularly, has significantly improved his reading ability.

Research and anecdotal evidence support the approach we used with Carlos and continue to use with many other male students in the clinic. Daly, Salters, and Burns (1998) report that gender-based identification with characters from stories is common among boys. A type of gender schema for boys tends to focus attention on textual personae and events that conform to their notions of appropriate male behavior. In the study by Daly and colleagues, middle school boys, as opposed to girls, had superior recall over story content with male protagonists, particularly when the character exhibited recognizable behavior. The opposite was true when stories featured female protagonists.

Bügel and Buunk (1996) had similar results to the findings of Daly and his associates (1998) but used informational texts in their study instead of stories. Passages with traditional male topics (such as science, sports, and cars) were reported by males as being easier to read than passages with traditional female topics (such as midwifery, fashion, and so on). In addition, males had superior reading comprehension of male-oriented text versus the female-oriented text; the opposite was true for females.

In spite of fears that encouraging adolescent boys to read more of what they like will strengthen gender stereotyping, concerns for listless and struggling male readers must take precedence for teachers and parents alike. Because of the diverse characterizations of masculinity found in the Jungian archetypes, books that are steeped in positive male archetypes may actually dispel stereotypical notions of what it means to be masculine. Garnering adolescent boys' interest in reading, keeping them reading, and channeling this reading ability into academic mastery must be a priority. Books with archetypal male characters are likely to accomplish all of this. Archetypal literature that resonates in the male psyche has the power to reveal the delight and the necessity of reading to boys. It provides a reflection on their burgeoning masculinity in the form of male characters who—even though they meet physical, psychological, and emotional demands—ultimately interact caringly with others and make good choices.

Although there is no quick fix for the complex problems that face adolescent males, I reiterate throughout this book that capturing boys' imaginations through books, texts, and other media is a critical element of improving their psychological, sociological, and academic health. Reading books that appeal to and affirm young men's masculine identities in positive ways may transform their sense of self and expand their academic possibilities. If middle school, junior high, and high school teachers carefully select and use engaging texts for boys, including those with positive male archetypes, they may help adolescent males view reading as acceptable and worthwhile.

BOY TALK

Gabriel, 15, Speaks of Men and Culture in Rudolfo Anaya's *My Land Sings: Stories From the Rio Grande*

A lot of people who don't know us think we're all no good. There's a piece of sidewalk on the way to school where someone wrote, "greasy spic." You can't erase it or anything. I even hear people say "wetbacks" and "beaners." They read in the newspaper and hear on television about Rodriguez or Garcia or Jimenez stealing a car or beating up his girlfriend or killing someone in a gang fight and can only think about us in that way. They don't know how rich our history and culture are. They think that because Jennifer Lopez or Ricky Martin are Hispanic Americans, everyone should like us. But people should respect us for more than that. We have worked hard to make Texas and the whole country a place that feels like home to us.

I felt proud to be Hispanic after reading *My Land Sings: Stories From the Rio Grande* (Anaya, 1999). These stories reminded me of how honest and good men of my culture are. It also reminded me that men in my culture do more than take siestas or act drunk or dumb.

In "Miller's Good Luck," Libor and Vidal are two wealthy businessmen arguing whether it was luck or hard work that made them successful. Libor thinks it's luck; Vidal thinks it's hard work. On the way to Santa Fe they meet a poor miller named Pedro Bernal. Pedro is hardworking and honest, so Libor and Vidal decide to use him in an experiment to decide who is right about how to be successful.

They give Pedro 100 pesos and tell him to do whatever he wants. Before Pedro can do anything, a hawk steals the money. They give him money again, but this time Pedro's wife accidentally trades the jar of wheat where Pedro has hidden his money. When the men come back, they think Pedro is lying about the money. Libor and Vidal go off laughing but throw Pedro a "worthless" piece of lead. This is when Pedro finally gets some good luck.

On his way home Pedro runs into a friend who is on his way to go fishing, but doesn't have a sinker. Pedro gives him the piece of lead, and his friend says he'll give him the first fish that he catches. Pedro's friend does, and Pedro's wife finds a very valuable diamond inside the fish. Pedro gets 175,000 pesos from the jeweler for it and builds a big mill business. When Libor and Vidal return, they find that Pedro has become rich. Pedro tells them the story of his good luck, so Libor thinks he has won the argument. But then they find the first sack of money in a hawk's nest and realize Pedro was telling the truth about what happened to the money. Libor and Vidal agree that it takes some luck, but that it also takes honesty and hard work to be successful.

I think this story has a lot of meaning for my people because many of my friends say they're going to get rich by winning the lottery or some sweepstakes, or getting on some game show. They forget that, like Pedro, you have to be honest and hardworking to really be successful. My family is big and doesn't have much money, but my father works hard and is always there for us; therefore, I want to honor him by not getting involved in gangs or blowing off school. I want to be a good man like Pedro and my father. If luck comes to me it will be a surprise. I hope I take advantage of it, but I am not going to hold my breath.

The story I liked the most was "The Three Brothers" because there are three boys in my family. My two older brothers are living their lives similar to the characters of Felipé and Patricio, who wasted their lives and were always looking for someone to take advantage of. My brothers aren't that bad, but one is a dropout, working as a carpenter's helper sometimes. The other is a senior in high school, but his grades are very low, and he has no idea what he's going to do when he graduates. I want to be like Ramon's character—honest, generous, and hardworking. He eventually becomes a prosperous farmer and marries his childhood sweetheart. Ramon talks to his children about not taking the wrong path in life like his brothers did. My father has told us that many times, but I am the only one who seems to listen.

CHAPTER 2

Literature and Positive Male Archetypes

So, you say, we have to change society first, and then boys will read good books. This is true. But if we can get just a few boys to read a few good books, we will have started the change. Cajole, coerce, do whatever needs to be done to get one book into one boy's hands, or back pocket. A book that he can make into a cave he can crawl into, roll around in, explore, for what's in there and what's in himself, you can do all by yourself, where no one can see you laughing or crying.

—Robert Lipsyte (as cited in
Literature for Today's Young Adults, 5th ed.)

Teen and preteen boys may be more inclined to read "a few good books" that serve as entry points into active literacy when teachers use literature with archetypal characters. These archetypes appeal to and affirm teen and preteen boys' unique masculine identities. This literature has the chance to capture boys' imaginations, bring them into the literacy club, and ultimately bestow hope for academic possibilities and life options.

What is this literature? To be sure, it consists of books that have not been written intentionally to depict these archetypes. Writers of young adult books do not usually plan to infuse their fiction or nonfiction with archetypes that celebrate the male psyche. Sloan (1991) keenly observes, however,

> In literature...certain elements and structural patterns are recurrent; this is evident in works both old and new, classical and pop. These patterns or models—fundamental and ancient—recur often enough to be recognizable as aspects of all literary experience; as such, they are archetypal. (p. 48)

Because the literature I share in this book has been written either for or about boys, male archetypes are found within it; moreover, this is good literature in which boys are likely to find something identity affirming and, above all, something worth pursuing.

In this chapter, I describe characteristics of positive male archetypes. A section immediately following each description provides examples of young adult literature in which these archetypes are found. These books, and the books used by the teachers profiled in the next chapter, entice adolescent boys into the literacy club while reinforcing a positive sense of masculinity.

Finding or Rediscovering Positive Male Archetypes

Positive male archetypes starkly contrast with the mass media's spurious and injurious conceptions of masculinity. Images from popular culture assault boys very early in their lives with tales of bumbling, shallow, and even monstrous men (Kipnis, 1994). Images of men and fathers all too often depict them as incompetent, lazy, or frightening (Hewlett & West, 1998) even though studies offer counter evidence that these stereotypes are exaggerated (Parke & Brott, 1999). So, where do we find or how do we become reacquainted with positive images of masculinity in a culture that has done much to tarnish those images and saturate popular consciousness with perversions of manhood? In answering this question, I return to the ideas of the brilliant psychologist Carl Jung, whose work has been enormously influential on modern conceptions of masculinity.

As stated earlier, Jung was one of the first to systematically investigate the uniqueness of the male psyche. According to Jung, archetypical models of maleness are inherent within the psyche of all men. For modern societies like ours, however, Jung describes a condition of "spiritual poverty" wherein we have lost the "historical symbols" of our fathers (deLaszlo, 1959). Jung observes,

> Our intellect has achieved the most tremendous things, but in the meantime our spiritual dwelling has fallen into disrepair.... For the artificial sundering of true wisdom creates a tension in the psyche, and from there arises a loneliness and a craving like that of the morphine addict, who always hopes to find companions in his vice. (deLaszlo, 1959, p. 300)

According to Jung, in order for a male to become a true man, he must rediscover his spiritual, inner self. This journey of rediscovery can be difficult, fraught with pitfalls and challenges. In the words of Jung, though, it "proves to be the indispensable condition for climbing any higher" (deLaszlo, 1959, p. 302). Jung continues, "The prudent man avoids the danger...but also throws away the good which a bold but imprudent venture might bring" (deLaszlo, 1959, p. 303). It seems that boys must be willing to endure hardships associated with a kind of "right inner passage" to become fine young men and honorable adults. Positive male archetypes are an adolescent boy's guides along the often dark and jagged way of this interior journey.

In support of Jung's theory on male archetypes, contemporary psychologists and sociologists (Arnold, 1995; Johnson, 1989; Moore & Gillette, 1992) have discovered that the qualities that most societies consider masculine are remarkably consistent. Cultures as diverse as those of Native North Americans, the island people of Truk in the South Pacific, the Mehinaku people of South America, the Samburu of Africa, the Samina of New Guinea, and many others, share an understanding of what it means to be a mature man. One example of a consistent model of masculinity is the "big man" of New Guinea, the "muy hombre" of Spain, and the "worthy man" of the Samburu who are all protectors, providers, and procreators. All show courage in the face of danger, are thoughtful risk takers when necessary, protect their families and communities, and exhibit extraordinary endurance to achieve laudable goals. They embrace these roles to nurture their families and build their communities (Gilmore, 1990). These different cultures share not only similar broad understandings of masculinity but also many specific male archetypes, such as Healer, Trickster, Prophet, and Warrior (Moore & Gillette, 1992).

The journey to manhood in almost all of these cultures involves, by design, inward and outward struggles that assure a new generation of men of goodness and strong spiritual connections. After exhaustive study of worldwide cultures, Gilmore (1990) concludes that manhood is a test in most societies. In these societies, manhood ideologies "force men to shape up on penalty of being robbed of their identity" (p. 221). He further offers "when men are conditioned to fight, manhood is important; when men are conditioned to flight, the opposite is true" (p. 221). Gilmore does not necessarily refer to male fighting from an antisocial standpoint, but, rather, states the importance of men remaining strong for their families and communities. Male flight, on the other hand, is prevalent in societies such as the United States, where there is remarkably high tolerance for divorce and paternal absenteeism. Male flight from communal responsibility is further conditioned in cultures, again similar to the United States, which accept definitions of men as loners and rugged individuals.

Our own culture, says Arnold (1995), is also responsible for "indoctrinated hostility to spirituality" (p. 12). Far from enthroning men, as many have argued, periods in the history of Western civilization such as the Enlightenment and the Industrial Revolution have disconnected men from their homes, their religions, and their inner selves. In Arnold's words,

> It is no exaggeration to say that modernity has created generations of Numb Men who cannot *feel* their own experiences, much less articulate them. Capitalism...has fabricated the Incredible Shrinking Man, a merely utilitarian robot programmed...to create capital. (p. 14)

Leaving children a legacy of economic prosperity is not enough. Children also must be shown how to lead lives of mission, purpose, and ideals. For boys, this means helping them persevere and thrive academically and imparting a positive sense of their uniqueness as males. The templates for this uniqueness are found in masculine archetypes of humanity's collective past.

Ten Positive Male Archetypes

An archetype, as previously stated, is an inherited idea or mode of thought that is derived from the experience of the race and present in the unconscious of the individual (Jung, 1955). Jung theorized that each man possesses a masculine soul, the *animus*. He found evidence for archetypes of the animus in the nearly identical motifs and tales of manhood that appear in widely separate cultures. Tribal stories, songs, poems, and fairy tales of different cultures—originating in antiquity before modern communications made worldwide connections possible—speak of manhood not as an entity, but as both an inner and outer test of courage. According to Jung, deep knowledge residing in the collective unconscious makes up the archetypal core of man. Exhumation of the animus is one result of archetypal study.

I present the 10 positive male archetypes to help teachers guide adolescent boys through the archetypal world of the male psyche. These images of masculinity, derived from the work of Jung (1955) and Arnold (1995), may be thought of as signposts along a boy's psychic journey to claim or reclaim an honorable masculine identity. The archetypes include Pilgrim, Patriarch, King, Warrior, Magician, Wildman, Healer, Prophet, Trickster, and Lover. These archetypes are the focus of the literature and teaching strategies presented here and in Chapter 3. Using archetypes to interpret literature is a very common practice in literary criticism (Cowden, Viders, & Lafever, 2000; Cutter, 2000; Garry & El-Shamy, 2005; Knapp, 1984, 2003; Schaum, 2000).

Pilgrim

The Pilgrim archetype is one of male wanderlust. He is a searcher and wanderer, filled with hope, faith, and the need to improve life. Deliberate pilgrimages are a featured practice of major ancient religions. A male's pilgrimage is a quest for spiritual freedom, which he reaches by seeking a special holy place. A Pilgrim endures great hardship across many miles, enacting this sacred ritual. In the process of pilgrimage, a man must give up the comforts of familiarity, because only through detachment from that which impedes his progress can he find his way to higher forms of selfhood. The Pilgrim's spirit is characterized by Jung as the "highest freedom, a soaring over the depth, deliverance from the prison of... timorous souls who do not want to become anything different" (deLaszlo, 1959, p. 303).

It is critical to a boy's consciousness to become reacquainted with his inner Pilgrim; if not, he may grow up to be like so many adult men in lockstep that leads to mental stagnation, emotional numbness, and spiritual starvation. Adults do boys few favors by turning a blind eye to undisciplined and habitual video watching. Recent reports suggest that the average 5 to 7 hours per day that children spend in front of television or computer screens, and with handheld devices, regardless of content, results in less intellectually stimulated and more emotionally disconnected adolescents and adults (Greenspan, 2000). Boys who are mired in this video morasse take fewer and increasingly limited flights of imagination and ignore their inner Pilgrim. Young boys need and crave, especially in their souls, meaningful and vibrant interaction with others who can keep them in touch with the wanderer within.

Wandering is meaningful for adolescent boys when it is born of intense needs or desires for life-altering experiences. In this way, Pilgrims search for great solutions to seemingly insoluble problems. Solutions may come at a significant price; however, this is part of the test of Pilgrims' commitment. As Jung suggested, these inner journeys are not for the cautious because they require bold action and risk taking.

Adolescence is itself a metaphor for a pilgrimage. Boys travel unfamiliar physical, emotional, and sociological terrain in this phase of their lives. Adult role models must help teen and preteen boys clarify the goals of their pilgrimages and support their pilgrimages to higher levels of selfhood.

A Pilgrim in Young Adult Literature. Adolescent boys will find an ideal Pilgrim in the character of Henry Smith in Gary Schmidt's (2008) *Trouble*. Henry's father has created a way of life out of running from problems, believing that one can live far enough away from Trouble, so that it never finds you. But Trouble finds the Smiths anyway, as Franklin, Henry's older brother and a prep-school rugby star is accidentally cut down by a pickup truck driven by Chay Chouan, a Cambodian who attends Franklin's school. Racial tensions against the Asian immigrant community flare both at school and in the town. As Franklin lies in a coma, Henry is forced to sort out his feelings for his "perfect" older brother who he learns may have also been an abusive, racist jock. Like all Pilgrims, Henry decides he must take a journey to understand his ambivalent feelings. He and a pal set out for Mt. Katahdin in Maine, which he and Franklin had planned to climb. Along the way, however, they meet Chay, who is on his own journey to cope with feelings of guilt for the tragedy he has caused. Together, these Pilgrims endure physical and emotional challenges on the path to the mountain that transforms them.

Patriarch

Patriarch, as well as King, is one of the most important archetypes of responsibility. The Patriarch represents the masculine form of care, nobility, and self-sacrifice. His energy provides a family with "emotional stability, sturdiness, firm correction, world-wisdom, constructive criticism, moral principles, and a sense of fun" (Arnold, 1995, p. 38). Like all other positive male archetypes, the role of the Patriarch has been tarnished by images from pop culture, but the archetype continues to burn within each boy. It remains there to be discovered or rekindled.

There would appear to be a need in our society for the reemergence of Patriarchal fathering and mentoring for young boys (Blankenhorn, 1995). Mead's (1969) scientific studies on fathering reveal phylogenetically (from an evolution perspective) that male care for offspring has been tenuous. Males have learned, however, to overcome their primal inclination to leave after impregnation and "commit themselves to their families and societies as nurturers and care-givers in a uniquely masculine fashion" (Arnold, 1995, p. 37). Patriarchal care is characterized by its firmness, consistency, dependability, and fairness. For thousands of years, Patriarchs—in their social roles as fathers, tribal leaders, and judges—have been responsible for creating orderly and lawful societies and institutions for the personal and aesthetic welfare of the community.

Feminists and other modern critics of patriarchy are not unfounded in their claims of its historical and current abuses. Rigid, violent, and misogynistic forms of male dominion have prevailed throughout the ages. I must agree with Arnold (1995), however, who argues "it is unfair, unscholarly, and unwise only to characterize a system by its abuses. One rarely hears an...account of patriarchy that also takes into account its vast contributions to human history" (p. 37).

Hewlett and West's (1998) *The War Against Parents: What We Can Do for America's Beleaguered Moms and Dads* asserts that one of the caustic messages of the 1990s was mass media's negative stereotyping of moms and dads. In a case of pop culture irony, say Hewlett and West, the television wasteland of the 1950s, which unrealistically portrayed U.S. parents and families, at least paid tribute to mothers and fathers by reaffirming the importance of parenthood. In subsequent decades, progressive sensibilities were offended by the patriarchal nature of stereotypical television families. Hewlett and West argue, however, that in dismissing the fantasy elements of television parenthood, parents have been dismissed altogether. Open season on parents, especially dads, is evident everywhere in the mass media, from talk shows and contemporary movies to popular songs, books, and magazines (Smith & Cook, 2008). This parent bashing sends a clear message that fathers no longer deserve the respect that once came with being a dad. Fathers, when they exist at all in popular media, are increasingly portrayed as dominant, disconnected, and even dangerous. This point is made vividly in Smith and Cook's (2008) report on gender stereotyping in films and TV where the following is revealed:

- Male characters are only half as likely as females to be parents. They are about half as likely as females to be married or in a committed relationship.

- The fathering and relationship picture is even bleaker for male characters of color. Among those male characters developed enough to ascertain their parental or relationship status, just over a third of nonwhites are parents, compared to more than half of whites; and less than a quarter of nonwhites (22.2 percent) are married or in committed relationships, compared to 45.3 percent of whites.

- Almost twice as many nonwhite males as white males are portrayed as physically aggressive or violent. Among male characters, 44.1 percent are physically aggressive or violent, compared to 36.9 percent of females. With three times more male than female characters, the actual number of physically aggressive males is much higher than the number of physically aggressive females.

As honorable masculinity declines in our society, the first qualities to fall away are, historically, the last to develop—namely, patriarchal responsibility and nurturance. Modern cultures eschew initiation rites of adult males, leaving boys with fewer reference points for responsible masculine behavior. Instead of expecting male irresponsibility to reverse itself by bashing or dismissing men, as is common, people should excite the consciousness of boys and restore a sense of masculine pride and responsibility.

In addition to being responsible for others, the Patriarch is generous and gracious. Arnold (1995) describes the Patriarch as "the archetype in the masculine psyche that offers to father those who are not so fortunate, who are orphaned or lost or helpless or who need guidance and wise direction" (p. 89). Exploration of this archetype teaches young men to understand what it means to be a father. Adolescent boys can also find expression for this fatherhood in ways that serve others just as powerfully as these boys will come to serve their own children. The ideals of the Patriarch, for example, can inspire boys to provide community service, such as helping homeless people, reading to patients in children's hospitals, and participating in beautification and cleanup efforts. Helping boys access this archetype makes *all* of society a better place.

A Patriarch in Young Adult Literature. Martin Conway from Edward Bloor's (2008) *London Calling* possesses many of the qualities that adolescent boys admire in the Patriarch. With an alcoholic father who has left the family and a sister who is an overachieving Ivy League graduate, Martin must decide who he is and what he should become.

One night, Martin meets Jimmy Harker, whose influence on Martin forever changes his life. Jimmy's strange accent and urgent request for help leaves Martin wondering whether their encounter is a dream. But Jimmy re-enters Martin's life over and over again and guides him through a wartime past set in London during the Blitz of WWII. In what seems like a dream, he sees his own grandfather, a statesman, standing outside the U.S. Embassy in London and awakes with knowledge about people and details of the Blitz that he didn't possess before the arrival of Jimmy. Demonstrating true qualities of a Patriarch, Martin discovers his gift for generosity and self-sacrifice in providing the help that Jimmy had been requesting by righting some historical wrongs and caring for the well-being of his own Conway family. And in so doing, Martin finds out what it means to live with honor and integrity.

King

The King embodies male greatness. He is trustworthy and wise, and he engenders excellence in others as well. Filled with spiritual generosity, dignity, and composure, the King accompanies people into places they do not wish to go, but must. Every male who wants to be a leader should explore this archetype to better understand generosity of spirit, difficult decision making, and equanimity.

At first glance, it would appear that most boys and men today would have difficulty identifying with the concept of King. As a boy, I was immersed in the adventures of courtly intrigue with Danish Prince Valiant, who appeared in the Sunday paper; the legendary tales of ruthlessness at the behest of King Henry VIII; or Daniel Dravot's cunning and illegitimate rule of Kafristan in Kipling's (1999) "The Man Who Would Be King." These images formed my model of kingly behavior. Most males develop notions of kingship from the popular conception of an all-powerful monarch, luxuriating in pampered, carefree living and exercising his prerogative at will. With this model in mind, it is little wonder that boys become overwhelmed by this grandeur; furthermore, U.S. boys are steeped in democratic ideals of representative government and self-rule, not in those of a monarchy. I distinctly remember my fifth-grade teacher, Sister Rose Thomas, vilifying King George III for his efforts to crush the insurrection of democracy-minded New England colonists. There is little room in the political and social milieu of the United States for this kind of King. Yet, as Arnold (1995) points out, "regardless of these conflicting attitudes, any man who finds himself in a position of power over others...needs to develop this archetype successfully if he is to govern well and keep from becoming a Tyrant" (p. 112).

Given the exceptional goodness of the King archetype, nothing could be more honorable than to encourage adolescent boys to imitate it, regardless of their personality. The qualities of King described in Psalms in reference to King Solomon—who, in spite of his riches, comforts, and power, saw it as his duty to tend to the needs of his lowliest subjects—are clearly worth emulating by all of us:

> He gives justice to poor people,
> And saves the children of poverty.
> He frees the lowly and helpless who call on him,
> He takes pity on the poor and the weak.
> The souls of the powerless he saves...
> Their lives are precious in his eyes. (72 Psalms 4, 12–14, New American Bible)

Modern-day figures whom boys can readily recognize and admire for their similarities to the King archetype might include the school principal who sets high standards of conduct and scholarship, personally knows his students, and works tirelessly on the students' behalf to help them achieve their potential; the boss who wins the trust of employees, cares about employees' well-being, encourages both the janitor and the highest executive to speak freely about their concerns, and brings about equitable pay for office staff; or the military officer who openly discusses problems raised by his troops and works diligently to provide affordable and comfortable accommodations for military personnel and their families. And consider former U.S. President Jimmy Carter who, with his bare hands, helps build low-cost housing for the poor and less privileged—now that is Kingly behavior.

A King in Young Adult Literature. On September 18, 2007, a computer science professor with Kingly qualities took the stage of a packed auditorium at Carnegie Mellon University to give his final lecture. The professor, Randy Pausch, called it "Really Achieving Your Childhood Dreams" and it is described and shared in Pausch and Zaslow's (2008) book, *The Last Lecture*. It was his last lecture because cancer was devouring his pancreas and would claim his life a few short months later. Nonetheless, Randy exudes dignity and wisdom, critical qualities of the King, as he exhorts those in attendance to celebrate their dreams and strive to make them a reality. With slides of his CT scans projected on the large screen behind him, Randy offers a humorous, intelligent, and inspirational message about the importance of surmounting barriers, of nurturing one's own and other's dreams, and of seizing the day.

Warrior

Lurking in the souls of all males is the Warrior. He is brave, edifying, and honorable. In defining the Warrior archetype, it is important to avoid using female passivity as the subordinate concept. The definition of the Warrior should contrast with male greed, selfishness, and lack of humanitarian spirit.

Violent males are not Warriors, although this image has been appropriated by U.S. movies as the most salient and the most profitable; furthermore, emotionally wounded boys find the Warrior archetype so compelling that they may join gangs to gain a sense of misguided self-respect. This cheapened form of the Warrior is built on violent, self-righteous retaliation and the duty to protect neighborhood turf. These modern perversions make it difficult for both males and females to embrace this archetype's glorification. The Warrior's true masculinity is based on self-control and moral courage, and has nothing to do with a lack of behavioral volition or the sway of impulse and rage (Jordan, 1995). The Warrior's sacred obligation, which is recognized in almost every culture, is to never act violently out of blind anger or revenge, but to deliberately and strategically plan and take full responsibility for actions. As in the past, today's Warriors should be initiated and educated in ethical codes of "personal honor, noble restraint, magnanimity to defeated rivals, and individual humility for one's deeds" (Arnold, 1995, p. 104).

Although most modern-day males rarely need their inner Warriors for physical combat, they still need the Warrior's strength for everyday psychological and psychic battles. Warriors find expression in steadfastly training the mind and body, girding themselves for the onslaught of naysayers and detractors, and courageously defending an honorable cause.

Understanding the origin of the Warrior archetype helps illuminate its importance. The paradigm was an outgrowth of the Paleolithic hunter, around whom mythology, rituals, ethics, and art were developed as an homage to this central role in early human societies. "Lauded by poems, songs, and stories, celebrated and sanctified by rituals, and blessed by the gods, the Warrior has come to epitomize the noblest qualities of masculinity: bravery, self-sacrifice, stamina, and skill" (Arnold, 1995, p. 101).

No archetype symbolizes the opposition to evil more powerfully than the Warrior. Today this opposition involves battling disease, attacking drug use, and waging war on poverty and ignorance. Teachers, parents, and others need to help teen and preteen boys discover their inner Warriors as a source of fortification for a variety of meaningful causes. As Connell (1989) discovered, however, this is not an easily obtained goal. In his study of the interplay between masculinity and school, the construction of masculinity for teens from homes with either unemployed or absentee fathers involved a process of "getting into trouble" or blindly fighting school authority. Following these teens into adulthood, Connell documented their confusion and frustration in developing a patriarchal masculinity based on the mixed messages they received from home and school. This resulted more often than not in the recapitulation of the cool guys, nerds, and wimps models of masculinity from their working-class communities. Those trying to help boys access the Warrior persona will confront similar blocked paths; indeed, it is the inner Warrior that emboldens people to accept the challenge in the first place.

A Warrior in Young Adult Literature. The best real-life Warrior is a man who goes to great lengths to avoid aggressive action, but when he must act, he does so with confidence, resolve, and honorable intent. Such is the Warrior power of Nelson Mandela, who is engagingly described by Hort and Brown (2006). Born in a thatched hut in a small village in South Africa, Mandela was raised by his uncle and attended a local missionary school. When he was a young man, he ran away to Johannesburg to work in the mines. Eventually, he was admitted to law school and began to recognize the need to fight the racism of his homeland. Mandela became the leader of the African National Congress in the 1960s, which was committed to dismantling apartheid and restoring social justice for people of every race. The South African government (comprised of only white people) arrested and imprisoned Mandela for his radical views on racial equality, and he spent over 27 years in jail. Due in large part to his efforts to raise international consciousness about the atrocities of apartheid, the stress of embargoes and other policies of economic isolation finally pressured the South African government to release Mandela and modify its constitution to give blacks full participation in the political process. Within four years of his release, Mandela was elected president of the Republic of South Africa. Similar to all honorable Warriors, Mandela withstood extreme physical and psychological hardships because of his devotion to the welfare of others. He was gracious in victory, imposing strict policies that criminalized reprisals against whites and forging stronger interracial relationships to ensure prosperous coexistence in South Africa.

Teen and preteen boys cannot help but become absorbed in Hort and Brown's (2006) moving account of a man whose conviction brought a nation and the world closer to the ideal of social justice and human rights for all. Mandela illustrates how boys can potently channel the Warrior archetype into socially constructive and peaceable causes.

Magician

The Magician evokes amazement through his intuition and cleverness. According to Nichols (1980), the paradigm of the Magician and his wand is extremely ancient. Ancient wisdom has it that the Magician is the first major psychological archetype out of 22 symbols and situations of people's collective unconscious (Pearson & Seivert, 1995). Pop culture has, unfortunately, reduced this archetype to sleight of hand hucksters for sideshow amusement or high-priced, glossy deception for television. These superficial renderings have little connection with the deeper level of the

Magician archetype. Within men's core, the Magician engages psychic resources. According to Arnold (1995),

> Many modern men are appallingly unaware of the tremendous psychic potential that lies within them unused; educated in a left-brain/materialistic worldview, they insist that things are just what they appear, that what you see is what you get, and any other viewpoint is just superstition and religious hocus-pocus. (p. 107)

Adolescent boys should be guided in the ways of prayer and meditation to nurture their intuition and conjure their inner Merlin. We think of intuition as a female trait; indeed, a common synonym is "female logic." Yet primal societies gave elevated status to men who, inspired by hunches or feelings in their bones, could locate the best sources of game, water, or shelter. Pearson and Seivert (1995) report that men who develop their inner Magician follow business hunches that pay off, perceive subtle changes in the emotional moods and needs of loved ones, and notice how coincidences lead to special opportunities in their personal lives. For some the Magician archetype connects them to the universal mysterious and pervasive force that guides all creation. This is the force that strengthens people to reconcile with their enemies, restores people's pride after defeat, and helps people recognize blind luck or good fortune as the handiwork of the Magician.

To access the Magician archetype, boys need to become acquainted with their intuitive selves. Teachers may help boys become comfortable with this archetype by finding both ancient and contemporary examples of males who have used their intuitive powers to improve their lives and the lives of those around them.

A Magician in Young Adult Literature. Imagine being orphaned as a 12-year-old and forced to survive on the streets of Paris. That's how we're introduced to Hugo Cabret, the main character of Brian Selznick's (2007) remarkable illustrated narrative, *The Invention of Hugo Cabret*. Crawling through the walls of a Paris train station circa 1930, Hugo maintains the station clocks and begs, borrows, and steals what he needs to survive. We learn through the artful blend of story and pictures that Hugo's clockmaker father has recently died, leaving behind a magical automaton figure that looks almost real as it sits at a desk, pen in hand as if it's about to write a message. Hugo, like his father, has devoted himself to bringing the human-like figure to life. Hugo pores over the notebook his father has left behind that describes and explains the details of the inner workings of the automaton. When he meets a mysterious toymaker who sits in his stall in the station and the toymaker's daughter, Hugo's life swirls with magic, excitement, and joy. The toymaker, we discover, is really a stage magician turned filmmaker, the real-life Georges Méliès, who is most famously remembered for his direction of the first science fiction film, *A Trip to the Moon*.

Boys will be captivated by this intriguing and cleverly designed book that is to be read and literally manipulated. There is plenty of mystery and action, along with several well-rendered chase scenes. Boys will also be drawn to the story and life of Hugo Cabret for the praiseworthy ways he pursues and employs magic to bring happiness to himself and those around him.

Wildman

The Wildman archetype is characterized by lustiness, unpredictability, and independence. He is the ancient male paradigm of one who yearns for freedom. He is the original man frolicking in the lush, beast-filled expanses of Eden. Arnold (1995) describes the Wildman as follows:

> He is a figure representing man's primordial connections with nature; in the myths, he dwells in the wilderness in swamps, caves, or lonely desert tracts. Totally liberated from the trappings of modern civilization...he represents male earthiness, that grubby and gritty manly energy radically free from the effete effects of deodorized and cosmetic modern male narcissism.... That's the Wildman—that dangerous and attractive fellow beckoning us out of our ruts and into the wilderness. (p. 35)

For many, the word *wildman* evokes a host of negative images, such as tattered and unshorn street dwellers or undisciplined or lunatic social rebels. People lock their car doors when they see the wildman hitching a ride with a makeshift duffel at his side. On city streets and in subways, people walk briskly past the wildman shuffling toward them with matted-down hair and an outstretched palm. How unfortunate that boys have so few opportunities to encounter the authentic Wildman, who resides deep beneath modern consciousness (Anderson, 1990).

If we could go back far enough in time, we would discover that all men were Wildmen. Primal man was as wild as the beasts he hunted. Enslaved by and in awe of natural forces, primal man explained the mysteries of birth and death through myth and paid homage to large unexplained forces in an attempt to contextualize his existence. With the invention of agriculture, however, humanity changed forever. Men, no longer at the mercy of indifferent natural processes, learned to exploit nature for their own purposes. This process has yet to cease; consequently, boys and men living in modern civilizations have become disconnected from the former natural order of things. Most are now estranged from their inner Wildman.

The Wildman remains alive within the male psyche, though. Introducing an adolescent boy to his inner Wildman can be a daunting experience. When I reflect on this process of reunification, I envision the flash of recognition not unlike the kind that sweeps over the spouse of *The Man With the Twisted Lip* (Doyle, 1930). In this Sherlock Holmes tale, a gentleman dons the disguise of a hairy, deformed beggar in an attempt to repay a debt from a poor investment. He panhandles by day and changes into proper clothes each evening, returning to his wife and children as if nothing were untoward. Through a coincidence, however, after his wife spies him in the window of a notorious opium den—his safe haven for changing out of his disguise—he goes missing and is feared murdered. Holmes, of course, gets to the bottom of the mystery by deducing that the beggar and the gentleman are the same man. In a public unmasking before his wife, the man with the twisted lip is forced to remove his disguise. The reader sees the line between man and Wildman disappear. This dualism is also evident in Stevenson's (1994) *Dr. Jekyll and Mr. Hyde* and other stories from the late 19th century.

Teachers and parents should be cautious, though, when choosing books that present the Wildman archetype. The authors of the narratives from the late 1800s were influenced by the burgeoning fields of psychology and psychoanalysis and the work of Freud and Jung, and their tales invariably reveal the dark side of the Wildman archetype—the destructive, wanton nature of wildness. Even real-life Wildman Chris McCandless, from Krakauer's (1996) *Into the Wild* and the movie by the same name (Penn, Linson & Pohlad, 2007), leaves boys with little to emulate. Although McCandless embodies many positive qualities of the Wildman, such as eschewing materialism and seeking a state of oneness with nature, his ill-fated adventure is nothing more than escapism, or a complete turning away from family and friends, into what one might characterize as a pathological drive to be apart from everything and everyone.

The Wildman archetype helps boys escape the demands of modern life and exploit the archetypal inclination to improve their families, communities, and society. The Wildman emboldens young men to challenge the status quo, and question their own and others' complacency, conformity, and popular ideologies. The voice of the wilderness is, today, the voice within that tells boys to reject false promises and replace them with genuine behavior. This voice also helps adolescent boys see through fads and strive for solid and permanent values instead.

A Wildman in Young Adult Literature. Wildmen look for adventure, although sometimes they get more than they bargained for. Such is the case with Arnold Spirit in Sherman Alexie's (2007) compelling semi-autobiographical narrative *The Absolutely True Diary of a Part-Time Indian*. Arnold is an intelligent 14-year-old born with a slight brain defect, which leaves him the target of bullies. But he loves to draw and says of his clever sketches "I think the world is a series of broken dams and floods, and my cartoons are tiny little lifeboats." Arnold's best friend on the rez (reservation) is Rowdy, whose name fits, and together they wallow in the decay of the reservation until a teacher convinces Arnold to think beyond the hopelessness of the rez and escape its suffocating mire of alcoholism and drug abuse. Arnold transfers to a wealthy white school and is soon alienated by his own community. Nonetheless, this Native American Wildman tries to make the most of his new opportunities by making friends and starting on the basketball team. When he plays against his old classmates from the reservation school, Arnold is forced to come to terms with issues of identity and community.

This fascinating story is likely to engross boys with its straightforward and no-punches-pulled style. Reading this book will help them learn of the Wildman's power to stay connected to family and friends. The book also celebrates the virtues of the Wildman by demonstrating for boys how superficial things in life like hairstyle and the brand of sneakers one wears lose importance when compared with the solid values of friendship and cooperation. Arnold's experiences ultimately give him the resolve to overcome poverty, reconcile with family and friends, and improve his life.

Healer

The Healer archetype is mystical, spiritual, and capable of bringing wholeness to people and societies that are incomplete and suffering. Rituals of healing are deep in the histories of mankind. Well before the arrival of Jesus, for instance, baptisms by water were common throughout the Hebrew culture because they were viewed as a ritual to cleanse impurities and heal the wounds of sinfulness. Weston (1997), a renowned authority on medieval legends, shows how the processes of birth and rebirth and sickness and healing were integral to ancient fertility rites. In the Fisher King myth, for example, the ruler of a land that has become barren must endure sickness and disease before life-giving waters return to heal him and restore the fertility of his land.

Healers are powerful archetypes in many worldwide cultures. They cure physical, emotional, and spiritual illnesses of their tribes or societies. Ancient healers regarded most afflictions as spiritual in nature. The work of the healer, therefore, was to cure disease and injuries by invoking good spirits who were more powerful than the evil demons who plagued the sufferers.

Remnants of the Healer archetype continue to reside in the male psyche. Unfortunately, it has become extremely difficult for boys and men to access the healing side of masculinity because of a pop culture that depicts men as violent and destructive. To become Healers, boys must first learn to heal themselves. This self-healing is distinctly masculine. Grim (1984) describes the process of a healer or shaman receiving his healing powers through a harrowing spiritual journey, whereby the young and vulnerable healer must endure and conquer physical and emotional trials that require him to marshal a great force of positive spirits. This rite of passage is viewed by cultural peers as a miracle not only for the individual, but for everyone, because the shaman can then devote his healing powers to lifetime service of the wounded and sick tribespeople.

Self-healing must be dealt with carefully for boys living in today's instant-cure world. As Arnold (1995) points out, "The healing process takes place in a much more mysterious, complex, and individual fashion than the spiritual salesmen would have us believe, in league with forces and on a timetable not amenable to our conscious direction" (p. 136). Teen and preteen boys need models of the Healer archetype that fit into their complex and high-tech worlds. Teachers should work to guide boys through the inward journey of self-healing while encouraging boys' outward acts of public service for those who are hurting.

A Healer in Young Adult Literature. Healers have special gifts that they use to heal wounds, make people whole, and bring people together. This power is illustrated by Connor, the main character in Neal Shusterman's (2009) novel *Unwind*. In a society where unwanted teens are salvaged for every part of their body, from their brain to their toes, Connor joins two other runaways to elude and ultimately to heal a system that has gone mad.

In this society, pro-life and pro-choice forces reach a compromise that is enacted into law as The Bill of Life. It states that human life may not be touched from the moment of conception until the age of 13. However, between the ages of 13 and 18, a parent may choose retroactive abortion of a son or daughter, provided the youth's life doesn't "technically" end.

The process of both terminating and yet keeping someone alive is called "unwinding."

Connor's parents want him unwound because he's always getting into trouble. Authorities are planning to unwind Risa, an orphan, to save expenses for her care. Lev's strict religious family has planned for his unwinding since birth as a form of human sacrifice to God. When chance brings these three teens together, they embark on a desperate and harrowing journey to elude the authorities until they turn 18. Along the way they meet and help others who share a similar plight.

Shusterman portrays Connor as a boy with classic powers of the Healer. While on his journey across the U.S. with Risa and Lev, Connor makes a spiritual excursion to find a new source of confidence and self-knowledge. He then attempts to use this new understanding of himself to heal wounds of fear and division between people. Connor possesses qualities that adolescent boys can recognize in their own lives, making Unwind a highly useful source for helping boys access their inner Healer.

Prophet

When people think of a modern-day Prophet, they might think about a self-ascribed, television clairvoyant who predicts love, fame, and fortune for gullible callers. Other people may envision a wizened man who can predict the future, utter divinely inspired revelations, and effectively speak for a cause or concern. The Prophet archetype embodies all these qualities and more. He causes controversy and piques consciousness. He is "a spiritual figure of great antagonism who insists on battling falsehoods and telling the truth to society without regard to his own safety, success, or welfare" (Arnold, 1995, p. 33). This archetype has no room for pretense or false commitment. A spiritual friend of mine described the Prophet archetype to me in a homespun way that makes clear this last point. He said, "The Prophet is like the ham in a ham and egg breakfast. Whereas the chicken makes a partial contribution to the meal, the pig makes a full commitment by giving his life. This is the Prophet" (R. Schmelzer, personal communication, December 29, 2000).

The Prophet's power to see and tell the truth makes him a most admirable paragon in the male psyche. He stands up to lies, is blunt, and possesses an intuitive lie detector. With these characteristics, why would anyone not want all adolescent boys to be guided by the power of this positive archetype? Like all of the archetypes I have described, the true Prophet is a very masculine figure. Endowed with a kind of spiritual virility, the Prophet stands up to assaults from people or societies in denial about conscience. Arnold (1995) says,

> Indicting, judging, accusing, attacking, exhorting, and exciting, his words sometimes wound and always irritate, and inevitably provoke and scandalize.... To the complacent, he hurls warning; to the desperate, hope. He tells us what we do not want to hear when we do not want to hear it. That is why society is always so intent on finding ways to eliminate him from its earshot. (p. 148)

It is rare to see someone in society speak as truthfully and lovingly as a Prophet does. Teachers should strive to find books that embolden male youth with this insight and the power of truth. Boys who have access to this archetype are capable of living and leading others to honorable and honest lifestyles. Providing boys with models of real-life men who love the truth, as well as examples of male literary characters who embody Prophet-like qualities, can help boys more readily access this powerful archetype for lifelong inspiration.

A Prophet in Young Adult Literature. *Prophet* is a heavy moniker. As evidence, consider its sparing ascription over the course of recorded history and particularly in modern times. To have Prophet-like qualities, however, does not automatically entail superhuman powers of prediction and uncanny insight. Perhaps the most ideal Prophets are those individuals who are not yet fully aware of their own gifts, but who pursue truth, justice, and goodness with innocence and humility. A unique fictional character in young adult literature who seems to embody the aforementioned qualities is Jeffrey Lionel Magee, better known as Maniac Magee. Jerry Spinelli's (1990) moving tale of the same name follows the exploits of a young man who wanders into a segregated Pennsylvania town and shakes the citizens out of their complacency forever.

Whether intentional or not, Spinelli imbues Maniac with characteristics reminiscent of biblical prophets. Maniac seems to appear in the small town of Two Mills almost out of thin air. Spinelli opens his book by describing Maniac in this way: "They say Maniac Magee was born in a dump. They say his stomach was a cereal box and his heart a sofa spring" (p. 1). Similar to John the Baptist, Maniac soon has the townspeople exchanging stories about his unusual feats, such as how fast and how far he can run, how in baseball he hits a "frogball" for an inside-the-park home run, and how many touchdowns he scores. His real accomplishment, however, comes in the form of challenging long-standing views regarding racial integration. The East End and West End of Two Mills are separated by an invisible line that segregates whites and blacks. Again, similar to the powerful biblical prophets, Maniac disrupts the status quo by being the first to cross that line, leading the community to a new level of consciousness.

With true Prophet-like strength, Maniac's color blindness and innocent courage show people a truth they had yet to glimpse. Boys have found and will continue to find *Maniac Magee* a story that piques their unique male imaginations. Using athletic prowess as the hook, Spinelli carves a figure of an adolescent boy who can also impress with his gifts of truthfulness and righteousness. Maniac Magee is an ideal model of the Prophet archetype for male youth.

Trickster

The Trickster archetype is irreverent, funny, and satirical. This archetype is the impish side of the masculine spirit, poking fun at pomposity, ostentation, and self-righteousness. His ancient role was to mock arrogance to make way for new, honest leadership. Shakespeare's jesters and sprites, such as Feste in *Twelfth Night* (Shakespeare, 1998) or Ariel in *The Tempest* (Shakespeare, 1994), express the aura of this archetype very well when they take advantage of interludes in the play's action to speak directly to the audience about the folly and overwrought emotions of the main characters, engendering satiric laughter.

This archetype lives on in the male psyche. The Trickster is the source of unconscious antics, as well as the spice and flavor in routine lives. The male Trickster is the office prankster who lightens moods; the teacher who is always ready to inject levity into the discussion of an otherwise turgid topic; or the buddy who teases in ways that remind his friends that life is not so bad, and that it does not hurt to laugh at themselves. The Trickster is the comedian, the political satirist, and the musical parodist who reminds people of their frailty and humanness in delightful ways.

The Trickster is a worthwhile role model for young men because he instills humility. For example, if a boy becomes conceited because of his athleticism during a baseball game, the Trickster finds a way to have him fall over his own feet on his way from third base to home and get tagged out. When a young man starts taking his sex appeal too seriously, his inner prankster makes certain that a piece of spinach is stuck in his front teeth when he tries to make a date in the lunchroom. Boys and men alike are equally susceptible to the antics of the Trickster, but they are also capable of exploiting that puckishness to bring themselves down to earth after their own arrogance balloons and induce a smile in the most churlish of peers.

A Trickster in Young Adult Literature. Most teen and preteen boys are familiar with the stories of *Willy Wonka and the Chocolate Factory* (Dahl, 1998) and *James and the Giant Peach* (Dahl, 2000). If so, they know the biting satire of the author, Roald Dahl. Dahl (1988) has also written an immensely entertaining autobiography titled *Boy: Tales of Childhood*, which colorfully re-creates his days growing up in England and Wales. What becomes clear in this enchanting tale is that the tricksters, pranksters, and practical jokers who abound in Dahl's creative works have their origins in the real-life misadventures of Dahl himself.

Like all effective Tricksters, Dahl zeroes in on those around him who behave pompously, contemptuously, or wickedly and makes them the objects of his acerbic wit or victims of his practical jokes. In the chapter titled "The Great Mouse Adventure of 1924," Dahl puts a dead mouse in the gobstopper jar at Mrs. Pratchett's candy shop to get back at her for her ill-humored manner toward him and other neighborhood kids. In another instance, the young Dahl finds a way to retaliate against his sister's smug fiancé by filling his pipe with goat dung.

Bringing truly nasty adults down a few pegs is a motif that runs throughout Dahl's fiction, as well as in these exciting sketches of his own life. Nowhere in his book is this more apparent than in his struggles with the blind and often brutal authority so wantonly displayed by headmasters at the various boarding schools Dahl attended. According to Dahl, the headmaster at Llandaff Cathedral School was particularly odious. Anytime Dahl attempted to expose the dark side of boarding school life there, he would get whipped on the back or ankles with a cane. Undeterred by these harsh punishments, Dahl, drawing on the full power of his inner Trickster, continued to find ways to defy school authority by deploying a clever array of practical jokes on both teachers and bullies.

Dahl's uncommon adventures are not meant to give legitimacy to irreverence or disobedience. Instead, they demonstrate how wit and trickery can be used to expose phoniness, hypocrisy, and arrogance. These are the Trickster's gifts, which Dahl possessed in abundance. Boys are sure to find his autobiography of childhood through adolescence funny and sometimes painful, but always interesting.

Lover

The Lover archetype is giving, caring, and intimate. Without love, human beings cannot go on. The Lover is the primal energy, passion, and appetite for all human hungers, such as for food, well-being, reproduction, creativity, and meaning (Moore & Gillette, 1992). Mostly, the Lover is the symbol of man's connectedness to all other people.

The word *lover* has been appropriated by popular culture to simply mean a sexual partner. This cavalier definition is detached from all deeper and aesthetic meanings, making it difficult to talk to young boys about the authentic and intimate nature of the Lover archetype. Love as a narcissistic urge to satisfy one's own primal hunger is an abomination of true love as embodied in the inner Lover of all males. Young men need to find expressions of love beyond the heat of romantic passion. There is love in generosity to friends or strangers, in the compassion of forgiveness, and in other acts of selflessness. It motivates us to form alliances, to place a common shoulder to the wheel, and to recognize that in helping others we are also helping ourselves. Goodman (1992), in reference to the importance of "connectionism" between people, says,

> Each individual's self-actualization can be fully realized only within a just and caring society. Individual goals must be balanced by deep and sincere attitudes of altruism, compassion, cooperation, and civic responsibility and the social structures that support them. Freedom within this context suggests nonexploitative psychological, social, and economic relations and the belief that our individual identities cannot be seen as separate from the organic, interdependent system of humankind.... (p. 9)

The Lover, then, has the capacity for deep empathy. He is profoundly sensitive to the pain and joy of his family and friends and to those in the community in need of assistance and caring. To talk about love in such terms may make this archetype difficult for most adolescent boys to access because these qualities are stereotypically feminine. So it remains highly challenging for many teen and preteen boys, whose notions of masculinity are steeped in popular culture, to connect with this sensitive form of masculinity. This does not mean, however, that boys are incapable of establishing or reestablishing contact with their inner Lover.

When young and mature men appropriately access the Lover archetype, they feel alive, enthusiastic, compassionate, empathic, energized, connected, and romantic about their lives, work, goals, and achievements (Moore & Gillette, 1992). This is because the Lover is humane and gives positive, meaningful purpose to the other masculine archetypes. All males, then, need to strengthen the Lover archetype throughout their lives to stay connected to those around them and to avoid slipping into isolation and loneliness. To radiate love, adolescent boys must love themselves and return the love of others. Teachers must find books that help boys learn to love in an honorable and uniquely masculine way.

A Lover in Young Adult Literature. Boys need palpable, contemporary depictions of men who love honorably, so that they can find connections between their own efforts to act in loving ways. A contemporary role model is this Lover of youth, the late Earl Woods (Woods & The Tiger Woods Foundation, 2006) described in his book, *Start Something: You Can Make a Difference*. In the foreword, youth are urged "to make a difference in the world, to reach higher and farther than you ever imagined. I challenge you to start something." From this simple yet essential message comes practical advice about how youth can learn to love themselves by acting in loving ways with others. Making a genuine difference in their lives and the world around them is a challenge for youth, but the benefits of actively seeking ways of improving the well-being of family, friends, and teammates, and their own behavior and achievement in school makes taking up Woods's challenge entirely worthwhile.

Woods's desire in this book is to teach youth many valuable lessons about reaching goals and believing that anything is possible. He stresses the need to make a difference in the world by reaching out to and caring for others. He demonstrates how this simple but powerful guidepost for a better life can be expressed in a number of ways, including helping to clean up a park, settling an argument peacefully, writing down one thing each day that one can be proud of, donating school supplies to a needy school, asking parents about their day, including the kid who always gets left out, or refusing to give up in the pursuit of these goals.

Using a golf analogy, Woods makes it clear that it's not how well you hit the ball, it's what kind of person you are that counts. This message comes through repeatedly. This wise and friendly manual for being a better friend, student, teacher, and community member is a valuable book for teen and preteen boys who are searching for honorable expressions of their inner Lover.

Exposing teen and preteen boys to books that embody the 10 positive male archetypes described in this chapter may not automatically transform them into active readers, although it is this kind of literature that has the potential to present boys with a reason to read. Archetypal literature provides a reflection on boys' burgeoning masculinity by depicting male characters who struggle with similar life choices. Teen and preteen boys concern themselves daily with questions about what it means to be a man. The images of masculinity they receive from popular media and their immediate surroundings may have little resemblance to authentic and archetypal masculinity. In his book *Reaching Up for Manhood: Transforming the Lives of Boys in America*, Canada (1998) says,

Our beliefs about maleness, the mythology that surrounds being male, has led many boys to ruin. The image of male as strong is mixed with the image of male as violent. Male as virile gets confused with male as promiscuous. Male as adventurous equals male as reckless. Male as intelligent often gets mixed with male as arrogant, racist, and sexist.... We must all spend more time trying to understand what happens to boys—and how we can help shape them into better men. (p. xiii)

Teachers who use books with positive male archetypes may improve their chances of reaching boys, of helping boys find entry points into active literacy, and of getting boys to think critically about text and about what it means to be a man.

BOY TALK

Jermaine, 12, Makes a Statement About Men and Slavery Based on Reading Ann Cameron's Adaptation of *The Kidnapped Prince: The Life of Olaudah Equiano*

My granddad says all of us have slaves in our past. Our people come from Mississippi. They moved to Texas to work on the farms, but mostly Mexicans do the field work now. I listen to Granddad and the other old men on Greenwood Avenue talk about when Corpus had separate schools and parks for black people, and separate places for them to sit in movies and restaurants. We were called "Negroes" then. I would have hated living at that time, but being a slave is the worst thing that could happen to a person.

I had never heard of Olaudah Equiano before I read *The Kidnapped Prince: The Life of Olaudah Equiano* (Equiano & Cameron, 2000). As I read, I found out that there are not many books by slaves because they weren't allowed to read or write. *This* book was written because Olaudah was a prince before he was kidnapped and forced to become a slave. This is like taking some rich guy's kid, making him work for free all day in the heat, giving him hardly anything to eat, and making him walk everywhere. The worst was when Olaudah was put on a ship and sent to the West Indies. Slaves were jammed into the bottom of the ship. There was no room to move, there were no lights, and it was dirty. The slaves also got seasick. If you made it out okay, you had to work in the sugarcane fields.

I'm proud to be an African American. Being a slave meant you were nothing. The people who forced Olaudah to become a slave didn't have any respect for him and whether he was a prince. They just thought, "You're black and you're strong, so you work for us or else." When he finally got out of slavery, he wrote this book, and a lot of people bought it. This was back in the 1700s. Somehow Olaudah kept his pride. My granddad says people can take a lot of things from you, but they can't take away your pride.

CHAPTER 3

Teaching Positive Male Archetypes With Literature

Properly, we should read for power. Man reading should be man intensely alive. The book should be a ball of light in one's hands.

—Ezra Pound, *Guide to Kulchur*

T his chapter provides descriptions of teachers using good books as vehicles for exploring the 10 positive male archetypes with their students. I chose to include these particular descriptions because of the teachers' creativity in structuring innovative, meaningful, and engaging learning experiences around excellent young adult literature.

Teaching the Pilgrim Archetype With Literature

Philena is a ninth-grade language arts teacher. She has 14 boys and 3 girls in her last-period basic English class. The gender makeup in this class is not dissimilar to her other classes for freshmen who have the lowest scores on the state reading achievement test. Philena works closely with the teacher of U.S. history, who has the same students, so as to help these struggling readers and learners use literacy skills to improve their understanding of subject-area content.

During the study of the Great Depression, or more specifically of the Dust Bowl, Philena's language arts class read *The Dust Bowl* (Reis, 2008) and *Children of the Dust Bowl: The True Story of the School at Weedpatch Camp* (Stanley, 1992) to complement their learning of the topic in history class. These masterly crafted books trace the history of southwestern farmers who were forced to leave their dust-ravaged farms in the 1930s in search of better land and a better life. Punctuated by archival photographs, these books tell the story of men striving to achieve lives of dignity for themselves and their families in the midst of economic despair. In an effort to sensitize her students to the power of the Pilgrim archetype in the lives of the men and boys described in both books, Philena employed some highly effective ideas.

Ideas for Using the Pilgrim Archetype

Philena asked students to compare how men in *The Dust Bowl* and *Children of the Dust Bowl* embody the Pilgrim archetype versus the way that the men in other books embody the Pilgrim archetype. Students identified traits and motivations of the Pilgrim in Inman, the main character in *Cold Mountain* (Frazier, 1997), which Philena had read aloud to the class earlier that year. Inman deserts the Confederate army and makes a long and treacherous pilgrimage to his home and his wife on Cold Mountain, escaping a war for which he no longer has any heart. Inman shares several similar traits with Elmer Thomas, a character from *Children of the Dust Bowl*, who is from Muskogee, Oklahoma, USA. In the manner of all good Pilgrims, Elmer seeks a better life for his family in a land of bounty (California) after escaping the ravages of drought. Students recorded their findings on a compare-contrast chart.

The class also engaged in a *storypath* activity (McGuire, 1997), in which students take on the identities of people from the era or place that they are studying, which in this case was the Dust Bowl in Oklahoma and California. First, students individually created their own storypath character by providing pertinent personal information, as in the following example:

1. Name: Amos Brown
2. Age: 45
3. Date of birth: 1895
4. Birthplace: Ada, Oklahoma
5. Distinguishing features: A long scar on my arm from getting it caught in a combine
6. Occupation: A farmer in Oklahoma but now trying to find work in California
7. Family: My wife, Erma; three daughters, Julie, Barbara, and Thelma; and two sons, Amos Jr. and Billy
8. Personality characteristics: Stubborn and don't want to take anything for free; I want to work and need to find a steady job
9. Leisure activities: Whittling, playing horseshoes, and singing

10. Interesting anecdote: Joined the army when I was 22 and was sent to Belgium to fight the Germans; guess I can say I've been to Europe

Once students created characters for themselves, Philena organized them into logical family, work, and community groups and subgroups (such as farm owners, laborers, children, and so on). Next, Philena had her students create a large, colorful mural that was taped to one of the classroom walls. The students' mural contained drawings of fertile farmland, tents and shanties, jalopies, mountains, big farmhouses, and a police station. The mural allowed students to translate images of community that they gathered from both the history textbook and their two young adult books into an identifiable context for storypath activities.

The real heart and soul of storypath teaching occurs once the characters and the setting have been established, and once the episodes are introduced. Episodes are issues and concerns that the teacher may inject into the storypath community; they are historically valid and relevant to the characters' lives. Teachers should design episodes to generate focused discussion and problem solving among students as they role-play their characters. Philena introduced the following episode to her class, asking them to call a community meeting to discuss it:

> The men earn 25 cents per hour doing farm work but can't support their families on that wage. In order to pay for just the absolute basics, such as food and clothing, they need at least 35 cents per hour. If they demand a higher wage from the farm owners they'll be fired. What should they do?

The students role-played a camp discussion from the perspectives of their characters to brainstorm possible solutions. One student, Wally, said, "We need to fight the farm owners to make them give us more money." To this remark, "Amos" responded,

> We can't forget that everything we do must be for our families. We have to make sure our kids have food to eat. Twenty-five cents isn't much, but at least we can buy food with it. If we go to jail or get kicked out of California, who will look after our families?

Teaching the Patriarch Archetype With Literature

It is not uncommon in high schools to find just about anyone teaching reading. Thankfully, this arrangement does not always have unfortunate consequences. Emory, the basketball coach and reading teacher in a midsize, racially mixed high school, has been able to help young people, especially males, approach reading with new enthusiasm. He does this in two critical ways: (1) by saturating his students with reading material and (2) by emphasizing the importance of boys as readers.

One book he reads with his students is Walter Dean Myers's (1999) *Hoops*. He knew that this book would be a hit from the moment he discovered it. After all, nearly all his male basketball players find themselves in his reading class. Many of the female "roundballers" are also in one of Emory's classes. First and foremost for Emory is finding reading material that his students will want to read and are likely to have success with given his supportive instruction. One of Emory's biggest goals is to supply his students with a steady diet of literature that provides them with adolescent and adult models worthy of emulation.

Lonnie, the central character in *Hoops*, is an outstanding basketball player who is befriended by Cal Abbot, a former professional player who is now a high school coach. When readers meet Cal, he has fallen from glory because of his involvement in a point-shaving scandal. As a coach, he dedicates himself to helping other promising young athletes avoid his mistakes. The story climaxes when Lonnie discovers that bookies have been pressuring Cal to bench Lonnie to ensure that his team will lose the tournament championship. As seconds dissolve at the end of the crucial game, both the reader and Lonnie wonder whether Cal has, once again, succumbed to the allure of easy money. In a display of patriarchal self-sacrifice, however, Cal repudiates his dishonorable past and sends Lonnie in to help win the game.

Many of Emory's black and Hispanic American basketball players do not live with their biological parents. Their families and community offer limited examples of men who honor their paternal responsibilities; therefore, Emory designed class strategies meant to emphasize the positive qualities of Cal Abbot, the principal adult male in *Hoops*. Some of Emory's class activities are described in the following section.

Ideas for Using the Patriarch Archetype

As they read the book, students kept a list of the ways in which Cal acts with Lonnie that are similar to how they would have wanted Lonnie's real father to act. (Lonnie was raised by his mother.) At the book's conclusion, students referred to this list to write letters to Cal, praising him for mentoring Lonnie. One student's letter read,

Dear Mr. Abbot:
Thanks for helping Lonnie reach his dream of being a basketball champion. He couldn't have done it without you. You told him to stay away from drugs

and alcohol. And you coached him on what it is really like to be a big-time player. At the end you showed Lonnie that you don't have to cheat to win.

Your friend,

Elton

Students also rewrote parts of the story into short scenes and in small groups presented them in a Readers Theatre format. Two students reenacted the last couple of minutes of the championship game. Another group acted out the scene when Cal talks to Lonnie about how professional basketball is high-pressure and how it requires more than just skill. A third group presented the conversation between Lonnie and his girlfriend, Mary Ann, as they talk about making it out of the projects.

Another activity the students participated in involved identifying men on television who had similar archetypal qualities to Cal Abbot and explaining *why*. Among the television men who the students said "were not superhuman" but were good role models for their sons and daughters were Frank Taylor (from the short-lived CW4Kids series *Kamen Rider Dragon Knight*) and Noah Bennet (from the NBC drama *Heroes*). The students said these men demonstrated the capability of honoring patriarchal responsibility.

Teaching the King Archetype With Literature

In an alternative high school in South Texas, USA, Ruben works with adolescent boys and girls who have been marked for failure. Most of these teens are already well acquainted with the criminal justice system. Virtually all of them have family histories that would make most people shudder. Yet Ruben believes that none of these students are lost causes and that literacy is the key to turning their lives around.

The school operates as a kind of academic boot camp with tight controls over students' freedoms outside the classroom. Inside the classroom, however, because the usual system has not worked for these students, each teacher is encouraged to employ innovative strategies and approaches, especially if they are successful in reaching these adolescents.

From experience, Ruben knows that his students' literacy skills and self-esteem are dismal. In an attempt to deal with these concerns simultaneously, he uses books and literature therapeutically. He has found that reading material with cultural appeal tends to be more successful in sustaining his students' attention. Ruben looks for fiction or nonfiction books that present Hispanic Americans as people worthy of emulation. One such book is titled *Cesar Chavez: Labor Leader* (Seidman, 2004). This simply told biography of an important leader in the Hispanic American community stirs his students' curiosity. The book also sparks controversy among his students because many of them have a heritage of migrants including fathers and grandfathers or older brothers and uncles who spent many hot days toiling in the citrus fields of South Texas. Here are some ideas with which Ruben found success when he taught *Cesar Chavez*.

Ideas for Using the King Archetype

Ruben and his class engaged in a discussion activity called *value lines* (Brozo & Simpson, 2007; Green, 2000). This approach to discussion is especially useful when presenting students with content that evokes strong responses and controversy or when you want students to take a stand on an issue. Ruben began by creating a symbolic line in the middle of the classroom by stretching a long strip of colored paper on the floor from one wall to the opposite wall. He told his students to listen to the statements he was about to read and asked them to move to the right side of the line if they agreed with it and the left side if they disagreed. Ruben's statements included the following:

- Cesar Chavez did the right thing by not using weapons and violence to lead our people.
- Good leaders like Cesar Chavez teach their people to fight with their minds, not their fists.
- When people are being treated badly by government or business they have a right to use nonviolent means to make things better.
- I have the kind of qualities that would make me a good leader of my people.

Once each statement was read, students moved to one side of the line or other. Then Ruben directed his students to face another person on their side of the line and discuss why they agreed or disagreed with the statement. After about a minute, he had students converse with someone across the line to share why they believed the way they did. At different times, Ruben asked pairs of opposing conversants to give their opinions and ideas for everyone to hear. As he monitored discussion, Ruben encouraged respectful disagreements and polite arguing.

Every statement spawned lively discussion in Ruben's classroom. For example, in response to the statement about possessing leadership qualities, Omar told Enrique, his partner across the value line, that because he led his gang in a war with a rival gang to settle a dispute over drug turf, and his gang won, he thought he could be a good leader. Enrique countered that holding on to turf wasn't good for their people if it meant bad drugs stayed in the neighborhood and more kids got hooked. Overhearing this exchange, Ruben did not ridicule this pair of students, but redirected their discussion by asking Omar and Enrique whether Omar's gang activity would have been endorsed by someone like Chavez. By using the value line discussion strategy, students in Ruben's class were able to look more critically at which of Chavez's qualities brought about nonviolent leadership and reflect on the appropriateness of their own leadership behaviors.

Another strategy Ruben employed was the display of additional books that depicted characters from fiction or real life who embody attributes of the King. These books typically vary in level of difficulty from easy (plenty of pictures and photographs) to more challenging (novels and historical biographies). Students were required to make oral presentations comparing and contrasting Cesar Chavez with a leader from the book they read. After reading *Jackie Robinson* (Schraff, 2008), Philipé shared how both Chavez and Robinson

> were told by Anglos they couldn't have what they had. And they both fought hard for their people and for respect. Robinson was black and Chavez was Mexican but the people looked up to them. After Robinson, black people could play baseball with white people. After Chavez, Mexicans had more rights.

Lupé, one of the more accomplished readers in Ruben's class, took on a much longer biography—*The Tall Mexican: The Life of Hank Aguirre All-Star Pitcher, Businessman, Humanitarian* (Copley, 2000). Lupé shared the following:

> Like Cesar Chavez, Hank Aguirre grew up in poverty. He had to make thousands of tortillas every day for his father's little restaurant. This must have given him a strong arm because he became a great pitcher. Aguirre was like Chavez because, even though he got famous, he never forgot about his people.
>
> This guy, Robert Copley, who wrote the book was a good friend of Aguirre, and he told a lot of really neat things about him. When Aguirre quit playing baseball, he wanted to help our people, so he set up a business called Mexican Industries. It made a lot of money, and he gave jobs to Latinos, blacks, and people of other minorities.

Teaching the Warrior Archetype With Literature

As a high school history teacher, Angie notices how the boys in her classes tend to show more enthusiasm for topics involving war. "Weaponry, bombs, blood and guts—all that stuff really turns them on," she comments. "It's as though nothing else happened in the history of civilization." These adolescent interests are likely fueled by the way popular culture portrays war and warriors; that is, war is often glorified, and the leaders are invincible. To help her students, particularly the boys, appreciate the multifarious nature of the Warrior archetype, Angie makes sure that they read about and explore what she calls the "nonwar Warrior." A book she finds particularly suitable is Laura Jeffrey's (1997) *Simon Wiesenthal: Tracking Down Nazi Criminals*. Following is a description of some different ideas she employed with this biography, as well as other books.

Ideas for Using the Warrior Archetype

One of Angie's strategies was to begin each semester in both her world and U.S. history classes by teaching lessons about the Warrior archetype. She found that this allowed her to use literature throughout the study of various leaders and their conquests. Angie also read *Simon Wiesenthal* aloud to her students. She engaged her classes in discussion about the characteristics of a warrior and encouraged them to identify past and present people who might fit this characterization. John said warriors have to be super tough and gave Dwayne Johnson, better known as "The Rock," as an example; Rachel said April Ryan from the game *Dreamfall* was a warrior; and Damien said Tyler Hansbrough of the Indiana Pacers, a U.S. professional basketball team, was the best warrior he could think of.

Picking up on Damien's example, Angie asked the class to consider the qualities that make Tyler Hansbrough a warrior even though his battleground is not filled with tanks and guns. This led to recognition that words like *fight, battle,* and, most important, *Warrior,* have figurative as well as literal meanings. Angie said that a popular movement in the 1960s called "the War on Poverty" could be thought of as a war and suggested that the people who fought it could be thought of as Warriors. Her dialogue with the class follows.

Angie: If we think about the figurative meaning of the word *Warrior*, how does that change our sense of who qualifies?

Derrick: With what you have said, all kinds of people can be Warriors. Like, people who fight for something that's not a fight like in

> the parking lot, you know, like a doctor who fights for a way to cure someone.

Carrie: How about people who try to save animals and nature and stuff?

Angie: I think those examples fit our definition, don't the rest of you? What do you think, Michael?

Michael: African Americans didn't have any rights until someone fought for them.

Angie: So the people who fought for civil rights for African Americans could be considered Warriors, couldn't they?

This kind of class discussion made it possible for students to expand their understandings of the Warrior archetype and its diverse forms.

When Angie finished *Simon Wiesenthal* with the students, which took no more than 3 weeks of reading 15 minutes per day, she asked students to research the life of a nonwar warrior of their choosing. She reminded them of the example Wiesenthal set as a warrior who struggled for justice for himself and others who were victims of Nazi war crimes. Angie also reminded her students that he fought these battles with only courage and moral conviction. She provided students with regular library time to gather print and electronic sources for their research presentations.

Angie had her students present their research using a variety of media and formats. As part of the presentation, she required students to provide a brief biography with pertinent information, such as birth date and place and family members; include at least one interesting anecdote; describe important professional accomplishments; and explain what makes them a nonwar warrior. Students also had to be prepared to answer questions.

Some students created Powerpoint slideshows of their nonwar warriors that included photos, video clips, and even sound of the person's voice from interviews, radio, and TV broadcasts. Others used websites such as Make Beliefs Comix (www.makebeliefscomix.com/) to present their warriors in a graphic novel-type format. Still others chose to present their warrior in a first-person manner, as though they themselves were the historical figures, using simple gestures and props, and behaving in a manner consistent with what they had learned about their nonwar warriors. They could use their scripts but were not allowed to read directly from them.

David's portrayal of Morris Dees, the cofounder of the Southern Poverty Law Center, was exemplary. Standing before his classmates in a blue, button-down shirt with the sleeves rolled up to his elbows and a stylish tie, he intoned with just a hint of a southern U.S. accent:

> Hello, students. My name is Morris Dees of the Southern Poverty Law Center. I was born in 1936 in a small Alabama town called Shorter. My father was a cotton farmer, and in high school I was named the Star Farmer of Alabama by the Alabama Future Farmers of America. When I graduated from the University of Alabama School of Law in 1960, I started a mail-order publishing business and opened a law office. My publishing business was very successful. I sold it in 1969. In the mid-60s, I began taking cases that were unpopular with whites in Alabama. In 1968 I filed suit to integrate the all-white Montgomery YMCA. In 1971 we set up the Southern Poverty Law Center. We don't work for a profit because we want to make sure the poor and minorities get justice.
>
> People always ask me why I gave up a business that was making a lot of money to run a nonprofit center. It came to me one night in a Cincinnati airport. I grew up in the South and every day saw how prejudiced whites were against blacks. I agreed with the Civil Rights movement but was not involved. Then, while I was sitting around in the airport because we were snowed in, I decided to do something to help my black friends. I decided to sell my publishing business and become a civil rights lawyer.
>
> I am a fighter. I don't use my fists and I don't carry a gun, but I work as hard as I can to help poor people and minorities get the justice they deserve. I also fight against racism, neo-Nazism, and all hate groups.

Teaching the Magician Archetype With Literature

"I want my students to enjoy the magic of science," says Terrell, "and one of the best ways to do that is to present the people who made and continue to make amazing scientific discoveries as Magicians." Only a few hundred years ago, the conjurer, alchemist, magician, and scientist were regarded by people as the same. Today, new scientific and technological breakthroughs and discoveries occur with such frequency that all of us, particularly young people, have become immune to the enchantment of science. Terrell's efforts to imbue his students with a sense of enchantment about science involve revealing the human stories behind the science. What everyday forces influence individuals who made and make important scientific discoveries?

When his ninth-grade class was immersed in the study of Newtonian laws of motion, Terrell read *Rocket Boys: A Memoir* (Hickam, 2000) aloud to his students. Homer Hickam used his magic, inspired by the inchoate U.S. space program, to construct his own rockets from the most improbable of launch pads—a 1950s West Virginia mining town. His rocket wizardry led to a gold medal at the National Science Fair in 1960, which is a feat unimaginable for a rural miner's son. This feat is all the more wondrous because of Homer's perseverance in the face of his parents' tense and contentious marriage, as well as his father's dim view of Homer's "impractical" dreams.

This book engaged Terrell's students not only because of its science content but also because of its poignant and inspirational coming-of-age tale, which depicts relevant adolescent themes. Here are some ideas Terrell used to help his ninth graders make connections between the text and their own inner Magicians.

Ideas for Using the Magician Archetype

Terrell asked students to keep a learning log throughout the reading of *Rocket Boys* in which they made daily entries in response to various prompts that Terrell provided. Terrell constructed these prompts around the categories of content-based writing inspired by the SPAWN technique (Martin, Martin, & O'Brien, 1984). The SPAWN acronym stands for *special power, problem solving, alternative viewpoints, what if,* and *next. Special power* allows students to change an event from history or a story, then explain the consequences of this change; *problem solving* poses a problem from the story that students must solve in advance of learning about the actual solutions; *alternative viewpoints* asks students to consider a story's topic, event, or scene from a fresh or unique perspective; *what if* lets students think up new consequences for alternative scenarios that they have been given by the teacher; and *next* urges students to predict what will happen next in a story based on what they have learned or read to that point. For example, one day Terrell's students entered class and were asked to get their logs (which Terrell kept on a classroom shelf) and write a response to the following:

> You have the power to change one aspect of your life to make it more similar to Homer Hickam's life. Write what you would change about your life, why you would change this aspect, and what you think would happen as a result of this change.

Based on this prompt, Eddie's entry read,

> If I could change something about me it would be so I would stick to something. I always start something then I give up. I would change this because I like how Homer never gives up making his rockets work. If I stick with science, you never know, maybe I would find a cure for AIDS or figure out how to end polution [*sic*].

Because *Rocket Boys* is a story about how Homer uses the magic of science to live out his dreams, Terrell created an assignment called "Using the Magic of Science to Solve Problems" to ask his students how they might do the same thing. After forming groups of three or four students, he gave them the following four-part task:

1. Identify a problem in the world that your group would like to solve. No problem is too big, so think big.

2. Formulate hunches about how you might solve the problem. Use your imaginations, and don't let negative thinking block your group's brainstorming. If you can dream it, it may be possible.

3. Research whether your hunches have been tried and, if so, how successful they have been. Identify possible solutions that your group thought of that have not been tried.

4. Describe what kind of time and resources it would take to implement your possible solutions.

One group decided to take on the challenge of finding a cure for cancer. The scope of this problem was just what Terrell was hoping his students would define for themselves with this assignment. In their hunch-forming stage, someone mentioned that he thought he heard that sharks are one of the only creatures that do not get cancer. The idea of investigating sharks for a cancer-fighting hormone or enzyme became a possible solution.

From there, the group members went about gathering information on research that might have been done with sharks. Using the Internet as their principal resource, they found articles and references to research done on sharks' livers by Eugenie Clark in the 1970s, although they did not find more current research than that. The group thought more research should be done because Clark's findings were inconclusive. They prepared a list of resources that they would need to study possible cancer-fighting properties of sharks' livers, including such things as a marine lab, various kinds of sharks, shark biologists, medical and genetics researchers, cancer researchers, and test animals such as rats and primates.

When the group completed their work, the students made a formal presentation to the class. The group members had created a PowerPoint presentation that identified the problem of cancer and its worldwide significance, explained hunches about possible cures, described the results of their research into sharks' livers, and detailed resources they would need for further study of sharks.

In another activity designed to reinforce the connection between science and magic, Terrell invited a local magician to perform for the class. The magician was asked to perform his usual tricks, but be prepared to slow down a couple of them, so the class could see how they were done. Terrell's students were required to think of scientific principles that could explain theses tricks.

Teaching the Wildman Archetype With Literature

To many boys, the name Will Hobbs is instantly familiar. Over the past two decades he has written numerous adventure tales set in the rugged mountain west of the continental United States, Canada, and Alaska. Hobbs's books, such as *Ghost Canoe* (1998), *Far North* (1996), and *Bearstone* (1989), have become favorites of teachers and students alike. Not as widely known to youth, though a writer of true adventure stories that have gripped the imaginations of all who read them, Robert Swan has turned his attention to the preservation of what he calls the Earth's last wilderness, Antarctica. The fictional Andy Galloway in Hobbs's *Wild Man Island* (2002) and the real-life Robert Swan in *Antarctica 2041: My Quest to Save the Earth's Last Wilderness* (Swan, 2009) seek to be one with the natural world and consequently develop a deep appreciation for what it takes to sustain oneself in it. Both embody qualities of the honorable Wildman.

A kindred spirit with Galloway and Swan, Toby spends most of his time in the wilderness each summer. During the rest of the year, however, he is a 10th-grade environmental science teacher. Leanne, his wife, is just as drawn to nature as her husband. Their schedules—Leanne teaches 10th-grade English in the same high school—make this shared avocation possible. Each year they braid as much of their curriculum as feasible, so as to reinforce expanded language and thinking skills and the content knowledge of the students they share. One such shared effort focused on modern Wildmen Andy Galloway and Robert Swan. During a three-week unit, Leanne's English class read and engaged in activities related to *Wild Man Island* while Toby's environmental science class explored *Antarctica 2041*.

Wild Man Island is a first-person account of Andy's struggle to survive on a remote Alaskan island. Andy joins a group of kayakers on an Adventure Alaska trip which he purposely chooses because it will take him near the place where his father died nine years earlier while studying caves for evidence of human habitation before humans had walked across the straits from Siberia. On the last day of the trip, Andy sneaks away from the group to try to make it to the place where he believes his father must have perished but finds himself struggling to stay afloat when a storm carries him far off course and destroys his kayak. He finally manages to make it to what at first appears to be a deserted island and waits in hope for a rescue plane. When a plane fails to show up, Andy must use what nature provides to stay alive. He finds shelter in the many caves on the island and eats seaweed, ferns, berries, and mussels. Andy is not surprised to find bears and wolves inhabiting the island but is stunned when he discovers a large black dog and a mysterious wildman lurking in the background. Eventually, he encounters this "primitive" man who is dressed in animal skins and tree bark and carries a Neolithic spear. Andy learns that in spite of his appearance, the man is well-educated and has an interest in archaeology. Who is he? Could it be his father? Andy's resourcefulness, his respect for nature, and his courage help him to persevere until he finds out the answers as he awaits rescue.

Robert Swan was the first to walk to both the North and South Poles. This book chronicles these and other adventures from his days as a restless youth in Britain in the 1970s to his current efforts to raise concern about and force action to preserve the deteriorating polar environment, as he sails around the world in his vessel, *2041*. Readers learn about Swan's first big adventure bicycling alone across Africa. They also learn how Swan was able to fulfill his childhood dream of repeating Captain Robert Scott's historic trek to the South Pole in 1912. Once he achieved his dream in 1985, he mounted another successful expedition to the North Pole in 1989. These achievements were all the more incredible because he and just a couple other men without radios dragged all of their provisions on sleds the hundreds of miles over rugged icepack and melting glaciers. The year 2041 in the title of the book and the name of his ship has significance because it is when the international treaty protecting Antarctica is set to expire. Swan reports on the work being carried out today as a result of his volunteer recruitment activity, such as gathering and removing tons of garbage from Antarctica. Youth are gripped by this compelling narrative that mixes exciting tales of death-defying explorations of the poles with environmental awareness.

To engage their students in meaningful reading and to help them better understand the importance of a modern Wildman in improving interspecies harmony, Toby and Leanne employed the following ideas and activities.

Ideas for Using the Wildman Archetype

To reinforce text connections and create multiple opportunities for practicing writing, Toby and Leanne created a class blog that allowed their students to compose dialogues between Robert Swan, the polar explorer and environmentalist, and Andy Galloway, the fictional adventurer in *Wild Man Island*, as they progressed through their respective books. Assuming the perspective of Andy, Trent posted this message on the blog.

Are you out there, Mr. Swan?

I've landed on this desolate island in Alaska. I'm soaking wet with no fire and very hungry. How did you survive those long cold months on the polar caps? Maybe you have some tips for me about how to get warm and find food.

Thanks for your help. Andy Galloway

Antonio posted this response to Trent's call for help:

Hey Andy. I'm here. And I want to tell you that after what I've lived through, I know it's possible to survive almost anything. Once in Antarctica a wind storm blew so hard we couldn't put up our tents. We had to curl up behind snow drifts and our sleds and wait it out. We didn't eat for two days. And that was during the summer! As to your problem, when I was riding my bike through the rainforest of Africa, it rained every day nonstop. Everything I had was wet, including my matches, so I couldn't make a fire. I was clammy all the time. Try looking for a cave or even a hollow log you can get into. If there's wind but not rain, you can hang your clothes in the wind. They'll dry out faster. Good luck. Robert.

After reading about Swan's growing concerns for the depleting ozone layer around Antarctica and the effect of climate change on its melting glaciers, Devon made this post on the class blog:

Hello Andy. All wilderness is worth preserving, even the polar environments. I've walked for days without seeing a single animal, only ice and snow. But that doesn't mean Antarctica is a wasteland that can be ignored. There are birds, penguins, walruses, and seals by the thousands on the coast of this continent. They need our protection. And big chunks of the glaciers are falling into the sea because of global warming. What are you finding on your island that needs protecting, Andy? Robert.

Evan attempted to respond to Devon's post based on what he has read about discoveries Andy is making in the cave where the wildman makes his home. He offered this entry:

I agree with you, Robert. I am discovering some amazing things on this island. Did you know my father was an archaeologist? He was an explorer like you, too. He wanted to find out if there were people living on the southern Alaskan coast before people crossed over from Siberia. And I think I've found evidence to prove he was right. I've been in this cave that has artifacts and paintings that must be much older than anyone thought. This island must be preserved and explored by scientists who can figure out how old these things are. The island also has so much natural beauty. Incredible forests, high mountains, and lots of wildlife. So if a bunch of researchers end up coming to this island, they need to make sure they don't hurt the environment here. Good luck with your work to preserve Antarctica. Andy

Toby and Leanne also took their students on a field trip to the nearby Smoky Mountains to learn more about the elk repopulation project. They wanted to bring students into contact with park rangers, conservationists, and scientists. Leanne and Toby structured the field trip so their students could gather research; afterward, the students were required to produce reports and PowerPoint presentations on topics related to environmental conservation and job opportunities in that field.

Leanne and Toby asked the students to generate questions in advance for the rangers, conservationists, and scientists. These questions could be related to the elk repopulation project, as well as to general occupational and environmental issues on which the experts were likely to have specialized information and informed opinions. Leanne and Toby compiled the students' questions to eliminate redundancy and organize them into logical clusters. This approach makes efficient use of everyone's time and avoids random topic-hopping.

During their trip and after their return, students also were required to answer questions about the elk repopulation project from Robert Swan's point of view. For example, Leanne and Toby asked the following:

How would he feel about this project?

What problems would he expect with such a project, and are they similar to those of the actual project?

What role would Swan want in the project?

Students kept all their notes and written responses in a science log, which they took on the field trip. The logs are spiral-bound notebooks with personalized covers; they were stored in Toby's classroom. Students responded to writing prompts every day either before or after a lesson. They dated these responses and made sure to write the prompt as well.

The final activity that Toby and Leanne created was based on their ability to combine their classes for occasional group activities. One of these activities was a mock trial based on the following premise: Wildmen like Andy and Robert have an important role to play in modern society. Toby's class was required to defend this position; Leanne's class had to disprove it. Students developed arguments, identified lead counsels and legal teams, obtained witnesses, and role-played a jury that rendered a verdict.

Attorneys for the opposition argued that Wildmen like Swan are out of touch with what most people want. Wildmen are free to do whatever they wish, these lawyers argued, but they do not have the right to pretend that they are better than everyone else, and they do not know what is best for others. To bolster their case, the lawyers questioned a student who role-played a scientist, who reported that many of the claims of environmental degradation are exaggerated.

In defense of Wildmen like Swan, defense attorneys argued that important discoveries in nature, such as certain medicines and findings about human history, like those Andy and his father discovered, would be missed without them. They also argued that new ideas emerge by questioning the way things have always been done. To support these assertions, the lawyers introduced a witness (a student dressed in outdoor attire) who offered impassioned oratory on behalf of the animals and the trees. The witness made it clear that humans are connected to all living things and reminded everyone that people like Swan and other field scientists who braved the bleak wilderness of the southern icecap discovered the gaping hole in the ozone layer. That discovery by Wildmen has led to serious international attention to ways of preventing further deterioration of the ozone layer and preservation of the last real wilderness on Earth.

Teaching the Healer Archetype With Literature

Peg made a very deliberate decision to introduce her 11th graders to Robert Lipsyte's (1992) *The Chemo Kid*. After fighting a successful battle against leukemia, Peg found that Fred Bauer's fictional struggle to overcome cancer resonated with hers. Peg's English literature class is structured around American themes such as multiculturalism, human rights, and biodiversity. One of her favorite themes is American archetypes. While recuperating from a bone marrow transplant, she read many books about healing. With this reading came the realization that the Healer archetype—one not previously explored in her curriculum—had been expressed in a variety of forms in U.S. literature (for instance, in Walt Whitman's *Memoranda During the War* and in William Gibson's play about Helen Keller's teacher Anne Sullivan, *The Miracle Worker*). Peg's search for a young adult book that featured the Healer archetype led to her discovery of *The Chemo Kid*, a contemporary tale of healing from the point of view of a young man, who happens to be in the same grade as her own students. To her delight, it proved to be a real hit with the students.

Although this intriguing novel is inherently appealing to adolescents, Peg made the power of the Healer archetype the focus of the students' examination of *The Chemo Kid*. Following is a sampling of Peg's ideas.

Ideas for Using the Healer Archetype

To introduce the archetype, Peg had her students fill out and discuss an "opinionnaire." An opinionnaire comprises declarative statements centered on a critical concept, such as friendship, technology, or in this case, healing. Peg's students responded to each statement using a format ranging from "strongly agree" to "strongly disagree." A "maybe" or "not sure" option was not included because Peg had found that many students chose it as an easy way out. White and Johnson (2001) discovered that opinionnaires are highly beneficial in furthering the goals of readiness for learning. When their readiness potential is fully exploited, opinionnaires can activate and build relevant prior knowledge for specific topics, build interest in and motivation to learn more about a particular topic, and help students set meaningful purposes for reading and learning. See Figure 1 for the opinionnaire that Peg used to introduce the Healer archetype.

When students finished responding to these statements, Peg asked them to form small groups to discuss answers. This brought out many different ideas, experiences, and opinions that reinforced, extended, and challenged the students' responses. Peg followed group discussions with a class discussion, listening to input from each group and facilitating student-to-student dialogue.

The students' principal assignment was the completion of the Healing Project, which required students to support the healing of someone in their lives (family member, friend, or a person in the community). Peg defined this healing in its broadest sense—making people and their living conditions better. The assignment required that students maintain a journal with regular entries describing how they supported healing, as well as the results of their efforts. The goal of this project is to help demonstrate the potential healing powers that reside in each person.

One student, Gilbert, took advantage of a program at a neighborhood community center for senior citizens where his mother worked. The center enlisted volunteers to visit and interact with severely mobility-impaired or bedridden individuals. Gilbert's mother introduced him to Alfonso, an 85-year-old man with severe arthritis, and the two hit it off immediately.

Figure 1. Healer Archetype Opinionnaire

Directions: After each statement, write SA (strongly agree), A (agree), D (disagree), or SD (strongly disagree). Be prepared to explain your answer.

1. Only doctors can heal the sick.
2. There are people who are not doctors who have special healing powers.
3. It is important to know how to heal yourself.
4. I can help a friend heal by just being supportive.
5. Healing can apply to more than sickness of the human body, such as the degraded environment, poverty, homelessness, and broken families and friendships.
6. When I have a physical or emotional need to heal myself, I can do it.
7. To heal is to make people and living conditions better.
8. Our society is sick and in need of serious healing.
9. Each of us should take care of our own healing.
10. If I had a serious disease like cancer, I could only be healed with medical treatment.
11. I spend time being supportive to friends and others who are trying to heal.
12. If I knew how, I would get involved in projects that support healthier living conditions for others.

Gilbert's Healing Project journal entry reflects his surprise at finding his conversations with Alfonso so enjoyable.

> October 23, 4:30—Healing Project Journal
>
> I had my first meeting with the guy at my mom's work. His name is Alfonso and he can barely walk because of arthritis in his leg joints. I talked with him for almost an hour. I discovered he used to play baseball on a black team in Florida. He told me about meeting Joe DiMaggio and Ted Williams when they played exhibition games with big league teams during the winter. He seemed happy to talk about those days, and I liked just listening to him.

Talking baseball was a good icebreaker, but by his third visit, Gilbert found Alfonso speaking more openly about things that bothered him. He complained about his legs; his children, who he said did not stay in touch; and being a poor man who was dependent on Social Security. Alfonso's reality challenged Gilbert to develop more resourceful ways of healing. Gilbert's entry describing his fifth visit reflects his efforts to be helpful and create a positive atmosphere for Alfonso.

Figure 2. Sample of a Healing Comparison Chart

The Healer	The Chemo Kid
Uses his gifts to make people who are in pain feel better.	Uses humor to improve his own and other people's recuperation process after receiving chemotherapy.
Helps restore all life to good health.	
Is equally concerned with society's physical, emotional, and spiritual health.	Becomes committed to eliminating environmental pollution by a local plant that's dumping chemical waste in the community's reservoir.

November 4, 4:30—Healing Project Journal

Alfonso's got a lot of problems that I'm not able to help him with. He seems to be in pain nearly all the time. He doesn't have much money. And just listening to him doesn't make him feel any better as far as I can tell. I got him to agree to sit in the cafeteria area and play checkers. It's open and bright in there with lots of windows. He doesn't go there too much because it's a long way from his apartment, and he doesn't have a meal plan because he says he can't afford it. Playing checkers seemed to take his mind off other things. He even beat me a couple of times. That made him feel pretty good.

Although the journal was a requirement, Peg encouraged students to document their Healing Project through other means, such as photographs, audio, or video, to enhance their oral reports on their experiences. Gilbert used several pictures—some of him and Alfonso playing checkers and some of Alfonso by himself—when he presented his report.

Peg also wanted to draw attention to the traits *The Chemo Kid* character, Fred, exhibits that are consistent with the Healer archetype, so she and the students created a large chart on poster board and attached it to the wall. She split the chart into two large columns. The class used the left side of the chart to list different ways in which someone might demonstrate healing. In the right column, the class chronicled the progression of Fred's behavior through the novel, noting instances in which his healing powers were applied. See Figure 2 for an example.

Teaching the Prophet Archetype With Literature

Seaward's self-contained classroom for students who have difficulty learning to read is one that other junior high teachers in his building visit

Figure 3. Word Map of the Prophet's Characteristics

often. He is the kind of teacher who decided early in his career to design curricula that was truly special for his learners. Instead of taking the view that his students' academic challenges required him to narrow teaching and learning possibilities, Seaward has embraced the charge from his principal to "Do whatever you can to help these kids make progress." *Innovation* and *meaningful learning* are the watchwords that guide his practice, and using language in all its forms is emphasized.

Seaward spent his teenage years in Detroit, Michigan, USA, assisting his parents in the fight for civil rights and workers' rights. His proudest memory is of meeting Dr. Martin Luther King Jr. at a union rally when he was 8 years old. During Black History Month in February, Seaward engaged his class of nine black boys and four black girls in a variety of activities designed to inform and uplift them. The unit emphasizes Dr. King and his legacy. Seaward described King to his students as the "brown prophet." Seaward filled the classroom with books about King and read several of them aloud to his class, including *Martin Luther King, Jr.* (Pastan & Levi, 2004) and *Who Was Martin Luther King* (Bader & Harrison, 2007 For his favorite book, *Martin Luther King: The Peaceful Warrior* (Clayton & Hodges, 1996), he designed several language and learning activities. What follows are other activities that Seaward used with his students during the study of Dr. King.

Ideas for Using the Prophet Archetype

To help his students recognize the power of Martin Luther King's gifts to inspire people to take positive action, Seaward had his class brainstorm the Prophet's characteristics. While students offered input, he drew a word map on the interactive whiteboard (see Figure 3).

In another activity Seaward demonstrated how students might use two digital storytelling options to present the prophecies of King. Stories for Change (storiesforchange.net/) using Windows Movie Maker, and StoryMapping (storymapping.org/) using MapBuilder and CommunityWalk software are outstanding resources that offer students creative and interesting digital formats for telling stories through video, photos, audio, and hyperlinks while orienting viewers to actual locations where important events took place. As Seaward read aloud from the selected informational books, he discussed critical events in King's life and time, as well as King's ideas and tactics for bringing about racial equality. Seaward asked students to identify prophetic statements made by King, then to consider whether they had been foretold accurately and what had come to pass.

Throughout the month, students then worked in pairs to create a digital story about King's prophecies. They used the Internet to scan for news reports and articles that dealt with issues related to human rights and racial and ethnic prejudice. One pair, for instance, searched for video of King delivering important speeches, such as his "I Have a Dream" address in Washington, DC, and the last one he gave before he was assassinated in Memphis, Tennessee. These clips were edited for statements related to the insights about race relations that Seaward and the class had discussed from the information books. The video was uploaded into the StoryMapping platform, and after each one the students included voice-overs while presenting news headlines that confirmed or refuted the Prophet's predictions. At the same time, they used MapBuilder to situate King geographically at the time of his speeches. The maps could be telescoped to pinpoint precise streets, buildings, and churches where the speeches occurred. By clicking on an icon, a brief description of the location was given, followed by the video and voice of King. Seaward and his aide worked closely with students in identifying appropriate Internet sites and sources, selecting video and sound clips, doing voice-overs, and providing other needed technical assistance for their digital stories about King. Using the interactive whiteboard, student pairs presented their digital stories. Seaward invited other teachers and school administrators to participate in these presentations. Afterward, each student was responsible for answering questions about the format of their stories as well as related questions about King's teachings. Tremayne and Mario created their digital presentation of King, the Prophet, using Stories for Change and included an article headline about the mistreatment of ethnic Uygurs by Han Chinese in the Xinjiang region of China. Their voice-over was "These people are beaten and even killed because they protest against the Chinese government for equal rights." When commenting on their digital presentation, Tremayne said, "Martin Luther King Jr. would be very sad about this, but he wouldn't stand around and do nothin'...he'd do whatever he could to help those people. He wouldn't use violence."

Teaching the Trickster Archetype With Literature

It would seem that some people are born Tricksters. I briefly described Roald Dahl's autobiography in Chapter 2, noting that, similar to many of his fictional characters, he was a habitual prankster. Hideki, a world history teacher, was playing practical jokes as far back as he can remember. When I spoke with him, he recalled with some amusement, if not pride, his best prank. Once, to get back at his Aunt Miko for chastising him for his bad table manners, Hideki mixed pieces of his mother's false fingernails with shaved coconut and sprinkled them on Aunt Miko's Jell-O. When she realized what she had eaten, she coughed and spit her dessert on the dining room table before running from the room.

Hideki's pranks continue. His students enter class every day alert for some new trick or gimmick. To begin a unit on medieval Europe, for example, he walked into class in a monk's robe and sandals, with what appeared to be a newly shaved head. He was actually wearing an actor's wig, but the effect induced considerable laughter and speculation among class members. He passed around a marvelous book that day, which captured his students' imaginations. The book was John Morressy's (1999) *Juggler*.

"The clown, jester, or trickster is a common figure from medieval times," Hideki explained. "His jokes and antics were entertainment, a way of making a living. But remember that more truth is said in jest. In other words, the trickster could use humor to disguise serious truths about royalty, society, religion, or particular individuals who thought too much of themselves." Beran the juggler must use all his willpower to survive the sacking of his village and the murder of his master, and overcome the Devil's contract on his soul. The teaching and learning ideas that Hideki employed in conjunction with *Juggler* are described in the following section.

Ideas for Using the Trickster Archetype

The class designed and published a medieval newspaper titled *Ye Trickster Broadsheet*. The newspaper had columns lampooning politicians and celebrities of today using pseudonyms of "olde," such as King George (U.S. President George W. Bush) and Lady Madonna (Madonna). Other sections

Figure 4. A Venn Diagram That Compares and Contrasts Medieval and Modern Tricksters

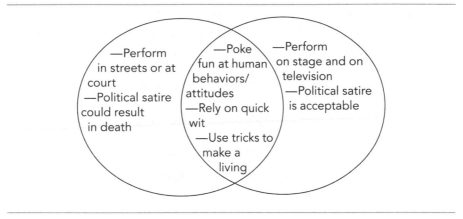

—Perform in streets or at court
—Political satire could result in death

—Poke fun at human behaviors/attitudes
—Rely on quick wit
—Use tricks to make a living

—Perform on stage and on television
—Political satire is acceptable

included jokes, classified ads, cartoons, and "The Trickster Calendar," which gave information and dates of upcoming performances by clowns, jesters, and jugglers. One classified ad read, "Wanted! Someone who can perform tricks, juggle, and entertain with the tongue. Must be capable of telling the truth in ways that amuse. Apply in person at Sir Phillip Funnybone's castle in North London." Another installment of the *Broadsheet* titled "The Merry Prankster Speaks," written by one of Hideki's class clowns, took aim at ostentation and arrogance by suggesting how certain innocent pranks might be employed to remind the guilty of their hubris.

Students also compared modern-day tricksters with those from medieval times. Hideki showed a video of political satirist Mark Russell and played the zany compositions of Harry Shearer. These men combine music and biting wit to poke fun at and raise consciousness about U.S. politics, as well as a host of social issues. Hideki also read excerpts from books (Radin, 1969; Willeford, 1969) that included descriptions of medieval tricksters. The students created a Venn diagram (see Figure 4 for an example) to compare and contrast modern and medieval tricksters.

Teaching the Lover Archetype With Literature

Love is the most prevalent literary theme. For Tonya, finding embodiments of the Lover archetype was not difficult, although selecting just the right book for her class of 12th-grade basic English students, most of whom were male athletes, posed a special challenge. She wanted a book that could hold the students' interest and offer a clear and forceful message of love, compassion, and doing the right thing. When Tonya discovered *Jack and Rochelle: A Holocaust Story of Love and Resistance* (Sutin, Sutin, & Sutin, 1996), she knew she had found the perfect book.

Jack and Rochelle Sutin are Polish Jews who escaped from Nazi labor camps. They tell the terrifying story of how they reunited and managed to elude and strike back at their would-be captors until they were finally liberated by the Russian Army in 1945. Above all, theirs is a story of love in the midst of intolerable conditions, both during and after the war, and while raising their family. The authors weave the theme of love of oneself and others into a gripping narrative of escape and survival. These exciting details engaged Tonya's reluctant readers, and Tonya, with her innovative teaching, made their experience with *Jack and Rochelle* more understandable and memorable. Examples of this innovative teaching follow.

Ideas for Using the Lover Archetype

Throughout the reading, Tonya explored what it means to love. In a class discussion to begin the book, many of her students, particularly the boys, had a difficult time speaking seriously about love or even using the word *love*. When the conversation stalled, Tonya asked students to record personal statements in which they use the word *love*. After the students wrote these in their journals, Tonya asked students to volunteer statements that she could write on the board, such as the following:

Greg: I love Tennessee football.

Tiffany: I love my Mom.

Josh: I love Faith Hill.

Vanessa: I love nature.

Brandon: I love Burger King Whoppers.

Dwight: Christ said to love your neighbor.

Tonya then asked the class to work with a partner and decide whether the word *love* was being used in the same way for each statement. Soon the class was abuzz with conversation. Students began to think seriously about the true nature of love and what it means to love something or someone. When Tonya brought the class back into discussion, the students told her of their revelations:

Josh: When I said I love Faith Hill, I didn't mean I actually love her. It's just that I love her music, you know, her voice and all. That's not the same as loving someone like my mom or grandma.

Greg: I think it's how strong you feel about something and what you're willing to do for it. I love Tennessee football, plain and simple. I'd love to play for that team someday, and I'm working hard now, so maybe that will happen. I love my mom, too. I work hard to make sure she's OK. I don't see any problem with that.

Tiffany: It's like nothing else or nobody else matters when you love something or someone. You'd do anything for that person.

Dwight: Christ's love ain't nothing like loving a hamburger. Those are two completely different things. It's silly to compare them.

Tonya followed this discussion by soliciting ideas about how people can behave in truly loving ways. As a result of the previous discussion and brainstorming activities, her students were able to provide more relevant responses. The list of behaviors the class generated included the following:

• Helping someone whose car has broken down

• Giving a homeless person clothes and food

• Helping the environment, so people can have clean air and water

• Forgiving someone and not holding a grudge

• Working with neighbors to solve a problem

To help her students appreciate the various expressions of genuine male love, Tonya used *Jack and Rochelle* in a way that made it possible for her male students to find connections between the text and their own lives. One activity Tonya had students engage in at several junctures in the book was reader-response writing (Brozo & Simpson, 2007; Petrosky, 1982). Students were given questions such as the following:

• At this point in the story, what aspect of Jack's love for Rochelle did you find most interesting or moving?

• What are your feelings and attitudes toward this?

• What experiences have you had that may help others understand why you feel this way?

Students worked with a feedback buddy during the drafting process. Tonya usually allowed up to three drafts before students were required to submit a paper for a grade. She also encouraged volunteers to share their compositions with the class to reinforce the need for people to connect with an audience when they write. Greg read the final draft of his reader-response essay to the class.

> At this point in the story, Jack and Rochelle are hiding in a swamp. The German soldiers are trying to find them. If they do, they will be killed. Even so, Jack is always showing concern for Rochelle and thinking about what he can do to make sure she survives even if he doesn't (even small things like telling her every day how much he loves her and saying things to keep her spirits up).
>
> This makes me feel good and bad at the same time. It makes me feel good because I think it's neat how much Jack loves Rochelle, so much that he would give his life for her. It makes me feel sad too because my mom and dad divorced when I was little, and I've never seen them in love or treat each other like people who love each other, like Jack and Rochelle. When you grow up like I did, never really seeing my father and mother together, you think it's the way most married people live. Most of my friends' parents are divorced too. But this true book says married people can love each other all the time and treat each other good.
>
> I hope I can be like Jack when I get married. And I hope I can find someone who's strong like Rochelle.

Tonya also reaffirmed the multiple ways in which mature males can demonstrate genuine love by inviting men from the community to speak to the students. These were men whom Tonya regarded as excellent models of the Lover archetype. She began searching for these particular guests by referring to the list of loving behaviors that she and her class had created just before they had started reading *Jack and Rochelle*. She then made her own list of people and various occupations that might fit these behaviors. Ultimately, four male guests were able to speak with the students to recount their unique experiences and answer the students' questions.

Tonya required the students to plan for the guest speakers by creating questions relevant to the speaker's occupation and background. A group of students was also responsible for filming the guests; Tonya granted them appropriate planning time.

The first speaker, Bernie, survived the Holocaust. He began by sharing his experiences in a concentration camp. The spellbound students, having just completed *Jack and Rochelle*, were brimming with questions. Bernie's most significant answer, however, was his revelation that he no longer harbored any ill will toward the people who mistreated him. This illustrated genuine love.

Wallace, a director of a homeless shelter, described who homeless people are, giving these "throwaway" people an identity, a personality, and a history. He went on to talk about how he became interested in helping homeless people, starting with volunteer work at his church's inner-city missionary project and continuing with his current full-time job of maintaining the church's shelter. Wallace told the class that he earned a college degree in hotel and restaurant management, but he decided to follow his calling and put his training to use in the shelter instead of starting a business.

Rodney is a nurse in the Doctors Without Borders program. His sobering stories of disease and starvation, as a result of poverty, famine, and war throughout the world, kept Tonya's students attentive, although uneasy. Rodney explained how a doctor, with whom he assisted in the university hospital, recruited him into the local program. In response to a question from one student about why someone would intentionally put himself or herself in the middle of mass suffering, Rodney replied by saying,

> There's a sense of duty about it. I'm a nurse, so I'm trained to help people who are sick and dying, but it's more than that. There's a story that's always stuck in my mind involving two guys who are talking. One asks the other, "Why did God make so much suffering in the world?" The other answers, "So you'll help ease it."

Rodney's anecdote helped the students understand his compassionate love.

Bryan's experiences as a volunteer firefighter have involved middle-of-the-night calls, smoke inhalation, irritated eyes, and the occasional surprise. Saving lives and limiting overall property damage are the two priorities of firefighters. Bryan made it clear to the class that as a volunteer he also had a regular job. He decided to volunteer because he wanted to guarantee that his family and those of his neighbors were protected in a fire emergency.

Tonya was pleased with each of her guests' unique expressions of forgiveness, generosity, and caring—all forms of genuine love. After their presentations, the men were asked to remain for a small in-class reception with food and refreshments, allowing the students one-on-one interaction.

The teaching ideas provided in this chapter demonstrate that books for teens and preteens that depict positive male archetypes can be used in many innovative ways to foster language development, critical thinking, and an expanded consciousness of what it means to be a boy and a man. The young adult novels, biographies, and informational books in this chapter may serve as entry points into active literacy for adolescent boys, especially those who have become reluctant readers. When teachers help boys find these entry points by using books that celebrate the goodness of the male psyche, they prepare boys for literary journeys toward honorable masculinity.

BOY TALK

Richard, 14, Relives an Experience From Will Hobbs's *Bearstone*

I didn't go to school until I was 8; my parents were into this thing about traveling the country like their Indian ancestors. My parents really were wild Indians. They rode Harleys first, then bought an old school bus when I was born. They didn't have me until they already had gray hair.

I guess I'm proud to be an Indian, but I don't think about it much. I look just like everyone else. Most people think I'm Mexican or something. My hair is black and straight, and my skin is a pretty brown color. Dad says we're part of the Tarahncua, the first people to live in this part of Texas. I still feel different sometimes, not because I'm an Indian, but because my parents are so weird. None of my friends understand me when I tell them I don't really have a place I can call home. I was born in Oklahoma, and I've lived in 14 different states. Before moving here, we were in Florida. Mom thinks we're going to stay here because our native roots are here. I hope so.

I kind of know what Cloyd was going through in *Bearstone* (Hobbs, 1989). He's the same age as me, and he's an Indian, but in a lot of ways we're very different. He didn't have his parents around, and he pretty much stayed in one place out in Utah. My mom says I stayed in Utah for a while, but I was just a baby, so I don't know where it was.

What's really weird is I had an experience a lot like Cloyd's, or I guess I should call him Lone Bear; at least, that's what he calls himself. The part I'm talking about is when Walter, the white guy who owns the ranch, finds out that Lone Bear can't read. I knew just what Lone Bear must have been feeling; that is, you wish you never had to look at another book again in your life or write another word. For me it happened when I went to my first school. It was in Arkansas, and I was in first grade. I don't like to tell this story too much because it reminds me of how much I hate my parents for doing this to me. Anyway, I was a lot bigger than the other kids. Most of them were only 6. The teacher passed out our reading books and called on kids to read. Thank God not everyone knew how to read, but some of the girls did, and they were pretty good too. When the teacher called on me,

I got real scared and thought I might get sick or something. I finally said that I couldn't read without my glasses and had left them at home. She was nice and didn't force me to try. At recess she asked me if I knew how to read, and I had to tell her that I didn't. I felt terrible because, even though I should have been in the third grade, I still didn't know how to read.

That first-grade teacher was never mean about it and always tried to help me, so I learned fast. I decided I would never be embarrassed in class again, so I worked real hard to catch up with the students who were my age. Since I've been in Texas, I've been able to be in the same grade as the other kids my age. I know that reading a lot has really helped me. I like to read after school and at home even though none of the guys I know do.

Lone Bear was lucky to have someone like Walter who didn't make fun of him because he couldn't read. I was lucky to have a nice teacher. Boys need adults who won't make them feel bad if they have trouble in school; they might just give up. I'm not saying I'd rather read than play football, ride my skateboard, or hang out with friends. But I like to read enough that if I have something really great, like *Bearstone*, I'll read it just to find out what happens in the end.

CHAPTER 4

Creating Successful Literacy Experiences for Boys

I would let [a boy] at first read any book which happens to engage his attention; because you have done a great deal when you have brought a boy to have entertainment from a book. He'll get better books afterwards.

—Samuel Johnson (as cited in *The Life of Samuel Johnson*)

A chieving a language curriculum with positive male archetypes is similar to using literature for the purpose of developing other themes and literacy skills. The critical difference, of course, is the choice of reading material used by teachers to expand students' literacy abilities. This is no small matter, however. Evidence abounds that language teachers are more likely to select and use narrative fiction that may be less appealing to boys. Simpson (1996) argues that many language teachers "reward particular kinds of literacy practices which girls take to like ducks to water" (p. 275).

The previous chapter described numerous teaching strategies centered on texts that are likely to appeal to boys—texts with positive male archetypes. This chapter will provide additional ideas, strategies, and suggestions to help teachers make text choices that are better for boys. This chapter is also devoted to establishing guidelines to help teachers identify, select, and develop teaching strategies around books with positive male archetypes. I have peppered these guidelines with descriptions of instructional strategies designed and implemented by teachers to help their male students become active readers. Drawing from my firsthand observations, I share these scenes of innovative and successful teaching for the benefit of other teachers attempting to create similar learning conditions in their own classrooms.

Curricular Guidelines for Teaching With Archetypal Literature

Discover Boys' Outside-of-School Interests

Guthrie (2008) points to a number of causes for student antipathy toward learning, such as lack of intellectual challenge or lack of understanding about how to apply their learning. Teachers who are able to reverse academic antipathy champion classrooms that promote active learning, employ a student-centered curriculum, and, above all, capitalize on student interests. Teachers will never make significant progress eradicating boys' difficulty with reading and learning unless they dedicate themselves to discovering boys' interests and acquainting boys with quality books related to those interests.

I admonish my student interns that it does not make sense to ask children new to our reading center questions like "What do you like to read?" More often than not, these children, who have had a history of reading failure, will have very little to say to such a question. Why? The majority of them would not be coming to the reading center if they enjoyed reading. Students who find reading pleasurable are already good readers and readily talk about favorite books, authors, and topics. Conversely, struggling readers are short on specifics regarding these preferences; therefore, the direct approach to discovering what a struggling reader likes to read may do little more than reconfirm the student's status as a weak reader or a nonreader. An oblique approach to finding appropriate books for struggling readers is better. Teachers, then, should first discover what adolescent boys' interests are outside of school to introduce them— particularly struggling and reluctant readers—to enticing literature. The following sections include strategies for learning students' outside-of-school interests, such as My Bag, companion introductions, interest journals, and interest inventories.

Another "My Bag" Success Story. The Texas Coastal Bend is not known for its beaches the way California, Hawaii, or Florida is. To a hardcore group of young sailboarding junkies, however, the wind-tossed waters off Padre and Mustang Islands offer an undiscovered paradise. Delfino's interest in windsurfing came to my attention when he shared his "My Bag" with me on the night when his reading tutor was absent. At the time, I was director of the reading center at Texas A&M University in Corpus Christi, Texas, USA, which provided diagnostic and tutorial services to children and adolescents from the local community.

I've been using the My Bag strategy for many years as a way of getting to know students. It allows them to showcase their strengths, loves, hobbies, and dreams. The strategy involves placing items in a bag or some other comparable container. (Delfino used his backpack.) The decision-making process used to select items for the bag forces students to think critically about themselves and about how certain items symbolize different aspects of their life.

I began working with Delfino that evening by sharing items from the My Bag that I keep in my office and update regularly. My approach is to take items from the bag and use them as prompts for other students to ask questions. I do this instead of a show-and-tell, to build questioning strategies and encourage students' displays of genuine interest in their classmates. Delfino asked me several questions when I showed my guitar pick, such as how long I had been playing, what kind of music I played and liked, and if I played in a band. He was especially curious about a photo of me running on the beach. After brief conversation that revealed how I try to stay fit by jogging and my fondness for jogging along the Mustang Island shore, Delfino said he knew that beach like the back of his hand. To prove it, he rummaged through his backpack and pulled out a photograph of teenage boys in wetsuits, standing next to their sailboards. Behind them was Bob Hall Pier, a landmark of that beach. Delfino was one of the boys in the picture. What happened with Delfino over the course of the semester only reinforces the power of the My Bag strategy to reveal personal information so critical in matching boys' interests with good books.

Once I found out how enthusiastic Delfino was about windsurfing, I knew the book he would have to read: *Lockie Leonard, Human Torpedo* (Winton, 1991). The remainder of items from Delfino's My Bag did not include a single book or magazine. In spite of his intense attraction to his hobby, he was not reading about it. I probed Delfino for details about his school life, as I do most young adults who come to clinic, only to discover that he could not remember a single teacher ever recommending a book for him to read besides his required reading. This is not an isolated story. I have evaluated numerous reading programs around the United States and have found (particularly at the secondary level where the problem is most acute) that it is rare for students to (a) use school libraries except for required projects, (b) be exposed to alternative text sources beyond the core textbook, and (c) be encouraged simply to read a book for pleasure.

When Delfino returned the following week, I had already decided that I would continue working with him. The anticipation of reading *Lockie Leonard* together, as a way of garnering Delfino's interest in reading, building his comprehension skills, and deconstructing aspects of teenage masculinity, was too much to pass up. I started by asking Delfino to keep a journal to track his responses to our discussions, as well as his personal reactions, questions, and connections, resulting in a kind of "my life–his life" analysis. Before we even began reading, we both responded to the following journal prompt: When do we feel happiest and most in control? I no sooner got these words out of my mouth before Delfino started writing. He wrote the following in a stream-of-consciousness format:

That's easy...for me there's nothing like boarding.... I don't like school that much and I don't like all this football and basketball jock stuff...but I love being on my board...there's nothing like it...you should try it Dr. Brozo...it's like nothing else matters when you're out there.... You know you can get up to 30 or 40 miles an hour...man that's fast and you feel it in every part of you.... But sometimes when the water and wind are just right, you could be floating on a magic carpet...that's the name of my board and rig, you know, Magic Carpet.

I handed Delfino his copy of *Lockie*, which had Lockie on the cover "hanging ten." A smile came over Delfino's face, acknowledging an instant connection with the book's theme. We read the inside cover together:

The sun was almost down as he caught his last wave, leaning and cutting across its orange glistening surface as it rolled toward the beach like the twist in a great monster's tail. It hissed behind him. His hand trailed in the smooth, faceless wall; he tossed his head back and hooted as the whole pitching funnel of his insides shot him down the line. He wasn't thinking of anything. He didn't need to. (Winton, 1991)

I then asked Delfino to compare what he had written with this description of Lockie's boarding experiences. He immediately drew a comparison between himself and Lockie by pointing out how he had written "nothing else matters when you're out there," whereas Lockie "wasn't thinking of anything. He didn't need to." "Only those of us who get out on the water on boards understand what we're talking about," Delfino said. Before we had read the first page, he was bonding with his water buddy, Lockie Leonard. Winton's books have had an equally powerful effect on many boys. Winton (1999) has reprised this character in at least one other novel, *Lockie Leonard, Scumbuster*. Other teachers have made Lockie Leonard books available to their students and have reported on the life-changing impact the books have had on youth (Sanderson, 1995).

As we progressed through the book, I asked Delfino to point out passages that resonated for him. For example, in the first chapter he read to me:

No joke. Lockie Leonard could surf. He was lousy at football. He could be counted on to entirely screw up a cricket match, and he wasn't even any good at Monopoly, but he could sure ride a board. Genuine surf rat.... (p. 12)

Delfino drew my attention to his journal entry again, pointing out how both he and Lockie felt disinterested in popular sports but knew they could handle their boards.

We spent a considerable amount of time each week critiquing other male images in the book. These males included Lockie's father, Sarge, and a variety of "bogans," which is Australian slang for teenage tough guys. We generated a variety of responses with these male characters: We listed their behaviors and qualities; we identified people we personally knew and people we knew from history and popular culture who were similar; and we discussed whether their male behavioral traits were worthy of emulation. Delfino characterized Lockie as wanting to be wild and free, much like himself, and not too complicated. I helped Delfino see that there was more to Lockie than this. For instance, Lockie demonstrates honorable qualities when he refuses to fight with the bogans, escorts his girlfriend away from trouble on the beach, and exercises self-control in the face of his girlfriend's sexual overtures.

When I think back to Delfino and our time with *Lockie Leonard*, I cannot help but reflect on the importance of connecting boys to books related to their interests. The French philosopher Rousseau (1979) says in *Emile, or on Education*,

> Reading is the curse of childhood.... A child has no great wish to perfect himself in the use of an instrument of torture, but make it a means to his pleasure, and soon you will not be able to keep him from it.... Present interest, that is the motive power, the only motive power that takes us far and safely. (p. 213)

Delfino, the adolescent boy who had equated reading to torture, became reacquainted with books after being introduced to the kindred spirit Lockie Leonard. Delfino also discovered honesty, humility, and innocence in this fictional Wildman—admirable qualities that he thought worthy of imitation.

Delfino's final journal entry epitomizes the power of books with characters and themes that interest the male reader. Delfino constantly mentioned how he was more eager to read *Lockie* each week than any other book he had ever encountered. This permeates his final response to the book:

> I still don't like to read much...but after Lockie Leonard, I like it more than I used to. This was the best book I ever read in my life. It was so cool to read about someone that was a lot like me. Lockie never made a big deal about how much he loved surfing and how good he was at it, but kids gave him a hard time anyway. Only my friends know I windsurf. Even my p.e. [physical education] coach thinks I'm no good at any sport...he hasn't seen me on the bay. I wish teachers would let students read stuff they're interested in. If when I was a kid teachers let me read books about surfing and stuff I think I would be a better reader now. I'm going to look for other books about

surfing and also tell our librarian to get books on surfing. The next book I'm going to read is the other Lockie Leonard book.

I have shared my experiences with Delfino to demonstrate how I selected *Lockie Leonard, Human Torpedo* through the My Bag strategy. Delfino's mother had already told me that he disliked reading, had low grades in English and most of his other classes, and did not read for pleasure. To have asked Delfino what he likes to read would have yielded nothing. With the My Bag strategy, however, I discovered Delfino's windsurfing hobby. Only teachers who are concerned about boys' lives outside of the classroom have a chance of successfully engaging them with text, because the texts these teachers choose will directly relate to the boys' life worlds, or lives.

Grouping for Reading Interests Using My Bag. Jared, an English teacher, supplements the My Bag requirement to ensure that he has a permanent record of his ninth graders' out-of-class interests. In addition to assembling bags to share in small groups, students must also make a written list of the items in their bags, with brief notations on each item's importance. After the bags are shared, Jared still has a list of the students' items on file. This allows him to share texts and other readings related to students' interests, or group students with common interests to explore texts related to certain class topics.

Jared's heightened concern for his male students compelled him to find reading selections with positive male themes and archetypes related to the students' interests (as revealed in their bags). For example, Jared formed groups around such interests as low riders (a type of car), football, music, and African American pride. Each group read texts that portrayed real-life or fictional male characters who were somehow connected with these interests.

One group of three black students had shared My Bag items related to their families and culture. Jared introduced this group to the comic and deeply moving novel *The Watsons Go to Birmingham—1963* by Christopher Paul Curtis (1995). Students in this group enjoyed the weird and hilarious world of Kenny Watson and his family. Living in Flint, Michigan, USA, in 1963, Mr. Watson decides it is time to visit Grandma in Birmingham, Alabama, USA. The story of their drive through the heart of the South, at a time when blacks were segregated, and their eventual rendezvous with one of the darkest and most turbulent moments in U.S. history—the bombing by white supremacists and death of three girls in a Birmingham church—made for a riveting literacy experience for Jared's students. Mr. Watson's strength and unflagging commitment to his family left a lasting impression on the three black teens. As stated throughout this book, images of men like Mr. Watson need to be far more commonplace in the lives of many boys of color. Young adult books that display images of positive masculinity for these boys and provide them with concrete, attainable models of honorable male behavior is a combination too powerful for teachers to ignore.

Companion Introductions. In addition to the My Bag strategies, there are numerous ways to discover boys' hobbies, loves, and dreams. The *companion introduction* is another successful approach to learning about students' out-of-school lives. For several years while I was on faculty at Texas A&M University, Patty Walters's seventh and eighth graders had established a buddy relationship with one of my undergraduate secondary reading classes. (Please refer to Chapter 5 for details on a special teaching unit conducted with one of Patty's classes.) This buddy relationship entailed at least two visits per semester to either Patty's school or my university classroom where the middle school and college students participated in joint learning activities. First, students from our classes paired up. To get to know each other and to share what each learned that day in the class together, partners first talked about their lives (family members, pets, role models, personal and career goals, proudest accomplishments, what they do for fun, and what they like most about school).

The unique aspect of this process came when personal introductions were made before the entire class. Students introduced their partners by role-playing one another. For example, when it was Ben and Ramon's turn, Ben sat silently while Ramon stood behind him and stated,

> Hello, I'm Ben. I'm a junior at Texas A&M University. I am majoring in history. I was in the army for three years. I was in Kuwait during the Gulf War. I am married. My wife's name is Roseanne. I would like to have a child soon. I have a dog named Jack. I like football and to fish and hunt. I've been around the world with the Army. The person I admire most is my father. My goal is to be a high school history teacher and football coach. I'm proudest of my military record.

When my partner Noe finished, we changed places, and I introduced him:

> Hi, I'm Noe. I'm 13 years old and in the eighth grade at West Oso Junior High School. I have three sisters and one brother. I have a small dog named Pepe. I love basketball and play guard for the Bears. The person I look up to is Michael Jordan. My goal is to make the high school basketball team and

maybe go to college and play. My proudest accomplishment was scoring 18 points in one game. I like p.e. the best because I can give my brain a rest.

My students and I always had a great deal of fun with these introductions, as well as other activities with Patty's students. Teachers can also conduct these companion introductions to equal effect within their own classrooms and just with their own students. An astute teacher gleans valuable information about students' interests from the introductions. Consider what the class learned about Noe. Knowledge of his fervent attraction to basketball alone offers a link to good reading material to match his interests. Appropriate for Noe would be *Shooting Stars* by LeBron James and Buzz Bisinger (2009), *Matt Christopher: On the Court with Yao Ming* (Stout, 2004), *Matt Christopher: On the Court with Shaquille O'Neal* (Stout, 2003), and Michael Jordan and Mark Vancil's (2006) *Driven From Within*. These books would likely motivate Noe because of their basketball content; they also present real-life sports figures who embody honorable masculinity. In an era when athletes repeatedly exhibit poor sportsmanship, adopt supercilious attitudes, or openly dismiss their responsibilities as role models, LeBron James, Michael Jordan, Yao Ming, and Shaquille O'Neal have conducted themselves with dignity both on and off the court. Displays of these basketball stars' generosity are apparent in their foundations that help disadvantaged children stay in school, provide scholarships that enable disadvantaged children go to college, and supply general relief for children and families in poverty, refugees, and victims of famine. These books demonstrate to boys like Noe that they can aspire to play basketball like the greats but should also learn the value of dedication and masculine largess.

Interest Journals. Another way to gain insight into the life worlds of teen and preteen boys is through the use of *interest journals* (Bromley & Powell, 1999; Wrobleski, 2004). First, a word of caution about journal writing in general: In spite of compelling testimonials that journaling helps develop students' writing abilities (Atwell, 1998; MacArthur, Graham, & Fitzgerald, 2005), using this strategy requires special attention to the unique nature of male propensities. Boys often find journal assignments requiring them to express feelings and emotions much more difficult than their female peers do. If teachers insist on this kind of emotive response only, writing may become a turnoff for boys in the same way that reading has become a turnoff when they are exposed to a steady diet of texts unrelated to their interests (Ivey, 1998; Taylor, 2004; Worthy, Moorman, & Turner, 1999). Alternative response modes are likely to yield a desired level of language production and keep boys interested in writing. It is critical to remember that any text that provides pleasure and engages boys in reading is good because novice readers learn through reading; thus, the same holds true for writing. Boys should be allowed latitude in journaling. If they desire to focus on a story's action rather than their feelings toward the story's characters, teachers should accept it. This does not excuse boys from delving into their feelings to understand characters' motivations for certain behavior, but it emphasizes that language production is the most important goal of journaling. Journaling based on students' interests is an inherent motivator just as reading books and other material related to students' interests is.

Simply defined, interest journals are a form of journaling in which students write about topics that interest them. Teachers who use interest journals often structure the activity in a way that allows peers or themselves to respond interactively to students' journals and entries. This approach makes journaling ideally suited to discovering boys' likes and dislikes. Tonja has been successfully using interest journals with her sixth graders for several years. She tells me there is no better way to get to know her students at the beginning of the year (while also supporting the writing habit) than with this form of journaling. One of her testimonials stands out.

Bo, a diffident, thin, and small boy, entered Tonja's classroom just after the Christmas holidays. His military father had recently been assigned to the local naval airbase, moving from Saudi Arabia to the Texas Gulf Coast. Bo's belongings had not yet arrived at their new residence, so he didn't want to share a My Bag with the class. Instead, Tonja got him started with an interest journal. Within a couple of weeks, Bo's journal entries revealed his fascination with airplanes (not surprising because his father is a navy pilot), computer games, baseball, and golf. Another clue to Bo's out-of-school interests was provided in the following entry:

> If I didn't have to go to school, I would play golf every day. Maybe in 2 or 3 years I could play like the greatest golfers in the world. So far, my dad has taken me golfing about five times but not in Corpus Christi yet. When he gets the time, he said he would take me. I also like golf because I love being outside on warm days. Hitting a good shot and watching it fly is really fun.

Armed with this knowledge, Tonja was able to supply Bo with books from the school library and her own collection, including Jimmy Roberts's (2009) *Breaking the Slump: How Great Players Survived Their Darkest Moments in Golf—And What You Can Learn From Them*, Jerry Roberts's (2005) *Roberto Clemente: Baseball Player*, and Ethan Edwards's (2008)

Meet Derek Jeter: Baseball's Superstar Shortstop. Not only are these books directly related to Bo's interests in baseball and golf, but they also depict men who are worthy of imitation.

Interest Inventories. *Interest inventories* are simple to construct and easy to fill in, making them useful tools for discovering students' interests outside of school. Generally speaking, the easier the response mode, the more likely it is that students will make the effort to complete the inventory. Figures 5 and 6 present two different types of interest inventories developed by secondary reading teachers. The sample inventory shown in Figure 5 asks students to circle a number between 1 and 4. These numbers correspond to the students' feelings toward a given activity. Notice that there is also space at the end of the activities list for students to add their favorite activities. The sample inventory in Figure 6 requires students to complete sentences regarding their activities and preferences outside of school.

Teachers like Hector, who teaches high school reading, survey their students' general interests with similar inventories at the beginning of the school year and once or twice during the term. These inventories give up-to-date information on each student's likes and dislikes. Preferences evolve in the ever-changing life of most adolescents, so that what may have been a

Figure 5. Interest Inventory (Circle a Number)

Directions: Circle the number that matches your feelings about the following activities.

Activity	Excellent	Good	Okay	Not Interested
1. Playing sports	4	3	2	1
2. Watching TV	4	3	2	1
3. Hunting/fishing	4	3	2	1
4. Playing computer games	4	3	2	1
5. Dancing	4	3	2	1
6. Surfing the Internet	4	3	2	1

Please add your favorite activities in the space below.

_____

_____

_____

Figure 6. Interest Inventory (Complete the Sentence)

Directions: Please complete each sentence to let me know what you like to do outside of school.

1. After school I like to _____.

2. My favorite thing to do on weekends is _____.

3. _____ is my favorite sports team because _____.

4. I really think the music of _____ is cool because

_____.

5. _____ is a movie I would see over and over again because

_____.

student's strong interest in September may be a lower priority by April, or earlier.

Antonio, one of Hector's 10th-grade reading students, could not spend enough time talking about bodybuilding during the fall. Hector learned of Antonio's obsession with weight lifting after reviewing his first interest inventory. So when Hector gave a book talk on Chris Crutcher's (1995) *Ironman,* you would have had to nail Antonio's feet to the floor to keep him from racing up to select that book for independent reading. By January, though, bodybuilding had been supplanted by wrestling as Antonio's new obsession. He had had such an enjoyable experience reading *Ironman* that he begged Hector to give him a good novel about wrestling. Hector was eager to oblige and plucked three books from his shelf for Antonio. One, Mark Kreidler's (2007) *Four Days to Glory: Wrestling With the Soul of the American Heartland,* is a story about the biggest high school wrestling tournament in the United States. Another book, Brian Shields's and Kevin Sullivan's (2009) *WWE Encyclopedia,* showcases the pantheon of popular television wrestlers (with whom Antonio was familiar) with colorful photos and short biographies.

Hector's selection of narratives about wrestling, because they would seem to celebrate traditional or even stereotypical masculine behavior, may leave some people uncomfortable. Simon (1987) reminds us that we should respect boys' reading preferences to avoid demeaning their lives; furthermore, when helping boys find entry points into literacy, we should always bear in mind that we had modest beginnings on our own literacy paths. For example, some of the most renowned figures in the United States, from novelists to Supreme Court justices, found entry points into literacy with such "artless" texts as those from The Bobbsey Twins and Nancy Drew series (Cooper-Mullin & Coye, 1998). The point is this: Only after years of traditional print explorations do we come to pride ourselves on our sophisticated and flexible reading abilities. Teachers should, therefore, resist the tendency to withhold what young men desire to read, because boys already filled with disaffection toward books cannot bypass the journey that we have taken to arrive at a point of active literacy and expanded consciousness (Young & Brozo, 2001). Ultimately, no one knows where a young man's first exciting print experiences will lead him.

The other book that Hector gave Antonio was John Irving's (1997) *The Imaginary Girlfriend: A Memoir.* This book tells Irving's own story of college wrestling. Devoid of the smoke and mirrors, loud threats, and bizarre outfits and makeup seen in televised wrestling, Irving recounts his wrestling experiences in pure and vivid images. He captures the atmosphere of the wrestling room and reveals through anecdotes that he and his buddies were not a bunch of "dumb jocks"; intercollegiate wrestlers expend a great deal of physical and emotional energy to be successful. Irving shows the reader how common sports themes such as fair play, graciousness in victory, and cooperation really do apply to life. This is a splendid book for adolescent athletes to enjoy and appreciate for its portrayal of honorable masculinity.

Hector allowed Antonio to do his 6-week project on the similarities and differences between professional and amateur wrestling. On a large poster board, Antonio created two columns. Each column listed information about the two forms of wrestling in parallel fashion. For example, a statement under the Professional Wrestling column read, "Every wrestler can fight any other wrestler." Directly across from this statement, in the Amateur-College Wrestling column, Antonio wrote, "Wrestlers are in weight classes and only wrestle guys in the same class." Antonio's major breakthrough, however, was his acknowledgment of the disingenuous nature of professional wrestling. One of his entries read, "Pro wrestlers never act afraid and only talk about beating the other guy," whereas the other column read, "College wrestlers never brag in public and often get really nervous and sometimes even sick in the locker room before a match." On another line Antonio included the following statements for each column: "Pro wrestlers know how each match is going to go and who will win." "College wrestlers have to be ready for any move from the other guy, and nobody knows who's going to win the match."

How many teen and preteen boys are passing through life without knowing that outstanding fiction and nonfiction books that speak to their interests are readily available? Antonio is one of the lucky ones. Hector made it possible for at least one male teen to be introduced to exciting books directly related to his interests. As a result, Antonio read three books, which is more than what he might otherwise have done. The benefit of reading is well documented in the professional literature; however, the boost to his self-esteem and reaffirmation of a positive male identity that Antonio gained from reading is of incalculable value. The lesson here is that it is essential for teachers to discover male adolescents' interests and involve themselves in an ongoing search for quality texts that will capture boys' interests.

Introduce Books Through Book Talks

Using the titles listed in the Appendix, teachers should have little difficulty finding books with positive male archetypes within the aforementioned genres. For example, Damien, a middle school reading teacher in a small town, allowed his class to form small groups around a novel of their choosing. He keeps an extensive collection of trade books in his classroom and reads most of them himself. Damien purchases many of his books at garage sales or discount bookstores for a fraction of their original cost. When students forget to return these books or lose them, Damien merely requires a donated replacement of another suitable book.

Damien introduces novels and other books to his students through *e-book talks* and then asks students to create their own. In this way, the students can discover more about a book their teacher and classmates enjoyed by simply accessing the digital archive of e-book talks stored on one of the class computers.

A book talk is a short, exciting glimpse of a book that is, in essence, a way of selling students on a book through a personal introduction. Think of a film trailer as an analogy: The film's most exciting or intriguing moments are packed into a highly condensed advertisement designed to lure audiences into the theater to see it. Likewise, an e-book talk that includes an audio track with an enthusiastic delivery, expressive reading of excerpts, and a cliff-hanging conclusion, as well as pictures, motion, and music, is especially enticing for reluctant readers.

Another powerful aspect of book talks, whether delivered in person or electronically, is that they allow teachers to demonstrate their concern for their students' literacy by reading books written especially for the students. This is no small matter, given evidence that the most common reason students give for selecting a particular book is that someone made a recommendation; that someone is often the teacher (Kragler & Nolley, 1996; Krashen, 2003).

Four boys, two who were football players, formed a group around a book titled *The Heartbeat of Halftime* (Wunderli, 1996), which they found in Damien's classroom collection. The book is based on Wunderli's own experiences coaching his son's peewee league team to a championship even though it was the underdog. The story revolves around Wing, a 13-year-old player on the Mighty Titans, whose football team has the longest losing streak in the conference. Determined to end the humiliation, Wing rallies his teammates to many long-shot victories as they complete their last season together before high school. In the midst of championship fever, Wing's father, who has been his mentor and private coach, becomes seriously ill, forcing Wing to decide what is most important to him. Wing's fight for a dad he truly loves and victory on the field casts him as an ideal Warrior.

As a former student of mine, Damien had become sensitized to the important role he plays for his teen and preteen students. He knows how rare it is for his students to interact with adult men who are also avid readers, so he takes great care to be a role model of active literacy. With this in mind, he took full advantage of the opportunity to acquaint his boys with the honorable displays of masculinity in *The Heartbeat of Halftime*. Damien and the group evaluated Wing's and other male characters' behavior against a standard of honesty and bravery. They also discussed what it means to "fight for a valorous cause." As described in Chapters 2 and 3, Warriors do not need to fight with their hands. Warriors can fight with their minds and hearts to improve themselves and the lives of those around them. Wing demonstrates this power when he fights against great physical and emotional odds.

Capitalizing on the theme of the honorable Warrior, the group created an e-book talk for Wunderli's novel. First, they gathered and created pictures and video to incorporate into the talk. Damien directed them to Internet sites with public domain images, such as Classroom Clipart (classroomclipart.com), Copyright Free Photos (www.copyrightfreephotos .com), and FreeFoto (www.freefoto.com). The boys also used the digital cameras in their mobile phones to take additional pictures and video clips of themselves and their teammates at football practice and during a game. Next, using the notetaking format in PowerPoint the students created a type of storyboard by inserting still and motion pictures in the panes and drafting text for the accompanying narration and other relevant notes, such as about a possible musical soundtrack and sound effects. For *Heartbeat*, they pulled musical segments from the high school football movie *Remember the Titans* (Yakin & Bruckheimer, 2000). Finally, they pulled all the pieces together using Windows Movie Maker software to create the book talk, using an external microphone for talking and excerpting. When completed, the entire e-book talk was only 3 minutes in length, but packed in that short amount of time was an exciting visual and auditory rendition of Wunderli's tale about how Wing and his teammates beat the odds and became champions.

Create a Guys' Rack

A remarkable man himself—born into poverty, he later became a paraplegic from a diving accident and is now wheelchair bound—Kenny is a constant reminder to his seventh-grade students, most of whom qualify for free or reduced-price lunches, that by dint of sheer effort, personal goals can be accomplished. Kenny is also a former student of mine. He invited me to his classroom to see the progress he had been making with his male students by using some simple but powerful strategies that made it "safe" for boys to choose to be readers.

I watched as Kenny maneuvered freely and competently throughout the room while guiding and cajoling his students to higher level thinking with *The Bomb* (Taylor, 2007). He handed me a copy so I could follow along with the class. As students were reading and discussing the action, I noticed the initials G.R. printed on my book's spine. When we finished that day's chapter, students dispersed throughout the room to work on projects, discuss compositions with the teacher, or find a comfortable spot for reading. I wandered to the long bookshelf at the side of the room and began perusing titles when I found what the initials on my book stood for. Three full shelves of paperback novels, nonfiction, informational books, and magazines were in a section labeled "Guys' Rack." I saw a couple of boys walk directly to these shelves, select a book, and flop down on a beanbag to read. I also saw at least one girl do the same thing.

I later pressed Kenny for information about these books. He told me that when he began teaching three years earlier, his male students were rarely self-selecting books because of fear of ridicule. If a boy chose something that other boys deemed a "girl's book," the book would likely be returned to the shelf, becoming a "pariah" among the males. Fear of ridicule was a powerful incentive for the boys to find "boys' books." Kenny said he wanted his male students to be able to select books without fear, so he decided to label certain books as just for boys. These became the books that formed the Guys' Rack. Boys in his classes now have no doubt which books are likely to be more interesting to them; however, neither males nor females are discouraged from choosing reading material from anywhere on the bookshelves. Kenny's female students do not feel disenfranchised by his system because they know they are free to read a Guys' Rack book as well.

To confirm Kenny's description of his male students' new attitudes about self-selecting books, I talked with 12-year-old Evan after watching him choose a magazine from the Guys' Rack. I sidled next to Evan at a reading table in the back of the classroom and asked what he was reading. It was a computer game magazine. He told me about his interest in computers and his ambition to become a designer of computer games. In response to my questions about choosing reading matter from the boys' section, Evan said,

> "The stuff I like to read is already in one place on the bookshelf...that makes it easy for me to find things to read. I don't look anywhere else because I know the interesting stuff for me is right there."
>
> "What was it like before the 'Guys' Rack'?" I asked.
>
> "It took, like, a long time to find things to read...at least for me."
>
> I probed further, "Did you ever pick a book that your classmates thought was not something a guy like you should be reading?"
>
> "Yeah, they give you a hard time and everything.... When the books were all mixed up, you know, the boys' and girls' books all together, you didn't know if you had a good book until you read some of it."
>
> "Can you remember any particular book when that happened?" I asked.
>
> "I really like baseball, and I found this book about baseball. When I started reading it, I found out it was about girls' baseball. [The book Evan was referring to is *A Whole New Ball Game: The Story of the All-American Girls Professional Baseball League* by Sue Macy (1995).] I didn't know. The cover said something like 'a new ball game' or 'a whole new game' or something like that, and it wasn't until Lucy, who sits next to me, told me it was about baseball for girls that I figured it out. But then she told some of my friends, and they were passing notes and laughing and stuff. I ended up not reading it."

It is important to keep in mind that even if Evan's decision not to read a high-quality and interesting book about women's baseball leagues during WWII because of peer pressure alone seems to be an unworthy excuse, the net result was one more boy choosing not to read. I have elaborated on this point in preceding chapters, but because time spent reading is linked to reading competence, boys like Evan are likely to fall behind academically (Anderson, Wilson, & Fielding, 1988; Mullis, Campbell, & Farstrup, 1993). The reverse, however, has been shown to be true; that is, people who have a hard time reading can become much more competent simply through voluntary reading in areas of personal interest (Fink, 1995).

Kenny's goal, then, was to create a classroom environment that would nurture interest reading and that would not hinder personal book selection. The Guys' Rack has made it possible for Evan and other male students to find reading matter of high interest quickly and to enjoy books without fear of ridicule. At the same time, boys and girls in Kenny's classroom feel entirely free to find something to read from any of the bookshelves throughout the room. Thus, this important tool for male students does not alienate female students.

Know and Locate Books for Boys

Know Books for Boys. As established earlier and throughout this book, boys need help finding books that are both pleasing and identity affirming. Nicolle (1989) chides his fellow school librarians for their lack of attention to preteen boys' reading needs. He asserts that there is virtually nothing for boys to read once they enter what he termed the "five-year void," which is the period between the ages of 7 and 12. Without apology, Nicolle stated that boys will not read "watered down, insipid, cloyingly sweet" (p. 130) books but prefer books with genuine action, adventure, and villains. Placing suitable books in teen and preteen boys' hands is also one of the goals of education officials in the United Kingdom. Trends similar to those we are witnessing in the United States show British boys reading far fewer books than girls and scoring significantly lower on measures of reading comprehension (Clark & Foster, 2005; Younger & Warrington, 2005). The concern among U.K. officials is that "teachers have not been choosing the kind of literature that would most interest their male pupils" (Hoffman, 1999, p. 12). Teachers have been urged to include in their language schemes "stirring tales which appeal to young boys," so as to avoid the "serious danger of developing the idea that reading is...not a manly undertaking" (p. 12).

I am pleased to report that the volume and variety of excellent books for teen and preteen boys has grown considerably over the past two decades. It is now easy for teachers to find books from a range of genres to match the unique needs of their male readers. Results of surveys and research studies that focused on adolescents' reading interests (Bauerlein & Stotsky, 2005; Coles & Hall, 2002; Gambell & Hunter, 1999; Hechinger, 2008; Hughes-Hassell & Rodge, 2007; Lenters, 2007; St. Jarre, 2008; Worthy et al., 1999) point unwaveringly to the following genres favored by males:

- Humor
- Horror
- Adventure or thriller
- Informational or picture
- Science fiction
- Crime and detective
- Monster or ghost
- Sports
- War
- Biography
- Fantasy
- Historical

Form Alliances With Librarians. I often speak to teachers about how to make reading and writing more lively and meaningful for their teen and preteen students. All teachers, regardless of subject matter expertise, need to be enthusiastic models of active literacy behavior to show their students the benefits and pleasures of reading and writing.

Once, I was speaking to a group of high school teachers on the importance of paying special attention to adolescent boys' reading habits. I displayed and described various trade books that had been found to be particularly appealing to boys, similar to those recommended by Baines (1994), Brozo and Schmelzer (1997), and St. Jarre (2008). Some of the books I shared included the following:

- Stephen Biesty's (1993) *Cross-Sections: Man-Of-War*
- George Sullivan's (1991) *Sluggers: Twenty-Seven of Baseball's Greatest*
- Isaac Asimov's (1994) *Isaac Asimov's Great Space Mysteries*
- James Robertson's (1992) *Civil War! America Becomes One Nation*
- Ron Schultz's (1992) *Looking Inside the Brain*
- Rupert Matthews's (1999) *Explorer*
- Bill Littlefield's (1993) *Champions: Stories of Ten Remarkable Athletes*
- Ted Wood's (1995) *A Boy Becomes a Man at Wounded Knee*

We were situated in the school's library. As I passed around and commented on each book, I noticed that someone had gotten up and was moving among the bookshelves, although I did not give it a second thought at the time. When I concluded sharing these books, a male teacher sitting in the back of the group confronted me: "That's all well and good what you're saying about encouraging boys to read, but we don't have those kinds of books in our school." Before I could reply, the person who had been roaming among the library shelves shouted, "Yes we do," and held up every one of the titles I had just mentioned. The person, of course, was the school librarian.

I tell this story to make the case that a teacher's best friends in the struggle against adolescent boys' aliteracy are librarians. Even in school libraries that have what some might consider paltry holdings, there are always books capable of speaking to boys' inner struggles, hopes, and lifelong goals. I was reminded of this when I toured the junior high school library of a small school district in South Texas and discovered a cache of those wonderful Stephen Meader books (see Chapter 1). These timeless books of adventure are sure to keep most young men riveted page after page. Because of her meager budget, the librarian had devised an ingenious way of giving these books new life. With the help of students, the librarian re-covered the lifeless aqua, brown, and red bindings from the 1960s with enticing laminated collages that suggested the books' themes. Students found that these fresh covers helped do away with the stigma of reading old, boring books.

Because of their vast knowledge of young adult literature, librarians can also save valuable time by finding and grouping material specifically for male readers (Doiron, 2003). Teachers can work with librarians to create special "just for boys" sections in the library, giving male students a place to search for reading material that matches their interests. These books can also be checked out of the library and kept in the classroom, where teachers can provide book talks and make the books available for sustained and self-selected reading. Teachers may also simply ask librarians to order books that appeal to boys by either requesting these books directly or sensitizing the librarian to the need for such books. In my experience as an evaluator of reading programs, most librarians speak regretfully about how unusual it is to receive order requests from teachers despite regular solicitations for such requests. Consequently, any teachers willing to take advantage of this opportunity to shape the character of the library's holdings will likely have many of their reading material requests met. Teachers choosing to act on any of these ideas will form a critical alliance with librarians in the struggle to engage all boys in active literacy.

Use Book Guides to Find Boys' Books. One of the first questions I get when talking with teachers about using quality books with honorable male characters is "Where do I find books like those?" The answer is, from anyone or any source that has this information. Good librarians are perhaps the best guides to finding these books because of their abilities to point teachers in the right directions, find the material quickly, and most important, to make themselves immediately accessible to others. This book is also a guide to books with positive male archetypes appropriate for teen and preteen boys: The Appendix provides a lengthy list of these books and will help teachers, parents, and other concerned adults identify and procure reading material that will motivate males to read.

Numerous other resources are available to help teachers find books that will appeal to teen and preteen boys. A list of what I consider to be the best of these guides appears in Figure 7. Although not all of these guides are specifically for boys, they index, categorize, and annotate a range of books. The astute teacher, however, will find countless titles within these guides to motivate their male students to read.

Invite Men Who Read to the Classroom

How else will boys become familiar with what male readers look like than to observe men reading? As noted, most teen and preteen boys rarely see fathers or any adult men reading anything at all. This situation is most prevalent among adolescents of certain minority groups. In their investigation of the causes for high unemployment and underemployment among black males, Sum et al. (2007) find that black males tend to have lower educational attainment and terminate formal schooling earlier than white males. One of the reasons for this pattern may be the absence of role modeling by fathers for many boys of color (Fashola, 2005; Noguera, 2008; Weber, 1993). Unfortunately, absent fathers are all too common in the black community, according to the U.S. Census Bureau (2008)—55% of all black households with children under 18 were headed by a single female. In large urban areas, as many as 40% of African American boys do not graduate from high school (Alliance for Excellent Education, 2007; Greene & Winters, 2006), and 40% of African American men have problems with literacy (Herbert, 2007; Nagourney, 2007). These disheartening facts clearly point to the importance of male role models in the academic and social development of male adolescents, particularly black teen and preteen boys.

This is why we brought adult men who were dedicated readers into the classroom as part of our Real Men unit at West Oso Junior High School (described in more detail in Chapter 5). These men read aloud from their favorite books and talked about the importance of active literacy. One splendid role model who had a powerful impact on the seventh graders was my former colleague Dr. Malcolm Booker. Here was a black man

Figure 7. A Select List of Book Guides

Adamson, L.G. (1998). *American historical fiction: An annotated guide to novels for adults and young adults.* New York: Oryx.

Ansell, J., & Holley, P.S. (2004). *What do children and young adults read next? A reader's guide to fiction for children.* Farmington Hills, MI: Gale Cengage.

Barr, C. (Ed.). (1998). *From biography to history: Best books for children's entertainment and education.* New Providence, NJ: R.R. Bowker.

Beers, K., & Lesesne, T.S. (Eds.). (2001). *Books for you: An annotated booklist for senior high students* (14th ed.). Urbana, IL: National Council of Teachers of English.

Bushman, J.H., & Haas, K.P. (2005). *Using young adult literature in the English classroom* (4th ed.). Upper Saddle River, NJ: Prentice-Hall.

CheckerBee Publishing. (1999). *Science fiction: A reader's checklist and reference guide.* Middletown, CT: Author.

CheckerBee Publishing. (1999). *Young adult fiction: A reader's checklist and reference guide.* Middletown, CT: Author.

Coffey, R.K., & Howard, E.F. (1997). *America as story: Historical fiction for middle and secondary schools* (2nd ed.). Chicago: American Library Association.

East, K., & Thomas, R.L. (2006). *Across cultures: A guide to multicultural literature for children.* Santa Barbara, CA: Libraries Unlimited.

Follos, A.M.G. (2006). *Reviving reading: School library programming, author visits and books that rock!* Santa Barbara, CA: Libraries Unlimited.

Matulka, D.I. (1997). *Picture this: Picture books for young adults: A curriculum-related annotated bibliography.* Westport, CT: Greenwood Press.

Nakamura, J. (1999). *High-interest books for teens: A guide to book reviews and biographical sources* (3rd ed.). Farmington Hills, MI: Gale Group.

Nilsen, A.P., & Donelson, K. (2008). *Literature for today's young adults* (8th ed.). New York: Allyn & Bacon.

Odean, K. (1998). *Great books for boys.* New York: Ballantine.

Price, A., & Yaakov, J. (2001). *Children's catalog* (18th ed.). New York: H.W. Wilson.

Rodriguez, M., Rasbury, A., & Taylor, C. (1999). *Sacred fire: The QBR 100 essential black books.* Chichester, England: John Wiley & Sons.

Sullivan, M. (2003). *Connecting boys with books: What libraries can do.* New York: American Library Association.

Sullivan, M. (2009). *Connecting boys with books 2: Closing the reading gap.* New York: American Library Association.

Tiedt, I.M. (2000). *Teaching with picture books in the middle school.* Newark, DE: International Reading Association.

Zbaracki, M.D. (2008). *Best books for boys: A resource for educators.* Santa Barbara, CA: Libraries Unlimited

with an exceptional knowledge of science education, who from the most humble beginnings achieved academic acclaim as a university professor and researcher. What Malcolm took the most pride in, however, was his personal and professional habit of daily, regular reading. He exuded enthusiasm for reading books and magazine articles, and provided a real-life example of the benefits of literacy. He was able to establish a special rapport with the African American and Hispanic American students because of his background of poverty, his unemployed and absent father, and his high school and college athletic prowess, which the boys found irresistible because of their dreams of basketball and football stardom.

Although Dr. Booker was raised primarily by his mother and had few male role models, research proves that any adult male role model can have a major effect on black men's academic achievements and career aspirations (Chung, Baskin, & Case, 1999; Fashola, 2005). Teachers, then, need to arrange for as many classroom visits as possible by adult men who embody active literacy and honorable masculinity. These men should come from all walks of life—blue- and white-collar workers, people from the local college or university, members of the clergy, workers from retirement centers, and so on.

Another male role model who I was particularly proud to have as a speaker was Al Townsend, a garage mechanic. I discovered that Al, who had become a friend of mine as a result of the numerous service calls I made about my aging car, had an insatiable appetite for books on virtually any topic. When my wife dropped me off at his garage one day, I found Al lounging in his grease-smeared, although commodious, old office chair reading David Guterson's (1995) *Snow Falling on Cedars*. We immediately fell into a long conversation about our mutual love of reading, finding we shared many interests in authors and genres. As we talked, I began to notice, among auto parts, tools, and engines in various stages of repair, numerous paperback and hardbound books. His loft above the shop was a veritable archive of literature he "simply couldn't part with." In our seventh-grade classroom, Al read from one of his favorite science fiction novels, *Lathe of Heaven* by Ursula LeGuin (1997), and said that his modest means as an auto mechanic did not prevent him from taking joyous flights of imagination through books. He said, "Reading, for me, turns my hot, greasy shop into a cool, fresh garden." Enough said!

It has been said that creativity cannot be taught. I'm not sure I agree. I do know that some teachers using unconventional methods find a way to engender a will to learn in their students.

The ideas described in this chapter reflect, if not purely original thinking, an attitude of openness about instructional possibilities for enticing boys to engage in active literacy. No one told Kenny about the Guys' Rack; this is an idea that leapt into his mind as a result of serious thinking about the needs of his male students. Patty's companion introduction is something she picked up at an in-service session several years ago, although she was able to give it special expression when used with both the students from the Real Men unit and my undergraduates. The point is this: Teachers who think seriously about their craft find ways to reach students. All teachers who work with teen and preteen boys should be prepared to become nonconformists if necessary and to advocate for their male students' rights and needs as readers.

BOY TALK

Nick, 16, Meets Nick Adams, a Hemingway Persona

Mr. Burns knew I wasn't into the Hemingway (1995) story in our literature book. It was called "The Short Happy Life of Francis Macomber." I just couldn't relate to it. I like to hunt, and the African safari thing would be cool, but the plot seemed kind of silly. It was like a 1930s thing with these rich Americans who don't have much of a marriage and the husband trying to prove he's a big man by killing a lion.

Mr. Burns and I can talk about most things. He likes to hunt too. In fact, we hunted deer last fall during deer season. He told me he was kind of a hippie when he was in college. Not really a hippie, more like a wanderer. He hitchhiked all across the country, living out of a sleeping bag and meeting up with all kinds of interesting people. He said what had inspired him to do this was reading *The Nick Adams Stories* (Hemingway, 1981). He gave me his copy of the book and told me to give these stories a try. He thought I would like them a lot more than the Francis Macomber story.

First off, my name is Nick, and when I started reading about Nick Adams it was almost like meeting someone I knew. He reminded me of Mr. Burns but also a little of myself. The story I really got into was "The Fighter." Nick sneaks onto a train and gets thrown off in the middle of nowhere in northern Michigan. But he can handle it. He has his bedroll, and he knows how to take care of himself in the woods. He's young like me, though, and when he comes upon a small fire and a couple of older guys, you don't know what might happen to him. One guy is a former boxer and talks to Nick about some of his experiences. But his mind's gone and that makes the scene a bit threatening. They give Nick something to eat, but soon Nick moves on down the tracks to get away from the crazy old fighter.

The story seems simple enough, but I got this feeling that it was important for Nick to have the experience he had—almost like when I shot my first deer. You can't wait to do it, but when it finally happens, you feel a little sick and weird inside. The sound of the rifle shot seems to ring in your head for a long time, and you wonder if it was worth it. But you've got to get over this if you're ever going to hunt again. Mr. Burns says hunting is excusable if you don't abuse it and use as much of the deer as possible for meat.

It's amazing how much more I liked these stories than I did the one in our literature book. There's really no comparison. *The Nick Adams Stories* are about someone my age who likes being in the woods and tramping around. Nick is free, young, and not afraid to do things by himself. That's how he's sort of like me. I have one good friend called Jared. Nick has one good friend, too, named Bill Wemmish. I only wish these kind of stories were in our literature book. I think many more guys like me would enjoy reading them instead of the Hemingway story that's in there now.

CHAPTER 5

Achieving a Language Curriculum for Boys: The Real Men Unit

A book must be an ice-axe to break the seas frozen inside our soul.

—Franz Kafka

When we implemented the Real Men unit over 10 years ago, most schools in rural and suburban America were still untainted by gun violence. Sadly, for several decades before the massacre at Columbine High School in Littleton, Colorado, USA, the scourge of violence in low-income inner-city schools had been all too familiar to students, teachers, and parents. It was within just such an environment that we conducted our unit built around issues of masculinity, gender stereotypes, and violence. Our goal was to deconstruct images of the macho male for our impressionable middle-graders and replace them with portrayals of healthy masculinity. To accomplish this goal we believed it was appropriate at times to employ approaches that would leave a lasting impression on our youth, such as using a toy gun in the book talk, described at the opening of this chapter, as the unit got underway.

Since the tragedy at Columbine High, which as you'll see impinged on the Real Men unit itself, new stringent policies to restrict the introduction of guns and weapons in U.S. schools have been instituted. These restrictions often cover imitation and toy weapons as well, so our inclusion of a toy handgun, even to make a critical point about gun violence, would not be possible today. Nonetheless, the powerful effect on the youth who participated in the Real Men unit merited inclusion of the full-chapter description in this second edition of *To Be a Boy, to Be a Reader*.

A toy gun lay in the middle of the desktop. Patty Walter and Teri Placker stood on opposite sides of the desk staring intently and angrily at one another. Fourteen seventh-grade boys and two seventh-grade girls looked on curiously as I read aloud from *Scorpions* (Myers, 1990). The scene was of 12-year-old Jamal, the main character, trying to decide whether to take a handgun, given to him by a gang member, to school.

Jamal's classmate Dwayne, who is taller and stronger, has been goading Jamal to fight him. Jamal knows the odds of getting beaten up are high unless he uses his newfound source of confidence—the handgun. I read just to the point before Jamal makes his decision, and Patty began reaching slowly for the handgun. Then I abruptly closed the book. The students were disappointed; they asked me to read on, but I refused. Patty and Teri reminded their combined classes that this was the kind of excitement they would experience over the next several weeks as we read *Scorpions* together.

The three of us were introducing a new unit that became affectionately known as Real Men. I had just finished a brainstorming activity with the students, resulting in a web of popular images and stereotypes of men, which I had written on the board. We followed that activity with a book talk on *Scorpions*, Walter Dean Myers's gripping, pathos-filled tale of young boys and gangs in New York City. It was the beginning to an exciting critical study of men and boys in today's society.

The unit developed and taught by Patty, Teri, and me was devoted to exploring what it means to be a man. We built activities around the book's events and characters, striving to make the seventh graders more aware of the prevalence of male violence and selfishness. These activities were also intended to help students reflect on their everyday experiences with other boys and men who accept violence and selfishness as necessary features of masculinity. We ultimately hoped that the students would become engaged readers and be more critical of their own attitudes about stereotypical masculinity.

We discovered that careful instruction and interaction with an exciting young adult novel that speaks to traditional male interests helped the boys as well as the two girls in class to become more engaged readers and learners (Brozo & Schmelzer, 1997).

The Students

The four students I highlight in my discussion of the Real Men unit are Ricardo, DeWayne, James, and Shantala. I included a female in this profile to make sure that teachers recognize the value of this unit (and others similar to it) for helping to clarify and transform girls' attitudes toward boys and men. Girls, especially those whose lives are filled with negative male images, are also in desperate need of positive male images. The following students who participated in the unit exemplify the worthwhile nature of our work.

Ricardo is a small-framed Hispanic American boy who was living with his mother, grandmother, and two younger sisters. His father moved back to Matamoros, Mexico, and rarely visited the family. Ricardo and his family lived in a cramped two-bedroom apartment in federally subsidized housing. The apartment complex is notorious for high rates of teenage pregnancy, delinquency, and gang-related crime. Despite this atmosphere, Ricardo had managed to keep himself out of serious trouble, although other boys had begun pressuring him to join their gang. He had a desire to take on the roles of protector and supporter for the females in his life but was still too young and without the resources to really make this kind of contribution. In response to the dream of a better life by Jamal, Ricardo wrote in his journal:

> For my future I want to live in a reg. hous [sic] and I don't know where I want to work. And my dream is to travel around the world.

DeWayne was a tall, lanky African American boy with alert eyes and a wide smile. DeWayne told us at the beginning of the unit that he lived with his mother, father, brothers and sisters. Within a few weeks, however, we discovered that DeWayne had actually been living for some time with a grandfather who was trying to care for all the kids. The grandfather characterized DeWayne's father as a "crack head," although he was eager to figure out a way to move DeWayne and his siblings out of his household. DeWayne's journal response reflected his desire for a carefree lifestyle with no restrictions:

> I want to have a nice car. I would put the top back and wear my shades and cruise for miles and miles. Maybe even right out of Texas.

James was a handsome, streetwise African American. He was the only student in the class whose father, although not his mother, lived with him; however, James's father, a hairdresser, wasn't often around during critical after-school and early evening hours to supervise his son. James told us about coming home from school one afternoon and mindlessly punching the television's remote control only to discover that the television, the stereo, and other household appliances had been stolen by his drug-addicted aunt, who had broken in through a window earlier that day. James's journal entry concerning his future reflected his dreams to become a high roller, surrounded by wealth and glitter:

> My dream is to become a business owner and have lots of money and a lot of sports cars. I would like to live in a manshion [sic] in Las Vegas. The kind of job I would want will be a casino owner.

Shantala was a tall, athletic African American girl. She was 13 years old at the time of our unit activities. Her mother lived in Houston, Texas, USA. As a little girl, Shantala was given to a woman who was not a family member. There was no father in the home, and Shantala does not know her real dad. She wrote the following about her dreams in her journal:

> What kind of future do I want? To be in the WNBA. In a big house. A good job, a job that pays a lot of money.

These four adolescents well represent the attitudes, desires, and life worlds of the seventh-grade classes. They were not unique in the sense that their home lives were not any better or worse than their 12 other classmates. Virtually all experienced the daily challenges that come with inadequate housing, not having two parents in the home, and limited financial resources. These factors, as I have advanced in previous chapters, clearly placed Ricardo, DeWayne, James, and Shantala at risk of failing to live out their dreams. We found, however, that by introducing them to activities and experiences designed to question masculine stereotypes spread by popular media, these students showed remarkable depth of sensitivity and understanding. They also demonstrated a heightened degree of enthusiasm for reading, about males both good and bad, as well as crafting written and oral responses to what they were learning.

The Genesis for the Unit

My relationship with Patty dates back to graduate reading classes she had taken with me several years ago. We discovered a mutual interest in creating learning environments for secondary students that broke the mold. Patty's keen and critical mind, her sensitivity to adolescents' desires and needs, and her vast reserve of active language strategies (rooted in her background in theater) made her an ideal collaborator. Her school had coincidentally been the site of other research I had recently conducted.

Teri had been an undergraduate student of mine, and I had not seen her for a few years until she was reintroduced to me during a teacher inservice workshop I had given at the same school. She had recently become a member of Patty's seventh-grade language arts team. When she showed up in one of my required reading classes for master's students, I immediately recognized in Teri another kindred spirit whose goals were to make learning for adolescents critical, stimulating, and personally meaningful.

By November of that school year, Patty, Teri, and I had agreed to teach a language unit for their seventh graders. Both Patty and Teri were well acquainted with my keen interest in boys' literacy development. They thought this should be the unit's focus because we shared concerns about masculinity and reading. By a twist of good fortune, they were teaching the same reading course in adjacent classrooms during fifth period. The class was for seventh graders who had difficulty reading, and not surprising, boys far outnumbered girls in these classes. By combining the sections, we were able to expose a larger group of males to our readings and activities while coordinating instruction as a team.

Planning the Unit

We focused on the goals of the project at our initial meetings. After considerable discussion we derived the following main thrusts for the Real Men unit:

- Use literature as a catalyst for critical explorations of masculinity
- Critically explore images of violent and selfish masculinity in popular culture and media
- Foster engaged reading and learning

With these guidelines, we got down to the business of fleshing out a curriculum. We decided to devote the last eight weeks of the school year, two days per week, to the Real Men unit, and that it would be taught by the three of us. We also agreed that, in addition to the use of magazine articles, essays, and stories dealing with masculinity, a young adult novel would be used as the students' core literature source.

Finding an adolescent novel that would be just right for these unique seventh graders would take some time. We wanted to be certain whatever we used as the primary reading source would engage the students' imaginations throughout the eight weeks. We were fortunate to be living in a city with a wonderful bookstore specializing exclusively in children's and young adult books. The bookseller, a former elementary school teacher, had been a good friend and invaluable resource to me and many teachers in the area. With her help, we selected Walter Dean Myers's *Scorpions* to anchor the unit. This book was chosen primarily because, similar to our students, the two main characters in the story are in seventh grade, and as one is African American and the other Hispanic American, they were also ethnic matches with our guys; furthermore, the events in the story take place in a Harlem neighborhood, where events are similar to the daily events that take place on the streets and alleys of Molina, Texas, USA. We recognized the book's potential for providing our students with an excellent focus for critical exploration of masculinity, as it is perceived by adolescents of minority groups living in poverty and without fathers or other positive male role models. Here was a book that could engage our barrio youth, while offering countless opportunities to deconstruct the negative images of masculinity within its narrative through other readings and activities. Using a small research grant, I was able to purchase a copy of *Scorpions* for each student participating in the Real Men unit.

Gradually, Patty, Teri, and I began detailing the strategies we would use in the unit. We built our activities around events and characters from different chapters, striving to reveal how mass media, commercialism, and everyday experiences with other boys and men who were poor role models can distort aspects of masculinity.

The next phase of planning involved making decisions about and developing documentation methods to assess the degree to which we achieved our goals for the unit. We agreed to gather data from several sources so we could determine the effectiveness of our project. These data sources are detailed in the following sections.

Responses to the "To Be a Man" Survey

We created the "To Be a Man" survey to have students reflect on statements based on issues and events from *Scorpions*. The students had to respond either *yes, no,* or *unsure* to the assertions about masculinity, particularly violent masculinity, inherent in each statement, then supply a reason for their choice. The survey, given to students before the readings began, served as a baseline for their attitudes on stereotypical masculinity and violence. The results of Ricardo's, DeWayne's, James's, and Shantala's preunit surveys are highlighted in Figure 8.

Teacher Anecdotal Logs

I have been involved in classroom-based research for many years, so I know that it is important for teachers to keep their own record of observations and perceptions of their work. This documentation serves as a reflection on teaching, offering crucial feedback on teacher instruction and student learning. Throughout the unit, Patty, Teri, and I used our own written records of classroom events and our responses to them as a focus for weekly discussions. The process of testing our perceptions against the students' perceptions ultimately led to a deeper understanding

Figure 8. Sample Preunit Responses From "To Be a Man" Survey

1. When a man is being hassled by another man, he needs to fight to get the man to back off.
   Ricardo's response—"Yes."
   Ricardo's reason—"Because the guy will keep messing with him."
2. Men who walk away from fights are sissies.
   DeWayne's response—"Yes."
   DeWayne's reason—"When you got to fight, you got to fight."
3. Men need weapons like knives and guns to show how strong they are.
   James's response—"Unsure."
   James's reason—"Men should be able to have guns and knives."
4. You can't really be a man unless you are in a gang.
   Shantala's response—"Unsure."
   Shantala's reason—"You got to be really tough to be in a gang."
5. Men like to fight because that's just who they are.
   Ricardo's response—"Yes."
   Ricardo's reason—"We're stronger than girls, so we have to do the fighting."
6. Men who go to prison are real men.
   DeWayne's response—"Yes."
   DeWayne's reason—"My uncle knows this guy who was in prison because he killed someone, and he thinks he's cool."
7. If a man killed someone, other men would think he was really cool.
   James's response—"Yes."
   James's reason—"Where I live, you got to fight because people always messing with you."
8. Real men protect their families by fighting.
   Shantala's response—"Unsure."
   Shantala's reason—"If you don't want to get killed there you better be a man."
9. As soon as a boy turns 13, he needs a gun.
   Ricardo's response—"Yes."
   Ricardo's reason—"People know you're serious with a gun."
10. Sometimes being violent is the only way for a man to make others understand he means business.
    DeWayne's response—"Yes."
    DeWayne's reason—"I've seen it."

of individual student behavior, as well as greater sensitivity to classroom dynamics as a whole.

Student Work and Unit Projects

Student projects revealed a great deal about their level of involvement in the strategies and activities that prompted these projects, as well as their evolving sense of masculine identity. Some examples of unit projects included movie posters, scene reenactments, clay figurines with descriptions, life-size posters of characters with descriptions, and a three-dimensional model of a setting in the story.

Compare–Contrast Essay

Students wrote a compare–contrast essay when they finished reading *Scorpions*. It was intended to elicit their ideas about how Jamal is similar to and different from a "real man." As an end-of-unit activity, we wanted to discover whether students could analyze the behavior of a boy who chooses a form of destructive masculinity by comparing it to the expected behavior of a male who expresses his masculinity in honorable ways.

Week One: Introductions and Predictions

Patty, Teri, and I concluded our book talk on *Scorpions* and handed out copies of the book while telling the class that the tragedy of handgun violence is only one aspect they could expect to read about in this novel. After the students had received their copies, they began thumbing through the pages to locate the scene we had just simulated in our book talk, as well as to gain a sense of the book's length. Prior to our book talk, we had administered the "To Be a Man" survey, asking both male and female students to complete it honestly. I present examples of postunit survey responses later in this chapter.

Following the book talk, the three of us explained the goals of the unit. I said we would be exploring the consequences of good and bad decisions through the novel, listening and conversing with guest speakers, writing, sharing, and reflecting. The ultimate intent of the unit, we stressed, was to help the class better understand and appreciate positive aspects of masculinity, so as to guide them in their own decision making about who they wanted to be and with whom they wanted to associate. I told the class when the unit was completed I wanted them to be able to recognize what a real man was. To this statement, James replied, just loud enough for me to hear, "I am a real man." The boys around him chuckled. I did not challenge him.

I led the students in a group brainstorm to discuss their attitudes, perceptions, and experiences related to masculinity. I used the "Television Man" and "Real Man" as the central images for two large webs, which I displayed on poster board. By using television's portrayals of men, I knew it would be easier to draw out the numerous stereotypes of masculine behavior from these media-saturated youth. First, I asked students to turn to their neighbor, discuss what men on television are usually like, and jot down brief notes on these conversations. The class quickly fell into animated chatter about television personalities from sitcoms, commercials, sports teams, and music videos. When I opened the discussion to the entire class, nearly everyone was eager to provide input. Figure 9 illustrates the web brainstorm of some characteristics and images of the television man. James was quick to point out that they "have a lot of money...they gotta be rich." Elton said a television man "always has a good car and a good job." "They're good looking and dress in suits," intoned Maria (to the hissing of several boys). James, in his supercilious and blasé manner, offered, "TV guys are tough; they use weapons like guns and do expensive drugs." Lalo, who often spoke with a sense of higher moral conscience, said flatly, "TV men are disrespectful of women and the law." Shantala's characterization of a television man was, "They immature, they always fighting and drinking, and they players, you know, they mess around on they women." Her last statement brought a great burst of laughter from the guys, although they did not deny that Shantala's perceptions were accurate.

Overall, I was impressed with the class's ability to think critically about stereotypical portrayals of males on television. To contrast these negative images, I asked the class to help me create another brainstormed web (see Figure 10) based on real men. Students were once again asked to talk it over first with a partner before they shared their ideas with the class.

Ricardo began with, "A real man is loyal and honest...someone you can count on, you know, you can trust." These words have special importance because Ricardo's father had broken his promise to buy Ricardo a hunting

Figure 9. Web of Class Brainstorm of a Television Man

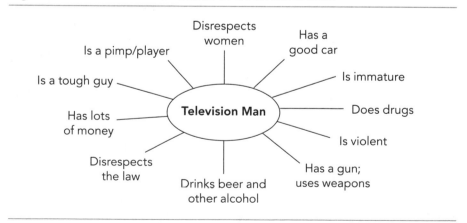

Figure 10. Web of Class Brainstorm of a Real Man

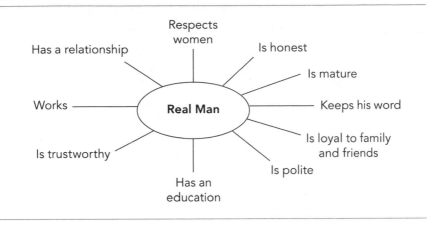

rifle after Ricardo raised his grades. Ricardo's father did not live in the same household with his son and has never been the kind of adult male Ricardo could ever "count on." John, a strapping, brooding 13-year-old who also lives without a father, added, "He's gotta keep his word." Willis and DeWayne agreed that a good man should "have an education." Shantala rejoined, "A good man dresses nice and is polite. He opens a door for a woman, you know, shows respect." "He needs to have a steady relationship," stated James, whose father's womanizing had been a regular source of annoyance for the cool seventh grader. He recounted on several occasions how for each new "squeeze" his dad would bring home, James was expected to act as though she might become his next "mom." Adding a last characteristic of a good man to our web, Tony suggested, "He should be able to find a pretty good job and keep it, so he can take care of his family and have a car." Tony's absent father had totaled his mother's car, which she depended on to go to the store, doctor's office, and the social service office. His father had neither insurance nor resources for acquiring another vehicle.

It became clear to Patty, Teri, and me that the seventh graders' perceptions of the qualities of real men reflected their own negative experiences with estranged fathers and other adult males. Fathers, and even mothers, behaving poorly were all too common in the students' daily lives.

Following the brainstorming activities, I shared a My Bag (see Chapter 4) to give the students a fuller personal introduction. I included items that reflected my traditional interests and hobbies, as well as my devotion to personal and social literacy and my commitment to my family. Students were very inquisitive about each item; while passing around photographs of my daughter and wife, students wanted to know their names, ages, favorite things to do, schools attended, as well as how long I'd been married, if I had any other children, why I had only one, and so forth. The class showed particular interest in the various books I pulled out of my bag. The greatest response came when I passed around a textbook that I had authored. DeWayne was amazed that I had written "such a thick book!" We told students they would have the opportunity to put together and share their own My Bags over the next couple of class sessions, which clearly pleased most of them.

Before the period ended, we invited questions about the day's activities. Students were eager to know more about the novel, barraging us with questions about the characters and the plot. We did our best to respond with answers that revealed little yet continued to pique their interest in *Scorpions*.

At the beginning of the next session, I was greeted by the students with smiles, nods, a "little skin," and letters of introduction that they had written. That night I lay in bed reading about their lives and felt hollow inside. The comfort of my new four-bedroom suburban home, although a mere 5 miles from Molina, must seem as far away and unattainable to them as Park Avenue appears to the characters of Jamal and Tito from their Harlem tenement. The crush of poverty, absent dads, and the dangers and discomforts that come with these conditions emerged from the still awkward hands of our young students' letters. Although heartrending, their stories reinforced the legitimacy of my work with them. Consider how James described the way things are on the streets where he lives:

> One thing I do not like about my neighborhood is everybody is trying to kill everyone. What I mean by this is you can be walking down the road and a car is coming...they will get in front of you and they won't move until you get close to them, and then they will move. Or they would carry guns or knifes [sic] around and threaten you, and the only thing you can do is run.

In her letter, Shantala included what had happened the afternoon and night before:

> I came home and my sister went in my room and pulled everything out of my dresser and my closet and messed up my bed, and I told my mom and she said don't worry about it and they will clean it up and they never did so I had to do it. And after I finisted [sic] I went in the kichen [sic] and their [sic]

were no food left for me, and my dad made it worstest [*sic*] because he came over and it never got better.

Among the items in DeWayne's letter was this small but revealing anecdote from the day before:

I was riding my bike and ran into a car. That was backing up and I hit it and I flew over the back end of the car. I hit the grown [*sic*] hard. Everybody was laughing at me, and they didn't help me up or nothing....

Finally, Ricardo's letter made me realize that the fiction we had created in our book talk is perhaps too real for some students. His words made my skin tingle:

I could relate to this book talk because it happened to my friend. He got shot sitting on the swings in the park. He was sitting on the swing with a gun in his pocket with the clip hanging out, and a gang drove by and saw it...he got shoot [*sic*] with a 357 magnam [*sic*].

The students' letters reminded me that countless boys enter school classrooms each day wearing the psychic and physical scars of their harsh worlds. That is why we allowed the students in this unit the safety and freedom to interrogate their own and others' conceptions of masculinity, look critically at pop culture images of maleness, and consider other possibilities of masculinity characterized by positive archetypal male traits, such as honor, commitment, and intellectual prowess.

We spent most of this day getting through the first couple of chapters in *Scorpions*. Instead of round-robin oral reading, we employed a simplified Readers Theatre, assigning the roles of narrator, Jamal, Tito, Mama, Sassy, and Mack. We had created simple stage flats (recall Patty's theater background) of a cityscape on large sheets of poster board and attached them to one of the classroom walls. Here students took positions for reading their parts while employing simple gestures. We rotated the male roles, so every boy in class had a chance to participate. Shantala and Maria, our only girls, traded off taking on the persona of either Mama or Sassy.

I was surprised to find students enthusiastically embracing their roles. I attributed this to the style of teaching the seventh graders had become used to with teachers like Patty and Teri, who exploited the theatricality of different novels and stories by having students participate in reenactments, impromptu dramatic interpretations, and Readers Theatre.

At the end of the period, students had to summarize what they had learned and make predictions in their journals about the action in subsequent chapters. Ricardo predicted the following in his journal:

> Tomorrow Jamal will probably join a gang. The gang he will get in is called the Scorpions. After he is in the gang he will sell drugs to buy a VCR and get his brother out of jail.

James speculated in his entry:

> What I think will happen is that Jamal is going to pressure Dwayne to join a gang, and Dwayne will. When he gets in the gang, he will start selling drugs. Dwayne will be making all the money, and he won't give it to Jamal. Jamal will kill him and brag about it.

DeWayne guessed,

> The problem will be about selling drugs. I think that Jamal will have pressure to join a gang. I think Jamal will join the gang and take a gun everywhere he goes. Jamal will probably kill someone and then go bragging to other people. He'll end up in prison like his brother.

The students' predictions reflect an uncomfortable level of familiarity with situations involving drugs, violence, gangs, and the criminal justice system. The students projected scenarios for the characters in *Scorpions* that approximated the lives of people who might live next door, down the street, or around the corner. These personal connections with the book's action and themes were what Patty, Teri, and I had hoped to achieve by using this novel. Another reason we chose the book was to have it serve as a reference for dishonorable forms of masculinity; that is, the central characters, seventh graders themselves, behave in ways we wanted our students to evaluate and ultimately disavow.

Week Two: Story Impression Writing and Skits

A strategy I found that worked extremely well with our seventh graders as a prereading motivator for the next chapter in *Scorpions* was story impression writing. Before students gathered their copies of the book, which were kept in a bookcase in the room, I wrote several words on the board. These words came directly from the pages we were about to read, and I asked students to use them in a short paragraph describing what was about to happen in the book. These story impression words helped the students form an impression of the action in the story, and their writing about that action served as a prediction of what they thought would happen next. As students read, they compared the actual events with their predictions. The aim of this strategy, then, is to hold students' interest for the duration of the reading and encourage careful reading.

The story impression words I gave the class in the order in which they appear in the chapter were *Jamal, bet, running, principal's office, Tito and Jamal, boat basin*, and *yacht*. Then, I helped students find a partner and directed them to write journal entries using each of these words. Students got to work quickly and fell into animated discussion with their coauthors as they crafted their entries. When they finished, I asked the students to share what they had written with the class. This gives all students a chance to ruminate on plot possibilities before learning what actually happens. Here is Ricardo and John's story impression:

> *Jamal* and another student make a *bet* for money or something. Someone sees it and goes *running* to the *principal's office* to tell. *Tito and Jamal* get kicked out of school and go down to the *boat basin*. They sneak onto a *yacht*.

DeWayne and James's story impression was by far the most elaborate and interesting; however, it revealed a knowledge about petty gambling and thievery that made me and the teachers uncomfortable.

> One day while *Jamal* was *running* to school he saw some kids in the back of the school rolling dice. They *bet* Jamal $5 that he couldn't roll a seven. Jamal said yes because he wanted to make some money to help his mama pay for Randy's new trial. As soon as Jamal picked up the dice, the principal came. All the other kids ran and Jamal was stuck with the dice. The principal told him to come to the office after first period, Jamal said alright. When Jamal went to the *principal's office*, the principal said you should be suspended for betting and bringing dice to school. Jamal denied it and said the dice weren't his. The principal didn't know Jamal was telling the truth so he suspended him and made him leave. Jamal met up with Tito after school and walked down to the *boat basin*. Jamal asked Tito to look out while he snuck into a *yacht* to try to find something to hock so they could get some money for Randy's new trial.

My goal with this strategy was to create a heightened sense of eagerness in the students to read the chapter. As we progressed through it, I asked students to indicate whether they found corroboration for their story impressions.

When we finished reading, I directed the class's attention to one of Jamal's statements from the chapter. In this chapter, the reader learns something important about Jamal that Patty, Teri, and I decided would serve as a critical source of reflection on how males should behave in the face of taunting. In the story, Dwayne, a tall seventh grader, is egging Jamal on and seems to have it in for him. About Dwayne's persistent harassment, Jamal thinks, "The only way to deal with somebody stupid like Dwayne...was to punch him out" (Myers, 1990, p. 60). We formed groups of three students, presented the students with this quote, and directed them to create short skits showing how interpersonal conflict can be resolved without fighting. Felipé, James, and Maria's skit was typical of the performances by the class. Felipé introduced the scene as follows:

Felipé: I'm asking a girl [*Maria smiles coyly*] to go to the movies with me, and this guy [*James nods his head*] says I'm messin' around with his girlfriend. So....

Felipé: Hey, Maria, you want to go to the movies with me?

Maria: What's playin'?

Felipé: It's a cool new Disney movie.

Maria: OK.

[*James walks up, pulls Maria to the side, and confronts Felipé.*]

James: [*with hostility*] You messin' with my girl?

Felipé: I wasn't tryin' to...

James: Where you two goin'?

Felipé
and Maria: We're goin' to the movies. You wanna come?

James: OK.

When the skit concluded, the class discussed how the three students were able to diffuse a potentially volatile situation by simply including James in their plans. James was angry and suspicious at first but was immediately calmed by Felipé and Maria's invitation to join them. In this way, James could see that Felipé and Maria were not attempting to conceal anything from him.

Another skit, however, was difficult for the class to accept as "something they would do." In the scene, John and Noe meet up after a football game; John challenges Noe to a fight. Noe walks away. John goads him by calling him a "sissy" and threatens to tell everyone that he "chickened out." In spite of these taunts, Noe keeps walking away until John eventually gives up. The male students could not believe the honorable way was to let John get away with his name-calling and threats. Noe best summed up this sentiment when he said, "He don't bother me in here, but if we were on the street, I'd jump him." With that, the two boys engaged in a mock fistfight.

Week Three: Anticipation Guide and Compare–Contrast Activity

I began the third week by taking the class through an anticipation guide for the chapter we were about to read. This strategy involves presenting students with statements related to the text they will read that day and asking them to guess whether the statements are true or false. This strategy increases students' interest and their desire to read the text closely to find support for prereading guesswork. Usually as students read the text, they refer to their anticipation guide statements for possible connections. This time, however, students could amend their initial hunches if they found that they were incorrect, although they had to be prepared to defend their pre- and postreading indications. Figure 11 shows the anticipation guide I presented the seventh graders. By taking a position on each of these statements about possible plot twists, the students were much more focused as we read Chapter 6 and eagerly checked their anticipation guides for accuracy or revision.

After rechecking students' anticipation guide responses in a class discussion, I pulled another line from the chapter to use in a compare–contrast activity of males who make good decisions and males who do not. In the book, Jamal, reflecting on his situation, reveals his sense of despair over the inevitability of a future marked by crime. He thinks, "If you were part of the life they were living, then after a while you did something and the police came and got you" (Myers, 1990, p. 117).

I asked students first to discuss these lines with their neighbors and think about whether people have control over their behavior and whether people (male and female, young and old) have the choice to make good

Figure 11. Anticipation Guide for Chapter 6 of *Scorpions*

Prereading			Postreading	
T	F	1. Jamal and Tito throw the gun into the river.	T	F
T	F	2. Tito shoots the gun in the park.	T	F
T	F	3. Jamal lies to Mama about getting in a fight.	T	F
T	F	4. Dwayne tells the principal about the gun.	T	F
T	F	5. The police arrest Jamal at his apartment.	T	F
T	F	6. Dwayne fights Jamal again.	T	F

decisions or bad decisions. After a few minutes, Patty, Teri, and I led the class in a minidebate. I was stunned to discover how many boys held sentiments similar to Jamal's. For instance, James commented that police stop people in cars just because they are black. Armando recounted a harrowing night when police with guns barged through his apartment's front door, believing the apartment was a crack house. They were all watching television, he said, and he was so scared he could hardly breathe.

We followed up the discussion by asking students to work in pairs to find pictures in magazines of males behaving in both admirable and reprehensible ways. Students made two columns on a piece of poster board and placed their pictures in the appropriate column labeled either "Positive" or "Negative." Not surprisingly, many students included a picture of a man and woman together, happy and in love, as positive. For example, Ricardo and John found a photo of smiling newlyweds and wrote beneath it, "This is a good man because he loves his wife." Lester and DeWayne also placed a picture of a bride and groom in their Positive column with the caption, "Is marrieing [sic] a woman he loves."

Other themes of honorable male behavior that the students chose included scenes of family life where the father is present. The caption of James and Felipé's picture of a father throwing a baseball around with his three sons read, "Good decision because the dad is spending time with his kids." Shantala and Maria also had a picture of a man holding his baby. They wrote beside it, "He is spending time with his child." Lester and DeWayne chose to portray positive male behavior through men who had jobs, particularly those with skilled professions. They glued a photo of a group of astronauts to their poster and wrote simply, "They have a good job." James and Felipé showed a man standing in the foreground with a proprietary look on his face, and a long cotton field and harvester behind him. They wrote underneath the picture, "Has a job and is a farmer."

Negative portrayals of men invariably involved guns and knives. There were several pictures of men and boys buying, holding, and shooting handguns and rifles. One ominous photo on Noe and John's poster was of a big man with his face in shadow; he was holding a pistol and his unbuttoned shirt revealed a long red scar running the length of his torso. They had written beside it, "He been cut so he have a gun." There were also pictures of men in prison garb. Shantala and Maria had a series of faces of infamous men, such as John Wayne Gacey ("He killed over 30 boys"), O.J. Simpson ("He killed his wife"), and even President Clinton ("He slept with another woman").

This activity and the minidebate showed Patty, Teri, and me that the students could distinguish between the media's portrayal of positive and negative male images even though they had been exposed to many negative male role models in their own lives. Like Jamal from the novel, they had definite notions about what constituted positive and negative behavior of boys and men.

Week Four: University Field Trip

This was a special week for all of us. The seventh graders were given a field trip to the university to explore the campus, and most important, to spend time with undergraduates from my content area reading course. The hour and a half was chock-full of activities, readings, and strategy demonstrations that kept everyone excited and involved.

Although only half a dozen miles from the junior high, this was the first time any of these adolescents had been on the campus of Texas A&M University in Corpus Christi. I watched with delight as the seventh graders gazed in awe at the large buildings and manicured grounds. The campus then was actually quite small and, because of hurricane codes, none of the buildings were over three stories. This field trip, nevertheless, was nothing short of an adventure for kids whose experiences are so circumscribed by their families' limited resources.

First, the students were to be guests in my university class. My undergraduate students had been prepared for their arrival, and as soon as the seventh graders entered the classroom, my university students greeted them, partnered off with them, and found a place to sit and visit. When everyone was settled, I introduced Patty and Teri. Patty reviewed what her students planned to do and gave directions to begin the first activity.

We began the class with companion introductions as a method of getting to know one another (see Chapter 4). Each junior high–undergraduate student pair went to the front of the room and introduced each other using the companion introduction strategy.

The next strategy began with the seventh graders assembling chairs in the middle of the room, where each took a seat. James suddenly stood up and said, "Jamal gets the job at Mr. Gonzalez's grocery store." Popping up right after him was Maria, who added, "He works after school and on weekends." She was followed by Noe, who contributed, "Jamal got paid after his first week and was real proud." John jumped up next and said, "Then Indian and Angel from the Scorpions came into the store, and Jamal got fired."

The students were demonstrating for my undergraduates a strategy known as *popcorn review*. Any student can begin the review by "popping" up to state a detail from the story. This detail begins a sequence of events, which entails the next person who pops up to correctly supply the following event and so on. Like popping corn, it is the random order in which students stand up to provide a brief description of the story's next event that gives the strategy its name. My undergraduate students were impressed, and we briefly discussed how they could use this strategy when teaching in science, history, English, and virtually any other content area. The seventh graders invited the undergraduates to take their places and demonstrate a popcorn review of their new learning. The four students in my university class who were kinesiology majors decided to give it a try and showed the rest of us how they could use the strategy to review bone and muscle connections. For instance, the first student stood up and said "radius," the next student said "ulna," the next "tarsal," and so on.

The following activity was the most enjoyable because it combined humor with review. Imagine a group of four students standing in a row in the front of the classroom. Each is wearing a long, white lab coat and a Groucho Marx mask with the fake plastic glasses, big nose, and mustache. Here is the context for the strategy known as Professor Know-It-All. The sight of these students in their ridiculous costumes was enough to ensure that all of us were paying attention. A seventh grader sitting among us asked the Know-It-Alls, "Where did Jamal hide the gun?" With this, the "professors" huddled in consultation, then turned to the class. They provided an answer in a complete sentence with each student saying one word of the sentence, and the last student saying the appropriate end punctuation. To the preceding question, the student know-it-alls replied,

DeWayne:	Jamal
Ricardo:	hid
John:	the
Shantala:	gun
DeWayne:	under
Ricardo:	the
John:	cushions
Shantala:	in
DeWayne:	the
Ricardo:	couch
John:	period.

The Professor Know-It-Alls fielded several more questions before a new team was asked to take over. This form of review along with the popcorn strategy takes a process that is usually predictable and unimaginative and gives it a fresh, humorous twist. By reviewing story content or other subject matter in these ways, students prompt and monitor each other instead of passively waiting for the teacher to ask questions and call on someone for an answer. Giving students the responsibility for review creates conditions in which they can become more invested in the learning process; it also increases their level of engagement with the strategies.

When class concluded, several of my students and I accompanied Patty and Teri's seventh graders to the university student center for drinks and snacks. This extra time gave the adolescents a chance to fraternize with college students and talk about campus life.

Based on residual conversation with the undergraduates and the seventh graders, that afternoon was a rousing success. One never knows the full impact of these kinds of encounters on either solidifying in a 20-year-old preservice teacher's mind that he or she chose a well-suited profession or exciting a 13-year-old's imagination to eventually realize a dream of attending college. Comments made to me by my university class, however, suggested a new resolve about teaching. One of my students remarked, "I really enjoyed those West Oso kids. I know that's a tough place to teach, but it would be really rewarding to work with students like that." The seventh graders also used words like *cool* and *neat* to characterize their field trip to the university campus. Felipé asked me, "You think I could get a scholarship to go there?," and I overheard James tell Noe, "I could be doin' that in six years."

Week Five: Columbine Tragedy Strikes at Our Core

Dear Jamal,

I know your [sic] having some hard times but just solve it not by violence, comprimise [sic]. You don't need a gun to protect yourself; just have God in your heart. So just throw the gun away, okay.

Your friend,
Tito

The preceding letter was actually written by Ricardo after we prompted students with the following question (which we asked them to respond to in their journals): If you were Tito, what would you say in a letter to Jamal about what he should do with the gun? From the time Jamal receives the handgun from Mack, *Scorpions* deals with Jamal's dilemma about whether to use the gun in a way he thinks his older brother Randy would respect or get rid of it. Javier responded,

Dear Jamal,

I'm sorry I'm convicing [sic] you to throw away the gun, but I dont want you to get heart [sic], but now I think you should keep the gun for pretaction [sic].

Tito

With the issue over the handgun coming to a critical point in which Jamal either gives the gun back to Mack and disavows membership in the Scorpions or continues to hold on to it until real tragedy befalls him, we decided the opportunity was ripe for an extensive and critical exploration of gun violence among young people. Just as we were initiating discussion and activities to help the class better understand the seriousness of this topic, Ms. Guerra, principal of West Oso, announced over the intercom, "Teachers and students, I have terrible news to report to you. In Littleton, Colorado, in a high school called Columbine High, two teenagers have just shot and killed several of their classmates and they have killed themselves. I would like all of you to join me in a moment of silence for the victims. Thank you."

The news stunned all of us. It was one thing to use a fake handgun as a prop for our book talk, to talk about gun violence in our streets, homes, and schools, but it was something entirely different to have that reality thrust upon us in such a horrifying way that day. Patty immediately turned on the television. We spent the rest of the period watching the ongoing news coverage of the chilling events in Columbine. In the 10 years since Columbine numerous school shootings have occurred in the United States and elsewhere around the world. And in most cases with just one or two exceptions, the perpetrators have been males (Time Line of Worldwide School Shootings, 2009). An outstanding novel for young adults on this topic that came out after our Real Men unit is Todd Strasser's (2002) *Give a Boy a Gun*.

Patty, Teri, and I lingered in a stupor after the bell rang, and the students shuffled out of the room. We could hardly bring ourselves to talk. At that moment, our lessons seemed so trivial beside this palpable tragedy of horrific proportions. For me, it brought on an uncomfortable, almost eerie feeling of déjà vu. Five years earlier, I was in this same school doing a lesson with a group of eighth graders when Ms. Guerra interrupted class activities to announce the shooting death of Selena, who was perhaps the brightest and most promising Tejano music star ever, and whose parents still lived in Molina, which made her death especially devastating to West Oso students.

Late on the night of the Columbine shooting, I called Patty to commiserate and seek fortification. I wondered if we should not close down shop, if our efforts were too insignificant to matter, if mere words like the Reagan-era mantra "just say no" could ever be enough. Could this really make a difference in the lives of disturbed youth or youth living in grinding poverty with out-of-control adults who could not provide any moral or behavioral compass for their children? Patty finally brought me out of my despicable state of self-pity by reminding me that our seventh graders were precisely the group in greatest need of our message of honorable masculinity. Incidents of gun violence, although increasing among white suburban youth, occur overwhelmingly in nonwhite, economically depressed communities like those where our students and families reside. She also reminded me that gun violence was hardly foreign to our students. Many of our students, like James who revealed the random shooting death of his best friend at the hands of local gang members, were already well acquainted with gun violence, crack houses, gang wars, and deadbeat dads. The Columbine incident would not change that. What might change that, she added, was our work in acquainting boys with positive masculinity to which they might aspire; thus, even if we gird just one young man with the confidence to stay clear of gangs and drugs, we might consider our work to have been a success.

With a new resolve, I began the next class session with a debate activity. The debate forced the students to focus on critical issues related to gun violence. I divided the class into two large groups, giving each instructions to adopt the perspective on their direction sheet and build an argument in defense of that perspective. The different perspectives were as follows:

> Perspective 1—You are a group of owners of gun stores. You have always followed the law, making sure the guns you sell go to people with proper identification and permits. A group of citizens wants to close your store because it feels your stores make it easy for criminals to get and use guns in crimes and homicides. Be prepared to defend your right to operate a gun store.

> Perspective 2—You are a group of citizens who wants to close local gun stores. You believe that because these stores make guns too easy to buy, guns get into the hands of criminals. All of you have had loved ones killed by criminals with handguns. Be prepared to argue why the gun store owners should close their shops or leave town.

We reminded students that the handgun in Jamal's possession could have begun its journey at a gun store, then to a law-abiding citizen, then to a criminal in a robbery, then to a pawn shop dealer, then to a gang member like Mack, and finally to Jamal.

Students were directed first to brainstorm ideas in support of their perspectives by working in pairs. This way, all students were likely to have something to contribute when we opened the discussion to the larger group. We prodded Perspective 2 students to think about what they knew of guns from personal experiences. We challenged students working with Perspective 1 to consider a person's legal right to sell and buy guns, and whether that meant they should be held responsible for someone else's reckless use of a gun. As the groups consolidated their arguments, we asked that each select a spokesperson. Afterward, all students were told to be ready to join in the discussion.

The debate began slowly as each side stated its position. As spokesperson for the gun shop owners, DeWayne said, "No one could put them out of business just because they didn't like guns." He went on to say, "We don't like that people use guns to kill other people, but it's not our fault." As spokesperson for the antigun citizens, James countered, "We don't want to have to put you out of business either, but it's your guns that killed my son, so we don't have no choice." Members of each group angrily joined in after hearing this statement. The students argued over whether guns or people shooting the guns were responsible for murder when guns were used. James even used the incident at Columbine to further his argument for the citizens.

After nearly everyone made at least one contribution to the debate, the dialogue wound down. We then asked group members to spend a few minutes talking among themselves about ways to reduce gun violence, assuming gun manufacturers and shops are not eliminated. Patty wrote students' ideas on the board as they shouted them out. The list of ideas included insightful recommendations:

- Parents should watch their kids, so they do not mess with guns.
- Parents should not leave guns lying around the house.
- Adults should help kids stay away from gangs because gang members always have guns.
- People who sell guns should be helped to make money some other way.
- Kids who bring guns to school should be kicked out for good.
- If kids kill someone with their parents' gun, the parents should have to go to jail too.

I reflected on our students' suggestions for reducing gun violence and wondered if any of them would fall victim to a criminal's bullets. Every day in the United States, children and young adults are killed by guns in homicides and in either purposeful or accidental self-infliction (Garbarino, 1999; Office of Juvenile Justice and Delinquency Prevention, 2006). These statistics rise precipitously in streets and alleys, tenements, and abandoned buildings of our inner cities, where poverty is high, education levels are low, and positive adult role models are scarce—situations similar to the lives of our seventh graders. Further increasing the chances that these boys will become victims of gun violence are statistics such as those cited in the Introduction, which indicate that 95% of all murders are committed by males, and males make up 70% of all homicide victims (Children's Defense Fund, 2009; Garbarino, 1999). Would James, for instance, one day find himself mistaken for a gang member and be gunned down while walking to the park? Would DeWayne awake one morning to find desperate crack heads pilfering his apartment and be forever silenced by a handgun? These are unthinkable notions but always on my mind as I slap hands with the guys exiting the classroom after another engaging lesson.

Week Six: Preparing for the Unit Projects

As we approached the conclusion of *Scorpions*, Patty and Teri began preparing the students for their unit projects. The students' options included movie posters, scene reenactments, clay figurines with descriptions, life-size posters of characters with descriptions, and a three-dimensional model of a setting in the story. Patty and Teri also invited students to propose their own projects, and at least a few students followed up on the offer. For instance, DeWayne asked if he could do an interview with a gang member or crack dealer (people from his neighborhood that he knew) and compare their lives with the life of either Randy or Mack from *Scorpions*. Teri was concerned about the liability for DeWayne's safety if something went wrong, especially if it were discovered that DeWayne was fulfilling a school assignment. I suggested that he might be able to get the information about a gang member through a secondhand source, perhaps a former gang member. DeWayne told us he could ask his uncle who had always said he used to be in a gang. James, meanwhile, wondered if he could match words from popular rap songs to the novel's main characters. Patty thought this was an excellent way to demonstrate appreciation of character and gave immediate consent. Noe, the student in our unit with the most advanced knowledge about computers, proposed a PowerPoint presentation with photos and graphics that covered the main story line. Although not an uncritical devotee of computer technology, Patty did encourage her students to use this medium for creating interesting language-based projects, so Noe's idea was also given approval.

Once Patty, Teri, and I received commitments from every student to do a particular project, we stocked the classroom with necessary resources, such as poster board and paper, markers, variously colored clay bars, shoe boxes, and other material to help students complete the assignment. Part of each class session was reserved for work on the unit projects.

One of the activities the teachers and I used during this time involved revisiting the pop culture images of boys and men. I brought in a dozen or so copies of *Men's Health*, *Esquire*, and *GQ* magazines, Patty collected an assortment of teen music magazines and local newspapers, and Teri gathered photograph books of movies and films. We distributed these sources to students and had them pair up to review them. Each pair of students was given a wide piece of poster board and instructed to divide it into four columns. In the left column (labeled "Male Images"), we asked students to keep a running list of how these magazines and books portray males (for instance, what the males are doing and what they look like). In the second column (labeled "Interpretations"), students were to write what these male images suggested to them (for example, physical strength, control, money, power, violence, authority with weapons, lady's man, and so on). In the third column (labeled "*Scorpions*'s Males"), students were to describe briefly similarities between boys from *Scorpions* and the male images in the first column. In the fourth and last column (labeled "My Behavior"), we asked the students to indicate their own behaviors or actions that coincided with male images in the first column. Before the period ended, the pairs shared their work with the rest of the class.

Exploring media portrayals of boys and men would appear to be an effective approach to take to help young men think critically about how gender stereotypes are promulgated by commercial advertisers. Langker (1995), a teacher of media studies in Sydney, Australia, reports on her success with junior high students as they deconstruct advertisers' images to reveal manipulations of young men. The students discovered that ads were replete with ethnic and gender stereotypes, portrayals of males as sexual objects, and messages that reinforce popular notions of the expendable man (such as fighting machine, soldier of fortune, and so on).

Felipé and Ricardo were the first to share their work with the class. Felipé held up one end of the poster board as Ricardo held the other, and they explained what they had written in each of the columns. The first image of a man in their Male Images column was Clint Eastwood as Dirty Harry, which was taken from one of the movie books. In the photograph,

Harry is holding his trademark long-barrel magnum with a caption that read, "Go ahead, make my day." Ricardo said,

> This is a man who thinks he's tough because he's got a gun. Mack and Jamal think they're tough too because they scare people with guns. Jamal scared Dwayne when he pointed it at him when they were fighting. I shot a rifle when I went hunting with my grandfather. I never pointed it at anyone.

Felipé and Ricardo both said they never shot a pistol, although they had both handled one.

DeWayne and John shared their poster and described an entry across all four columns. DeWayne explained,

> Here's a picture of [NBA basketball player] Charles Barkley, and it say next to him, "You gotta have protection." He so big he don't need no protection, so if you ain't big like him, you gotta get protection somewhere. In *Scorpions*, Mack says the same thing to Jamal when he give him the gun.

At this point, John broke in to say something about the last column. "My little brother, Carlos, was gettin' picked on by these older boys, so I had to walk him to school and tell them that if they messed with Carlos I would get 'em. They didn't touch him after that."

Shantala and Maria, who often worked together as they were the only females in class, had a different take on the assignment. Their poster identified several images of men either driving fast, expensive sports cars or in the company of adoring women. Describing one of the male images on their poster, Maria said,

> There's this man sitting at the table with a real pretty girl and some fancy food there. It say underneath "impress her with do-it-yourself gourmet." We thought this guy is only a player [slang for someone who acts slick around women]...he not cookin' to be nice but to get this girl 'cause she ain't got no ring on or nothin'. He just a phony. We couldn't think of nothin' from *Scorpions* like this, but my mom told me my dad used to do stuff like that, you know, then he left us anyway.

James and Noe found a picture of a man in a red convertible. The man was wearing sunglasses and had a very attractive woman sitting next to him. James explained,

> He was going real fast because the road is all fuzzy and everything, so we thought guys like him have cool cars they can get pretty girls with. In the book no one has any money, but everyone tryin' to act cool anyway. There ain't no girls in there except Mama and Sassy. On my street, guys in low riders act real cool and always have girls hangin' around 'em.

When Patty, Teri, and I had the opportunity to reflect on that day's activities, we agreed that the students seemed to have a fairly critical understanding of the spurious nature of mass media's images of males. Talking about false men is one thing; however, avoiding the everyday traps that entice men to behave in false ways is something entirely different. This is also true for the two females in our class. It might be easy for Maria and Shantala to say to their teachers and fellow students that men who do things to impress women may have dishonorable motives. Will they, however, be able to resist the wiles of an insincere man? Young girls in Maria's and Shantala's neighborhoods are getting pregnant at alarming rates, with little expectation or hope of the fathers sticking around to offer financial and emotional support. What does this say about Maria's and Shantala's futures?

We concluded our reflective session by ironing out the details on the end-of-unit activity—a school party to celebrate positive masculinity. It was only two weeks away. I had made arrangements with numerous male friends and colleagues to attend the party and share their personal feelings about being both men and readers. Patty and Teri were attempting to invite the students' fathers but held little hope that they would show up; after all, only James lived with his dad, and his father worked during the day. Teri would make arrangements for refreshments. Our agenda included teacher introductions, brief presentations by the male guests, one-on-one visits between students and guests, and student presentations of their projects, each of which would be displayed. Patty, Teri, and I also agreed to re-administer the "To Be a Man" survey after the party instead of at the book's conclusion.

Week Seven: End-of-Book Journal Entry

Students worked busily on their unit projects as they finished the last couple of chapters of *Scorpions*. Right after we read aloud the last word of the story, Patty asked students to open their journals and write a letter to Walter Dean Myers, telling him what they had learned as a result of reading his book. Ricardo wrote,

> Dear Walter Dean Myers,
>
> By reading your book named "Scorpions" I learned that life has many osticels [sic] like gangs, drugs, and other things. In the story Jamal is asked if he wants to be in a gang that his brother Randy was in. A friend of Randy's was named Mack and gave Jamal a gun. Just like in this story, I may or may not be asked to join a gang. But I am going to be on track and won't pick the same decission [sic] that Jamal had picked.
>
> Your reader, Ricardo

DeWayne reveals a very different reaction in his letter. His words left us all with the sinking feeling that despite what we had done in the unit, despite the message of honorable masculinity that pervaded the unit, despite the school's intolerance of fights and other violence, the logic of "street justice" may prevail for some of these kids.

> Dear Mr. Myers,
>
> I liked your book. I'm glad you had Jamal keep the gun. Dwayne could have messed with him again. The next time Dwayne might have a gun and try to scare Jamal and then Jamal could just pull out his gun and shoot Dwayne. Jamal needed the gun so the next time he go [sic] to the Scorpions hideout and a man tries to mess with him, he can either shoot the man or shoot at the man's ear.
>
> Your reader, DeWayne

The seventh graders pressed the issue of the surprise ending. Everyone sensed that Jamal's decision not to give the gun back to Mack or throw it in the river would lead to nothing but trouble. Jamal agrees to meet with the Scorpions in a remote area of the park late one night in what seems to be a bold statement, rejecting any thoughts that Jamal will be walking in his brother Randy's footsteps. Despite Tito's entreaties, he refuses to take the gun with him. This leads readers to conclude that if anyone gets shot, Jamal will not be the perpetrator. Two shots do pierce the air that night in the middle of a violent confrontation between Jamal and two members of the Scorpions. The students eagerly finished the last pages to find out which character had been holding the gun that fired those shots.

Week Eight: Real Men Finale

Although it all seemed to be over far too quickly, the unit's finale had arrived. The teachers and I had set up for the party in the back of the cafeteria. Student posters adorned the walls, and clay figurines and three-dimensional models covered a long table. Another table held several copies of *Scorpions* and a variety of student work created during the unit. Punch, cake, and cookies covered a third big table.

When I arrived, Patty pulled me aside and told me softly that Ricardo would not be joining us because he was suspended from school. She handed me a folder and said, "Read this." I tucked it into my briefcase. Later that morning, I opened the folder Patty had handed me, which held two pages of her project notes. I began reading and found that Ricardo apparently had been a lookout for a friend who had been caught stealing money from a teacher's desk. Soon after, Ricardo was in trouble again for hitting a boy in the jaw. His home life was not good either. Both his father and sister were in jail, and his grandmother, with whom he lived, had recently become ill. Patty spoke with Ricardo about this incident and discovered that Ricardo thought he had been justified in punching the boy.

Patty tried to reason with Ricardo by speaking about Jamal's actions in *Scorpions* and connecting Ricardo's actions to Jamal's. She asked Ricardo whether Jamal had been right to pull a gun and if Jamal could go to jail for his actions. Ricardo responded just as Patty thought he would because Ricardo knew Jamal's actions were wrong and knew the consequences Jamal could face because of these actions. She ended their conversation by asking Ricardo,

Patty: So do you really think hitting that boy was the right thing to do?

Ricardo: [*after a long pause*] No, I guess not....

Patty: What could you have done?

Ricardo: Told you or another teacher, or just ignored him....

Ricardo's behavior represents the difficulties of helping young men adopt new expressions of masculinity, which is a challenge everyone faces when trying to pry open the grip popular culture and media have on youth. Envisioning new ways of being boys and men was particularly challenging with the children of Molina because of their familiarity with the violent masculinity that dominates their community and lives.

Patty did, however, seem to get through at some level with Ricardo. One of the more challenging boys in the seventh grade and growing up in circumstances that would require every bit of his willpower to surmount, he was brought to notice parallels between his troubles and those of Jamal. Ricardo seemed to understand that punching a classmate was a poor decision. This realization also acknowledges the emptiness of his own macho bravado toward the incident. His duplicity in stealing money was obviously very serious and demonstrated the fine line that Ricardo and many other seventh-grade boys walked daily between self-discipline and delinquency. I will always remember Ricardo for his ability to evaluate his actions and those of his partner critically—much the same way he learned to evaluate critically Jamal's behavior throughout the novel.

Patty's notes brought a kind of joy that reinforced the satisfaction I felt over the celebration of the unit's finale, which had just ended. The party in the cafeteria began with Patty speaking about the unit's goals, what we had done along the way, and what we hoped to accomplish within the next hour. With her cue, students approached our male guests to form teams for personal introductions. We allowed these groups to converse for a few minutes, then had the group share what they learned with the whole class. We chuckled as our adult guests stretched their short-term memories to introduce the seventh graders within their groups.

After companion introductions, the students presented their unit projects. DeWayne held up his three-dimensional model of Jamal's apartment and described the scene in which the preacher prays with Mama, Jamal, and Sassy for the older brother Randy, who was injured in a prison fight. James made clay figurines of the main characters. He displayed these while supplying character sketches of each, then answered questions about the characters. Ricardo's life-size poster advertising *Scorpions* was on the wall. Because of his suspension that day, Teri pointed it out to the group and explained what Ricardo had intended with his picture of a scorpion above the words *Scorpions are back!* Shantala and Noe reenacted the scene from the novel when Sassy discovers the hidden gun in the sofa cushions. They rewrote the book's dialogue and memorized their lines. They also used simple props, such as a toy gun and a pillow on a folding chair.

When the students completed their presentations, Patty invited them to partake of the refreshments. Afterward, she asked our male guests to share some of their thoughts about being male and being a reader. Dr. Chuck Dugan, a kinesiology professor and former all-American gymnast, began by reading an excerpt from the poem "I Celebrate Myself," which is from one of his favorite books, *Leaves of Grass* by Walt Whitman (1993). He read the following lines:

> I celebrate myself, and sing myself,
> And what I assume you shall assume,
> For every atom belonging to me as good belongs to you.
> I loafe and invite my soul,
> I lean and loafe at my ease observing a spear of summer grass.
> My tongue, every atom of my blood, form'd from this soil,
> this air,
> Born here of parents born here from parents the same, and
> their parents the same.
> I, now thirty-seven years old in perfect health begin,
> Hoping to cease not till death.

Chuck went on to explain his philosophy about health: To be totally healthy, people must be both physically and intellectually active. He warned that the biggest mistake is to become imbalanced, forgetting to stimulate either the body or the mind. "Reading," continued Chuck, "is the best way to guarantee that our minds stay in great shape. That's why I read every day...it's a kind of mental exercise."

Another marvelous male guest was Dr. Malcolm Booker, whom I mentioned in Chapter 4. Malcolm candidly described his humble beginnings in rural Louisiana, his basketball scholarship to a state college, and, the pinnacle of his academic efforts, the completion of his doctoral degree in education at the University of Florida. He emphasized that life's circumstances give people plenty of reasons to avoid the difficult steps, to seek to "feel good" only for the moment, and to find excuses for bad behavior and decisions, which are truly within their own control. Despite the many questions students had about his exciting college basketball career, Malcolm adroitly refocused his answers on the importance of disciplining oneself, setting goals, and becoming as highly literate as possible. For example, after Felipé queried him about whether he ever played basketball with Michael Jordan, Malcolm laughed and responded, "I had dreams of playing big-time roundball, but when I broke my ankle in my junior year, and it never healed properly, my playing days were over." He went on to say,

> I knew many guys who were convinced that nothing would stop them from becoming pros...but when they got injured or flunked out, they had no backup plan, no Plan B. My best advice to all of you, especially if you like sports and think you're really good: Keep playing hard, work on your game to become as good as you can, but work just as hard on your school lessons, so if one plan doesn't work out, you'll have another ready to go. The one sure way to be ready is to be a reader.

Malcolm concluded his presentation by reading passages from Martin Luther King Jr.'s "Letter From Birmingham Jail" from *Why We Can't Wait* (King, 1963). Looking out on the diverse group of young adults, he intoned,

> Moreover, I am cognizant of the interrelatedness of all communities and states. I cannot sit idly by in Atlanta and not be concerned about what happens in Birmingham. Injustice anywhere is a threat to justice everywhere. We are caught in an inescapable network of mutuality, tied in a single garment of destiny. Whatever affects one directly, affects all indirectly. Never again can we afford to live with the narrow, provincial "outside agitator" idea. Anyone who lives inside the United States can never be considered an outsider anywhere within its bounds. (p. 34)

After brief presentations from our last guests, the final day of our Real Men unit drew to a close. Rene Zamora, a successful investment banker, revealed his love of books from the thriller genre. Doug Horner, a local actor, read dialogue from *A New Way to Pay Old Debts* (Massinger, 1910), an Elizabethan play that was being staged in town. Doug said, "It has everything to do with choices young men make to be deceitful and unkind or decent and honorable." The lines he read that stuck out in my mind were those from Lady Allworth to her son:

> You are yet
> Like virgin parchment, capable of any
> Inscription, vicious or honourable. (p. 869)

The point, of course, Doug observed, is that even though boys are vulnerable to external influences, they must strive to reject the vicious and emulate the honorable.

All the guests were perfect. Each uniquely embodied the characteristics of honorable masculinity and clearly stressed the importance of active literacy in shaping their personal and professional lives. When the bell rang ending the class period, the finality of the moment hit me. I hoped that these young people might take the memory of this unit with them and make good decisions as they enter adulthood.

Revisiting the "To Be a Man" Survey

Although the unit officially ended, Patty, Teri, and I still had a great deal of work to finish. It was time to re-administer the "To Be a Man" survey to the students and compare the results from two months earlier to determine any self-reported changes in attitude toward stereotypical male behavior.

Demonstrating this change in attitude using self-report measures is similar to research conducted by Farrell and Meyer (1997). In their study, they examined the impact of a school-based curriculum designed to reduce violence for sixth-grade students from inner-city Richmond, Virginia, USA. At the beginning of the school year, students completed a survey reporting the number of incidences of assaultive violence in which they had engaged. Farrell and Meyer re-administered the survey after an 18-session violence prevention program. Results showed highly significant reduction in the frequency of violence and several other related problem behaviors for boys. Most of these differences were maintained through the end of the school year.

We were heartened after reading our students' responses to the postunit survey. (The results of Ricardo's, DeWayne's, James's, and Shantala's surveys are highlighted in Figure 12.) Students' responses suggested that the unit was a success; however, it is impossible to know whether their responses reflected a genuine change in attitude or a desire to tell us what we wanted to hear.

Figure 12. Sample Postunit Responses From "To Be a Man" Survey

1. When a man is being hassled by another man, he needs to fight to get the man to back off.
   Ricardo's response—"No."
   Ricardo's reason—"Because they can talk it out."
2. Men who walk away from fights are sissies.
   DeWayne's response—"No."
   DeWayne's reason—"Even if you're stronger, what's the use of fighting."
3. Men need weapons like knives and guns to show how strong they are.
   James's response—"No."
   James's reason—"If they're going hunting or something, that's OK, but they don't have to use them [guns and knives] to fight."
4. You can't really be a man unless you are in a gang.
   Shantala's response—"No."
   Shantala's reason—"You're a man, staying out of gang."
5. Men like to fight because that's just who they are.
   Ricardo's response—"No."
   Ricardo's reason—"We have control of what we do."
6. Men who go to prison are real men.
   DeWayne's response—"No."
   DeWayne's reason—"That don't sound cool to me."
7. If a man killed someone, other men would think he was really cool.
   James's response—"No."
   James's reason—"You protect them better by having a good job and a good house."
8. Real men protect their families by fighting.
   Shantala's response—"No."
   Shantala's reason—"Prison ain't no place to prove you're a man."
9. As soon as a boy turns 13, he needs a gun.
   Ricardo's response—"No."
   Ricardo's reason—"A boy only needs a gun for hunting."
10. Sometimes being violent is the only way for a man to make others understand he means business.
    DeWayne's response—"No."
    DeWayne's reason—"There are other ways, like what you say that let's people know you ain't messing."

Intangible Effects of Real Men Unit

What I cannot adequately recount in my description and analysis of the Real Men unit are the small, everyday exchanges that took place with these young men—the facial expressions, the body language, the sighs and guffaws, the sarcasm, and most important, the occasional and fleeting glimpses into their souls. On the other hand, to tell all would somehow be cheating, like revealing a secret. Only those of us who lived this unit can ever know the full impact of the experience; furthermore, it is impossible to know whether the unit will have a lasting effect on the students. Experienced teachers accept the fact that their protégés will rarely, if ever, visit them in the future to show them who they have become and to tell teachers how much they meant to them, personally and professionally.

Someday Patty, Teri, or I may hear from one of our students from the Real Men unit. That student may have good news about his life, the honorable choices he has made, how he has kept out of trouble, how he stayed the course in school, and how he has come back to acknowledge the contribution that our instruction has made to his life. Far more likely, however, we will go on with our hopes for these young men, knowing that we humbly tried to make a difference by shifting their thinking about males and themselves in less stereotypical directions.

BOY TALK

Adrian, 17, Discovers His Father's History in Elizabeth Becker's *America's Vietnam War: A Narrative History*

At one of my dad's veterans' rallies, I found out something really interesting (at least to me). You know how most people think vets are all messed up on drugs, live on welfare, and are screwed up in the head and everything? Actually, that's not true. Most vets are very successful. Most of them have good jobs and families and have gotten over their war experiences without committing suicide or turning into monsters like the movies always show.

My dad's a good example. He went to college when he got out of Vietnam. He started working for a Xerox company, and now he owns Kinkos, the copy place out near the mall. It's because of him I've always been interested in history, especially war history. When I read *America's Vietnam War: A Narrative History* (Becker, 1992), I felt like I was getting the true story of how the war started and why we fought it in the first place. As I was reading it, I talked with my dad about the stuff I was learning. He gave me his understanding of the facts, from how he felt when he was first drafted and later when he studied the history of the war.

Chapter 6 about the Tet offensive is right at the time my dad was in Viet Nam [*sic*]. He was near Khe Sanh when the North Vietnamese attacked. Every week the news would show the number of dead American soldiers and Vietnamese [people], but it could never tell the real story about guys getting blown up and tortured or families getting burned. The real massacres happened in Hue. Becker talks about how many people were slaughtered after the city was taken over by the North Vietnamese and Viet Cong. They killed 1,000 innocent civilians and 3,000 other people. Many of them were Americans. When the Americans finally recaptured the city, they found mass graves where the thousands of people were buried.

Dad said he had orders to go to Hue. Many of his buddies had gone and been killed there. But when the North Vietnamese were pushed back, he didn't have to go. What a lucky thing, too, because at least 10,000 soldiers died there. He could have been one of them.

My dad doesn't think of himself as some kind of macho man for fighting in the war. And he doesn't totally agree with why we fought the war in the first place. But he agrees with Elizabeth Becker when she says Vietnam veterans have unfairly become "the symbol of lost American innocence twisted into madness" (p. 3). Dad says all wars are a form of madness, but the men fighting them don't have to come out crazy.

CHAPTER 6

Alternative Texts and Practices to Engage Male Readers

I suggest that the only books that influence us are those for which we are ready, and which have gone a little farther down our particular path than we have yet got ourselves.
—E.M. Forster, *Two Cheers for Democracy*

The overarching theme of this book is that boys will become more engaged readers if they're exposed to and have engaging literacy experiences around texts of interest. I've made the case that texts with positive male archetypes can capture boys' unique imaginations, sustain attention, and lead to more thoughtful reading. And yet, we know that every day, in classrooms across the United States and elsewhere, teachers are using a variety of texts and strategies in creative ways that contribute to successful and enjoyable reading and writing events for boys. This chapter, therefore, is devoted to alternative texts and practices that, while not specifically focused on archetypes, are motivating boys to read and learn all the same. These alternative texts include digital media, graphic novels and comic books, and other youth literacy sources.

Simply stated, alternatives to traditionally formatted print texts have an important place in any language curriculum for boys because that's what they enjoy interacting with outside of school. If boys are ever to develop the skill and will to master the demands of academic literacy and become lifelong readers of diverse texts, teachers will need to find ways of bridging boys' outside-of-school and inside-of-school literate practices. Whatever teachers do to eliminate barriers between boys' competencies with outside-of-school texts and classroom practices will increase their engagement in learning and expand literacy abilities (Sturtevant et al., 2006).

Recognizing Boys' Out-of-School Literate Practices

If understanding teen and preteen boys in today's society requires a large degree of openness the same might be said about coming to know and learning to value boys' literate practices beyond the school walls (National Literacy Trust, 2001). These practices pose new challenges for teachers, especially those who hold to traditional notions about reading and writing. What it means to be literate is undergoing perpetual revision in this age of digitized media, rapidly evolving vernacular, language hybrids, and global communication. And adolescent boys are inveterate purveyors of these new literacies, including but not limited to (a) playing and reading about computer and video games, (b) reading comic books and graphic novels, (c) interacting on websites devoted to their hobbies (skateboarding, collecting, sports), and (d) listening to or playing music and reading/writing song lyrics.

Teachers who recognize and understand these new literate practices and who have crafted successful language and literacy curriculum for male youth also understand how the boundaries of literacy have been stretched. For instance, Hawkins (2004) asserts that

> "literacy" is not simply the ability to encode and decode print. [It is] the requisite knowledge and skills to send and interpret messages through multiple media and modes in local and global contexts...[C]hanges in communication design, function, and mode in our rapidly changing world...[require] constant re-design of our means and methods of local and distance communications, [and] re-think[ing] what communicative skills it will take to participate successfully in that world. (p. 19)

My call for schools to honor the literacies and discourses of boys derives from the realization that they, like all of us, now live in a "mediasphere" (O'Brien, 2001), "a world saturated by inescapable, ever-evolving, and competing media that both flow through us and are altered and created by us" (Brozo, 2005, p. 534).

Adolescent boys may be the most active participants in the mediasphere, using and creating forms of discourse that could be acknowledged and appreciated in school settings. School is where youths' multiple literacies could be exploited and allowed to find expression to help them grow as readers and thinkers. To do so, teachers need to find ways of exploiting the multiple literacy competencies adolescent boys bring to school (Knobel, 1998), such as the ability to communicate through digital means and social networking (e.g., texting, Facebook, blogging, twittering); create hypertext documents; and interpret and think critically about music CDs and videos, video/computer games, and websites. Within traditional reading and language arts programs room will need to be made for boys' out-of-school literacies in order for teachers to build on their strengths, develop academic knowledge and skills, and promote lifelong independent reading and learning (Coles & Hall, 2001; Hinchman, Alvermann, Boyd, Brozo, & Vacca, 2003; Hull & Schultz, 2002).

In addition to digital media, boys are also drawn to alternatively formatted text, such as graphic novels and comic books (Bitz, 2004; Hatfield, 2005; Jacobs, 2007). In the United States, Hughes-Hassell and Rodge (2007) report on the leisure reading habits of 1,340 students in grades 5 through 8 at an urban middle school in a large northeastern city. In their findings, 54% of male students ranked comics as the favorite leisure reading choice.

Recently, I brought this point home to a skeptical freelance writer who contacted me while researching an article about boys and reading. What are they reading?, she wondered. I told her to go to her nearest bookstore on a Saturday afternoon and conduct an informal observational survey to find out. I suggested she first position herself near the young adult book section for an hour, and document the number of adolescent boys who browsed there. Then, I had her reposition herself near the graphic novel/ comic book stacks and do the same thing. "Call me back and let me know what you find," I asked. But I knew what her observations would reveal before she told me how surprised she was to discover only one or two boys in the young adult section but piles of boys in the graphic novel section, sprawled on the floor, leaning against the shelves, talking excitedly with buddies about the newest discovery.

As with other youth media, comic books have traditionally been spurned by teachers and librarians. Perhaps because adults tend to hold these texts in such low regard, boys have spent a considerable amount of their outside-of-school leisure time reading nothing but comics. When in 1992, Art Spiegelman's (1986) *Maus I: A Survivor's Tale* was awarded a Pulitzer Prize, comic books and graphic novels gained newfound respect (Brozo & Simpson, 2007). They now come in numerous genres and are quickly becoming recognized as an engaging resource for classrooms and libraries (Chandler-Olcott & Mahar, 2003; Mui, 2004; Weiner, 2002). Many teachers are now supplementing lessons on the Holocaust with graphic novels like *Maus* and teaching about the current state of Arab–Israeli relations with Joe Sacco's (2001) *Palestine*.

Furthermore, it has been shown that graphic novels and comic books are excellent resources for motivating reluctant readers (Cho, Choi, & Krashen, 2005; Schwarz, 2002; White, 2005). The illustrations can provide the needed contextual clues to the meaning of the written narrative, especially for struggling and visual learners (Chun, 2009; Gorman, 2003; Norton & Vanderheyden, 2004). These features may be particularly attractive to boys, who have demonstrated higher competencies with text formatted in nontraditional ways (Brozo et al., 2007).

Bridge-Building Texts

In most classrooms a core textbook continues to be the primary source for reading and learning. Yet, unless boys are able to relate to these texts on an engaging and meaningful level, they may not take from them as much as we know they should. Thus, even if these required texts are "readable," they may turn boys off to reading. Teachers, therefore, need to recognize the value of connecting text sources from boys' everyday worlds to required course readings and topics (Brozo & Brozo, 2009; Larimer & Schleicher, 1999).

The goal of this bridge-building process is to take advantage of boys' relative strengths with language and literacy outside of school by transitioning them into challenging academic texts. Another goal is to motivate reluctant and disinterested male youth to read required academic texts. Bridge texts are not only more interesting to boys but also help put knowledge bases in place for academic tasks. Furthermore, alternative sources, when linked to academic texts and given legitimacy in school settings, are likely to engage boys in meaningful reading and learning that can lead to elevated achievement (Brozo, 2006; Bushman & Haas, 2006).

Teachers who learn to use sources from the everyday worlds of boys as embellishment to core text sources will find their male students reading with greater interest and enjoyment (Guthrie & Wigfield, 2000; A.J. Martin, 2003). Consider, for instance, the science teacher who prepared her class for a study of the laws of physics by first exploring the website Skateboard Science (www.exploratorium.edu/skateboarding/) as a bridge to reading and studying laws of physics. Boys' reading comprehension is likely to be greater with high-interest materials because interesting material maintains students' attention more effectively (McDaniel, Waddill, Finstad, & Bourq, 2000).

Teaching Shakespeare With Manga

Ursula's male students in her ninth-grade general English class could only groan when she said they would begin Shakespeare's *Romeo and Juliet* at the start of the new grading period. Their expressions of displeasure turned to curiosity, however, when she told them they would prepare for the play by first reading the manga version (Shakespeare, Appignanesi,

& Leong, 2007). The art in manga graphic novels is highly stylized, originating in Japan, and the books are widely read by teens. This version of the play offers students a unique and highly readable complement to the one in their literature anthology.

Set in modern-day Tokyo, the authors combine *manga*-style art and abridged dialogue to re-create the themes of the play. Although the richness of Shakespeare's original language may be sacrificed, the script preserves the spirit of the story, including all the major speeches. The layout and characters are well-rendered in the typical gray-scale art of manga texts. By situating the play in modern Tokyo among rival *yakuza*, or organized-crime families, the authors present adolescent boys with a world they will recognize. And these features along with the engaging illustrations help boys comprehend the story, which prepares them for the original Shakespeare.

Ursula employed a kind of impromptu Readers Theater to read the manga text. Groups of students went to the front of the room with their books and read parts. A new group took over after 5–10 pages. Students were expected to use simple gestures and actions to accompany their readings. In between groups, Ursula engaged the class in discussion about the plot, characters, and theme, and then helped her class make connections between the 21st-century storyline from Japan and its original setting in Renaissance Italy. The boys were especially enthusiastic about this approach, because the illustrations and modern context made the story much more accessible than if they had launched the unit with Shakespeare's original heartbreaking tragedy. With the manga version, the boys were able to understand and follow the storyline, making it easier to appreciate the teenage heroes, the scheming and villainous adults, and the overarching theme of star-crossed lovers.

When the time came to break open the literature anthology and begin reading *Romeo and Juliet*, Ursula's entire class, especially the male contingent, was much more enthusiastic about taking on the Bard. Her students now had an appreciation for the drama and excitement of the play. They took full advantage of the compelling illustrations in the manga version to envision scenes of teenage romance; family feuding; fights over honor between Tybalt, Benvolio, Mercutio, and Romeo; and even suicide. With each scene, students were asked to compare the Shakespeare text, events, and characters with the manga version. Ursula had students rewrite scenes using everyday language, create their own cartoon panels, and perform impromptu dramatic interpretations, which they did with greater competence and accuracy as a result of the bridging experiences with manga.

Youth Media

As demonstrated by the work of Ursula, creative teachers find ways to honor youths' outside-of-school media while bridging them to the concepts and information in the classroom. An obvious source for enlivening school-based learning for boys is popular media and music (Knabb, 2003; Pailliotet, 2003). Because today's male youth live in the mediasphere, it makes good sense to find as many linkages as possible between the images and music with which they are familiar and topics under study in the classroom.

Music, as a medium of identity construction for boys, is a viable alternative text form that is underused by most teachers (Newman, 2005; William, 2001). Scaffolding for new understandings means working with what boys bring to the classroom, including their interest in and knowledge of popular music (Morrell & Duncan-Andrade, 2002).

Teaching Word Families With Rap Music

Derrick, an eighth-grade special education teacher with mostly boys in his self-contained English class, had been frustrated by his students' lack of engagement in the lessons and readings, until he began tapping into their media and music for teaching aspects of language and composition.

For instance, when preparing his class for a study of word families, he first found out what his male students had programmed on their iPods, MP3 players, and other portable music devices. He then tracked down the lyrics from some of these songs and raps and found they possess a variety of words that could be studied as families and then could be used as models for other similar words in school texts and in their own writing. With his students' own music as the text for learning word families, Derrick noted the boys in class were eager to participate in the lessons, remembered more content, and gave more thoughtful responses.

When studying the /ch/ and /ck/ digraphs, Derrick invited students to bring in lyrics with these elements. As long as the song or rap lyrics met acceptable school standards (no profanity, excessive violence, or degrading messages about women and girls), students were allowed to work with them in their analysis. With a partner, first students were to create a t-chart listing all the words that had either the /ch/ or /ck/ element. One pair of African American boys brought in and analyzed the rap lyric "I Love to Give You Light" by Snoop Dogg. The boys found many words with the word family elements (see Figure 13).

Derrick then directed the students to generate new words with the /ch/ and /ck/ sounds and add these to their t-chart. The pair with Snoop

Figure 13. Words from "I Love to Give You Light" With /ch/ and /ck/ Sounds

ch	ck
such	background
preach	jackers
church	glock
teachin'	block
watchin'	locked
each	black
preachin'	
reach	
beach	
child	

Dogg's rap lyrics added *catch, match, reach,* and *bunch* to the left column and *socks, locker, backpack,* and *stick* to the right column words. Each pair of students completed activities with the song lyrics they had brought to class to analyze.

With their new words, students were then asked to write lyrics based on the genre of music they analyzed. The lyrics had to contain the new words they generated to match the /ch/ and /ck/ sounds. Thus, the boys working with the Snoop Dogg rap wrote their own. While one kept rhythm on his desk top, the other one read the rap:

> I put my *socks* in my *backpack* when I go to school.
> I put my *backpack* in my *locker* or I look like a fool.
> I get my *socks* from my *backpack* when I go to gym.
> Where I *catch* the ball then *stick* it in the rim.

Derrick witnessed a new level of enthusiasm for learning among his students, especially the boys, doing word study work with their own song lyrics. The best result, however, was that his students' enthusiasm translated into genuine learning. Derrick noticed their ability to recognize many of the same words and those with the same word family elements in their own and their classmates' compositions, and as they read stories and other texts. This level of application and transfer occurred because Derrick eliminated barriers between outside-of-school interests and literacies of his students and classroom practices. And his male students were the special beneficiaries, as their engagement in reading and learning as well as their language competencies increased.

Teaching Business Contracts With Tejano Music

The eight boys in Marta's fifth-period business class were the toughest to keep on task, and she was always on the lookout for approaches that would be especially appealing to them. So one day when she observed her male students enter the classroom, she became inspired by an obvious way the topic of writing business contracts could be linked to their real-world interests and desires. Many had Tejano music pulsing from their earbuds, which led Marta to consider how her students' love of this Mexican American musical hybrid could form the basis of a fun and meaningful lesson.

Marta formed pairs of students, one to represent a recording artist and another a record company. Each pair was asked to create a fictitious name for both the company and the artist. For example, two students created the Tejano singer, Lil' Mario, and recording company, Sanchez Records. Marta sent students to the computer lab with links to access required Internet sites. At these sites students obtained background on the language and format of contracts in the music recording business, as well as actual business contract templates for recording artists. Students had to download templates of recording contracts and negotiate the details from the perspectives of recording artists and record companies. Marta provided the class with a series of questions they would need to address to satisfactorily complete the contracts; these included such matters as the effective dates of the contract, the deliverables by the artist and the company, compensation, and contingencies.

Student pairs completed their contracts in preparation for a fishbowl discussion activity. With this technique, a small group of students goes into the "fishbowl" to discuss an issue or problem while the other students look on. The outside group must listen but not contribute to the deliberations of the students in the fishbowl. When the fishbowl discussants conclude, students looking in can ask questions and react to the discussion they observed. When finished, another group of discussants can enter the fishbowl to start the process over again.

While one pair of Marta's students demonstrated how they hammered out a contract, her other students looked on; then the roles were switched. At regular intervals, student observers were given the opportunity to share reactions to and ask questions of the pair of negotiators they were observing. Contract contingencies seemed to bring out the most animated discussion. For instance, Lil' Mario wondered what would happen if just before a big concert he broke his fingers and couldn't play his guitar or lost his voice due to a cold and couldn't sing.

Once Marta's students completed the business contract activity, she held a small reception in class, with Tejano music on the CD player, fruit juice, and pan dulce (traditional sweet breads), before continuing to explore information in the textbook on business contracts. The boys in her class were very enthusiastic about this activity and performed well on her unit test.

Teaching Allusion With Digital Media

Alejandro decided to administer a questionnaire to his 10th graders at the beginning of the school year to try to gain insights into ways of structuring learning that would be more appealing to them. One of the strongest suggestions came from most of his male students who were univocal in asking for more choices and options, particularly in the ways they are assessed. Another recommendation that came mostly from the boys in his class was being able to use the computer and Internet for class assignments. Using this information as a guide, Alejandro created a range of different ways students could demonstrate understanding of newly learned content with digital media.

One striking example of how Alejandro took advantage of his male students' input was the approach he used to teach about allusion in literature. Allusion is a difficult literary device for students to appreciate, because it's a reference in a literary work to a person, place, or thing in history or another work of literature. Allusions are often indirect or brief references to characters or events, but if readers don't know the events and characters to which an author alludes, then the allusion loses its impact.

To help sensitize his students to this literary device and bring them to appreciate its significance, Alejandro gave the class its initial exposure to allusion through a YouTube video clip from *Shrek 2*, a popular animated film for youth. The three minute clip includes several visual allusions to other films and film characters, both real and animated, with the song "My Boy Lollypop" as the soundtrack. As the clip played, Alejandro asked students to note any images that referenced other movies or movie characters, and then held a discussion afterward. This visual approach, using media from his students' everyday lives, proved quite successful, as they were able to identify several allusions in the video. Alejandro was especially pleased with the involvement and participation of his male students in this activity.

Next, Alejandro guided his students through a class blog he had established. He indicated where they were to make entries and respond to their classmates. His assignment to them was to find examples of allusion in their own media—books, films, games, music, etc.—and post it on the blog with an explanation of the allusion. Each student was required to post two examples on the blog and write two entries in response to their classmates.

Alejandro was overjoyed to find the range and depth of student responses to his assignment when he checked the site a couple of days later. What pleased him the most were the contributions from his boys. They were at a level of sophistication and reflected a level of involvement he was sure he wouldn't have seen if the assignment had been framed in a more traditional way, as these examples attest.

"Evan"

The avant garde music group Mr. Bungle modified the Warner Brothers' logo into their own creation. By simply flipping and turning their record's label (Warner Brothers), they made an already existing logo into something brand spanking new. This is an allusion to the band's label, so it is kind of like a self-promoting allusion.

"Jung-Hee"

My allusion is from the anime *Lucky Star* (which no one has probably heard of, but is the only one I can think of at the moment). In one of the episodes, the main character, Konata, cosplays (dresses up) as a character from another anime, Haruhi from *The Melancholy of Haruhi Suzumiya* at a cosplay café. The function of this allusion, in a way, is self-promotion because the writers of *Lucky Star* also wrote *The Melancholy of Haruhi Suzumiya*.

"Fareed"

In a *Jimmy Neutron—Boy Genius* episode, Jimmy goes to find out why the Bermuda triangle has so many problems. On his way into the ocean to search for an underwater entrance, the viewers see a small pineapple. As all Nickelodeon viewers know, Spongebob Squarepants lives in that pineapple. This was the producers' way of saying "Hi" to the cast of Spongebob.

"Carlos"

I found one from *Family Guy*: This is an allusion to *The Ring*, like how when you watch the cursed video in the movie *The Ring*, you'll die. In *Family Guy*, the cursed video is *The Simpsons*, which is their rival. And if you watch it, they're basically [saying] *The Simpsons* is bad for you.

From here, Alejandro transitioned his class into looking for and uncovering allusions in traditional print texts, which they did with far greater success than his students had in previous years. With this assignment, Alejandro was able to take advantage of his students' competencies with media and literacies outside of school to achieve his goal of motivating reluctant and disinterested male youth to read and respond on a more thoughtful level to required texts in his classroom. Of course, the most pervasive popular medium in youth's lives is the computer, so it's a natural entry point.

Teaching Science Vocabulary With Video Games

One of Becky's sixth-grade science students, Ubikway, was a daydreamer. She would catch him during class staring out the window, blissfully disengaged from the flow of instruction. When confronted, he would apologize and refocus, only to fall back into his private reverie at the next available moment. Although the school year was new, Becky sensed that Ubikway was a bright young man, capable of accurate and thoughtful work, but wondered what it was that distracted him during her lessons.

Becky decided to talk with Ubikway after class. She asked for an honest response when she questioned him about how she could make her science class more interesting to him. Without hesitation, Ubikway said he was thinking about his new Star Wars video game, and if he could use video games like that or others, he would pay much closer attention in class. To Ubikway's delight, Becky asked him to bring the video game to school to show her how it's played.

Becky discovered as Ubikway helped her move through the game, talking strategy and using terminology animatedly, that science concepts and vocabulary were plentiful. After a more thorough review of the game, Becky decided to incorporate it into an approaching unit on space exploration. She knew this approach would be enthusiastically received by Ubikway and the other boys in his class.

Becky gave each student a chart with keywords to be studied during the unit (see Figure 14). She directed students to fill in definitions of the vocabulary terms based on their contextualized definitions within the Star Wars video game. She then projected the game on the screen and allowed different students to come up and play it while the class looked on. Becky would pause periodically when the game narrator, intoning like Darth Vader, uttered a term from their chart. Using the visual information, students were to write what they thought the word meant. This process was repeated for each of the terms from their charts.

Figure 14. Keywords for Space Explanation Unit

Star Wars Words	Your Definition	Textbook/Glossary Definition
Galaxy	the stars and planets	a cluster of stars, nebulae, planets
Meteor	a rock from space	small matter in the solar system
Planets	like the earth	a body that revolves around the sun
Space station	a station that floats in space	
Booster rockets	help the ship go faster	

Afterward, Becky discussed the same terms as they appeared in the class textbook, helping students use context and the glossary to determine word meanings. She then asked students to fill in the third and final column of the chart.

To reinforce the acquisition of the new science vocabulary, Becky next had students work with a partner to write their own Star Wars story using the words in context. One pair of her male students wrote,

> Luke Skywalker sat in a space station. It was in our galaxy. He was going to set off the booster rockets so he could travel to a planet. The planet was going to be hit by a meteor and Luke had to save it.

Throughout the unit, when students earned free time, Becky allowed groups of two to three to play the Stars Wars game she had set up in a computer carrel in the classroom. Thanks to Ubikway and his video game, Becky's class remained actively involved in learning the content and vocabulary of the unit on space exploration and demonstrated their heightened understanding on the unit test. This positive outcome for learning and memory as a result of playing video games requiring strategic thinking has been confirmed in recent research (Gathercole & Alloway, 2008). Noticing that her boys were especially engaged by this approach to learning, Becky has continued to find ways of incorporating their interests in alternative texts and media into her science lessons.

Boys' Book Clubs

Book clubs and book discussion groups designed to increase reading engagement and time for boys are occurring in schools, classrooms, and libraries around the country. Greater critical discourse about books (Geraci, 2003), improvement in reading and writing skills of linguistically diverse learners (Kong & Fitch, 2003; R. Martin, 2003), elevation of self-esteem (Jaeger & Demetriadis, 2002), greater leadership and independence (Bond, 2001), and tolerance of diversity (Raphael, Florio-Ruane, & George, 2001) are just some of the important benefits of book club membership documented in the literature.

In addition to these benefits, the opportunities afforded boys for structured, group conversation in book clubs should not be diminished. Schwarzschild (2000) points out that family mealtime talk, which he has shown promotes important conversational skills, more extensive vocabularies, superior ability to conceptualize, and adeptness at articulating meaning in spoken and written language, is a rare occurrence in the lives of many struggling readers and learners today. Book clubs might serve as surrogates for this family ritual that was once taken for granted.

Book Club as Reading Curriculum

Middle school teacher, Jeanne, had become frustrated with the growing number of male students entering her remedial reading classes. She noticed in her classes a trend that has been occurring nationwide—boys are three to five times more likely than girls to have a learning or reading disabilities placement (Zambo & Brozo, 2009). She was convinced their reluctance to participate, disinterest in the stories and books offered, and even hostility toward her would only be reversed if big changes were made.

During Jeanne's search for ideas and suggestions that would help her improve boys' reading skills and attitudes, she came upon a couple of articles I had written (Brozo & Schmelzer, 1997; Brozo, Walter, & Placker, 2002) and the first edition of this book, *To Be a Boy, To Be a Reader* (Brozo, 2002). Before long, I found myself exchanging e-mails with her to answer questions about my research into literacy and masculinity, and share strategies that might improve her male students' literacy.

In the end, Jeanne decided to organize a book club comprised of seven seventh-grade boys, whom she selected based on her experiences with them in sixth grade. Each was reading two or more years below grade level and had negative attitudes toward reading. With the help of the guidance counselor, Jeanne managed to place all seven boys into her second period remedial reading class. Nara, Colin, Ricardo, Jaimi, Michael, Renard, and

Esteban represented a similar ethnic mix to the overall school population: 46% Hispanic, 22% African American, 22% Caucasian, and 9% Asian.

Jeanne then invited me to participate in the club as a cyber member. From over 600 miles away in another state, I read the books the boys read, contributed my responses to the books, and engaged in electronic discussions with the boys in the club. My participation in the book club taught me three important lessons: focus on boys' interests, give boys options for responding to books, and have fun with books.

Link Book Club Selections to Members' Interests. Student book clubs should determine selection of reading material solely on the basis of what club members like. The quickest way to undermine enthusiasm is to assume the book club serves as a mere proxy for the regular reading curriculum. The material really does matter and can make or break a successful book club experience. Students who are disaffected readers in part because of the kinds of books and other print material they're required to read in reading class will need "free rein" (Bond, 2001) on all matters related to what will be read in a book club context.

To ensure she was making the most interesting possible books available to her boys, Jeanne gave them a questionnaire to determine their outside-of-school interests. The most popular activities were (a) playing on the computer, (b) playing sports, (c) watching TV, (d) making things, and (e) telling jokes. Along with this questionnaire, Jeanne also asked the boys what they would like to read, and their responses were (a) books that are funny, (b) books that are action-packed, (c) mysteries, (d) books about "boys like us," and (e) books that tell you how to do things. These patterns of interest are not unlike those for similar young men documented in other research (Chance, 2000; Doiron, 2003).

Armed with this knowledge, Jeanne and I were able to identify various books that would match the interests and book genres the boys revealed through the questionnaires. For example, to connect with the strong interest the boys had in computers, we introduced them to and had enjoyable reading experiences with *ChaseR: A Novel in E-Mails* (Rosen, 2002). In it, Chase's family moves to the country, but he remains in touch with his friends back in Columbus, Ohio, USA, by exchanging funny e-mails. Chase learns to create pictographs through the clever combination of various keyboard symbols. The boys in book club had fun reproducing these interesting keyboard figures while conversing with me via e-mail. Esteban wrote to tell me about *ChaseR* and the book club:

> I'm very happy to be in this class. The thing about a class full of boys is a
> good thing because we talk about our things, like girls and basketball and

stuff. Not saying having Ms. C [Jeanne] is a bad thing but it is hard to like talk about boy stuff. I like the computer so my favorite book was *ChaseR* by Michael J. Rosen. It's about a boy who moved from the city to the country. He lived 60 miles from the city. The book is about e-mail messages that Chase writes to his new and old friends. Chase has a sense of humor because he expresses it in his e-mails because of his signs, and Jokes. When he writes he writes about what's happening in the country and what he hates about the country. My favorite part is when he makes signs. Here are some examples. \0/ / / / / / > that's a Cicada. It's weird. He says cicadas are very loud and annoying. They make a lot of noise with there wings by pushing them together. At the end of the book Chase writes about what he likes about the country. So he changes. But he keeps his friends by writing to them on e-mail. I miss my friends in Mexico but they don't have computers. If they did I would write e-mails to them.

Allow Book Club Members Multiple Modes of Expression. Typically, students are allowed a limited range of response options based on what they read. Answering the teacher's or the anthology's questions is most common. To help reluctant male readers become more engaged with text, creative response formats should be made available to them. These might include drama, electronic presentations, art, and making real-world connections.

Michael wrote to tell me how much he had enjoyed *Death Walk* (Morey, 1993), the book the club just completed, and to get my reaction to an idea he had for a project.

Death Walk is my favorite book so far. Do you like it? I thought it was so weird how Joel gets into a fight at school. Then because he was so afraid of his father, he ran away from home and ended up in Alaska. Then he has the snowmobile accident. Did the book make you feel helpless like Joel who is stuck up there because it snows all the time and the planes can't fly. That's how I felt. I thought Donovan was a cool trapper. He saved Joel. But Joel has to walk all those miles in the snow to that house where the guy has a radio. This book made me think if I could survive a long trip by myself. It is the coolest adventure.

Mrs. C. [Jeanne] says we have to talk about the book in some interesting way. I'm glad because last year all we could do were book reports. I'm thinking about doing this project on Death Walk using the computer. I want to show the route Joel takes from Seattle to Alaska and then to the cabin of the radio operator. I was going to read a little bit from the book that describes the places Joel goes. What do you think?

In subsequent e-mail exchanges with Michael I offered suggestions for his project, such as useful websites and downloadable software, to enhance the presentation. Jeanne told me she had never seen him more enthusiastic in reading class than while preparing for and delivering his book project. One obvious explanation for Michael's enthusiasm is choice—choice of books to read and choice in deciding how to respond to gratifying books (Turner, 1995). This holds true for most reluctant and struggling readers, boys and girls.

Make Having Fun With Books a High Priority in Book Clubs. When reading is difficult and unappealing for boys one of the best antidotes is to immerse them in experiences with simply told stories that are very funny (Scieszka, 2003). To make sure the boys never grew too weary of the selections for the book club, even when they were related to their interests, Jeanne made humorous books available throughout the year. After reading the first in the series of Jon Scieszka's Time Warp Trio books, the boys couldn't get enough of them. During conversation about the Trio books we read in the club, Colin, a low-achieving reader, effused,

> Hi, Dr. B. How do you like the Time Trio series books? I read three already. That's really good for me because I don't finish many books. There really exciting, aren't they? My favorite book is *Viking It Liking It*. I can't read fast like Nara but I don't care if books are long when there [sic] good. The Time Trio books make me think about how fun it would be to travel in time. I like to dream about neat things like that.

Nara, who began reading books from the series on his own, wrote to tell me,

> I have read another book written by Jon Scieszka. The book's name was *2095*. It was funny. The Time Warp Trio meet their great-grandchildren. I like the part when they didn't have the number to pass the robot. His books are good. I really like his books. They are also funny.

Humorous books helped Jeanne's book club members sustain their efforts to read, discuss, and respond to all selections. Exposure to this genre also impelled some of the boys to seek similarly zany books to read on their own.

This book club experience reinforced my convictions about the kinds of books adolescent boys will read and why, when given the prerogative and support. When Renard, a genuine nonreader at the outset of the year, wrote me in May to say, *It's like okay to read even if other kids don't because reading is only one thing you do,* I realized just how successful the boys book club had been. The book club, as an alternative to the traditional remedial reading context, offered Jeanne a way of honoring boys' unique literacy needs. And when her boys found entry points to literacy because their interests were matched with pleasurable books, their reading skills improved, too. Five out of the seven boys passed the state test for reading that year. Jeanne was disappointed she couldn't take all seven over the top but was cheered by the very real hope that her boys will remain engaged readers throughout their lives.

Boys in Literacy Initiative

In Northern Virginia two teachers, Rob and Jodie, have established a highly successful boys' book club called Club BILI or Boys in Literacy Initiative. Targeting middle school boys, the club is unique in that it's fluid, accepting any young man who would like to participate, regardless of achievement level or school success. The founders explain this policy by stressing that all male youth, whether academically successful or not, need to develop the reading habit now if they are ever to become lifelong readers.

Another unique feature of Club BILI is that it's organized around monthly topics, genres, authors, and themes that the club members themselves agree are interesting to them. To find out boys' interests, a simple interest inventory is distributed at the start of the year to all the boys in the school. Boys identify their top five areas from a long and ever-growing list of topics and genres that include such perennial favorites as sports/athletes, supernatural stories, humor and funny stories, how-to books, and spy stories, as well as topics like gaming, computers and technology, art and artists, and music and musicians. This information is compiled with the most popular areas of interest rank ordered and used to inform the club's monthly themes and reading selections. Successful themes have been science fiction month, Cirque du Freak month, and sports month.

The Cirque Du Freak month was particularly exciting for the boys in Club BILI. Darren Shan's Cirque du Freak series is the compelling saga of a young boy's journey into a dark world of vampires. The first of now 12 books, *A Living Nightmare* (Shan, 2002), begins with Darren, who is the narrator and main character, sitting in the toilet and concludes with a wild and hair-raising graveyard crescendo. This proved to be prime pre-teen fare, according to BILI organizers Rob and Jodie.

Survival was another BILI theme that was a real hit. The boys read two books during that month, *The Boys' Book of Survival: How to Survive Anything, Anywhere* (Campbell, 2009) and *Born Survivor: Survival Techniques From the Most Dangerous Places on Earth* (Grylls, 2007).

The Boys' Book of Survival, in style and format a throwback to yesteryear, deals with every manner of important survival challenges for boys from pimples to zombie invasions. Filled with useful practical information such as orienteering without a compass and taking care of an injury in the wild, the guide also covers those rare but just-in-case situations, such as escaping from quicksand or keeping zombies at bay.

Born Survivor is the firsthand account of Bear Grylls's putting himself in the most unforgiving conditions on Earth and showing the reader how to stay alive. The boys learned how to cross a piranha-infested river, find fresh food in any environment, build a bush fire, and fend off grizzly bears. From a desert island in the Pacific to the snowpack of Greenland, Grylls taught the boys how to beat the elements and survive the wild.

The culminating event was a "Survival Night" in the school cafeteria, where survivalist food was served and the boys could watch nonstop TV episodes of *Man vs. Wild*, in which Bear Grylls demonstrates for the camera how to stay alive under extreme and threatening conditions, most of which are described in his book.

Rob and Jodie attributed the success of BILI to its focus on members' interests and to reading experiences in the club that encouraged social engagement and active learning. For these reasons, book club meetings do not resemble most other classrooms with strict seating arrangements and formal rules of behavior. Instead, the boys are reading and talking, but often walking around from group to group, identifying their favorite parts of the book, or re-enacting a particular section. Club meetings are often busy and loud but are always productive and focused on reading.

Cross-Age Reading Buddies

Since the start of 11th grade, Elton wanted to quit school. His older brother had dropped out, and his 17-year-old sister was receiving homebound instruction after having a baby. Ruby, the literacy coach at Elton's school, saw another possible future for this young man. She took particular notice of him while observing his history class one mid-September morning.

The class had been reading and learning about civil rights in America, and the history teacher had asked his students to find articles that dealt with some aspect of civil rights either in the United States or anywhere around the world. Students went to the long table in the back of the room which was stacked with newspapers and current events magazines and rummaged through them. Ruby watched as Elton spent more time than the others looking carefully for something that interested him. Back at his seat, Elton was reading very closely an article from *Jet* magazine as Ruby stopped by to visit with him. He explained to her in animated terms how the article was about white people who now believe that because Barack Obama is president African Americans no longer have to struggle for civil rights. The author, Elton went on to say, was warning that blacks should not let down their guard or stop fighting for civil rights that are still being denied or infringed upon because of race. Ruby was impressed with Elton's passion for the topic and his sensitive, critical reading of the article. When it was his turn to give an oral encapsulation of his article for the class, he did so with the same level of enthusiasm he had exhibited when sharing his reactions with Ruby.

Elton was just the type of young man Ruby was hoping to recruit for a new cross-age tutoring program she was instituting, which targeted students at risk of dropping out due to poor academic performance, low ability levels, or difficult home circumstances. The overall goal of the program was to improve reading skills for struggling students and keep them in school by tapping into their sense of responsibility to younger students. Keeping boys like Elton in school and raising his academic performance and self-esteem were her highest priorities. She had made arrangements with the neighborhood elementary school, which was only a short walk away from the high school, to host tutorial sessions twice weekly involving second and third graders and high school reading buddies.

Ruby spoke with Elton and several other boys individually about participating in the program, and when she had commitments from eight of them, began preparing them for their roles. The students were all members of the same third-block English class, so Ruby was able to use that time for group training sessions. More important, the English teacher agreed to allow the tutoring activity to count toward students' grades. This would be an important recruitment incentive for Ruby. Elton and the other tutors learned techniques for finding out the children's interests. They were taught simple read-aloud and vocabulary strategies. They learned how to facilitate writing in response to reading, and how to make books. And reinforced throughout was the expectation that these male youth would be encouraging of their younger buddies' reading and writing efforts and would help them see that these activities can be enjoyable. Above all, Ruby hoped that by developing literacy strategies for helping younger male readers less able than themselves, these adolescent boys would, in fact, expand their own reading and writing skills. The literature, at least, left open this expectation (Boyd, 2000; Brozo & Hargis, 2005; Fisher, 2001; Jacobson et al., 2001).

Elton's reading buddy was Angelo, a second grader, who was already experiencing difficulties with grade-appropriate reading materials. Elton was an ideal reading buddy for Angelo because it has been shown that gender- and culture-matched role models have the strongest positive effect on educational outcomes for their mentees (Zirkel, 2002).

In their first meeting, Elton discovered that Angelo lived in an adjacent apartment complex to his own building. He also learned that Angelo "loved" football and, because his father lived in New York, wanted to play for the New York Giants when he grew up. Angelo also told Elton what he wanted most was a computer so he could play "cool games." Elton made sure to tell Angelo about his interest in football, too. After getting to know each other a little while longer, Elton read some pages he had practiced from a short biography about LeBron James. Before long it was time to walk back to the high school. Elton reassured his new younger buddy that he would return in a couple of days. It was a hopeful start of what was to become a significant experience for the two of them.

Over the next few months, the tutoring program experienced attrition of three boys who couldn't keep up the commitment. They became impatient or didn't want to plan reading and writing activities for their elementary partners or, in the case of two of the students, eventually dropped out. Elton didn't give up, however, and came to enjoy his newfound status as a role model and "expert" reader for Angelo.

Because Elton and Angelo both had a strong interest in football, much of what they read and wrote about was on that topic. Ruby helped Elton find appropriately difficult, high-interest reading material. They enjoyed biographies of great New York Giants players from the past, such as Harry Carson, Frank Gifford, and Lawrence Taylor. They kept a scrapbook of the Giants' performance that season, reading newspaper stories and cutting out pictures of their favorite players. Along with these, they wrote captions, statistics, and bits of trivia from players' records.

While cutting out a magazine photo of the Giants' premier running back, Brandon Jacobs, also known to fans as The Beast, Angelo seemed in awe about his powerful 6'4" 265-pound physique, wondering out loud how he got so big. Using the Internet, Elton looked for more information on that topic. Because the cross-age tutoring sessions were held in the elementary school's media center, computers were available throughout the large open room. Ruby helped get their search started using descriptors such as "football players training," and they found pages of sites concerned with body-building and fitness. What caught Elton's eye, however, were references to performance enhancement drugs. Ruby helped them locate sites with straightforward, objective information about these supplements, which they printed for reading later.

Ruby made suggestions to Elton about the best way to share this information with Angelo. Her concern was that it wasn't presented in a way that could unintentionally glorify drug use. Elton assured her he was going to "set him straight about that junk." Under Ruby's watchful eye, Elton planned how he would read, write, and talk about performance-enhancement drugs in the next few sessions. Her own research yielded a book on the topic for young adolescents titled *Dunks, Doubles, Doping: How Steroids are Killing American Athletics* (Jendricks, 2006), which she found in the high school's library. The information in Jendricks's book is presented in a colorful, easy-to-understand format, with many illustrative photographs. She helped Elton develop strategies for sharing selected content from the book that would help Angelo begin to appreciate the drug-free ways of building muscle and stamina for athletic competition.

It was Elton, however, who came up with the idea of a digital activity related to the topic. Aware of Angelo's keen interest in computers, he developed a plan for taking a closer look at the characters from popular computer games. His plan was inspired by reading that one of the most common pastimes among many American football players when on the road or during the off-season was playing such games as *True Crime: Streets of LA* (Activision) and *WWF Wrestlemania* (THQ). Typically, the heroes and villains in these games are exaggeratedly muscled in ways that football players and body builders must envy and, perhaps, strive to resemble. Demonstrating once again for Ruby his ability to reason critically, Elton saw how these images might influence certain athletes to do whatever it takes, including using drugs, to achieve unusual physiques.

With Ruby's help and assistance from the elementary school media specialist, Elton and Angelo used the Internet to find pictures of popular computer game figures from *Take No Prisoners* (Red Orb), *The Hulk* (Vivendi-Universal), *Army Men: Sarge's Heroes* (3DO), and *X-Men: Mutant Academy* (Activision). These pictures were then downloaded and altered using popular image-modification software. Elton and Angelo learned how to rework the main characters' physiques, reshaping them in ways that were more proportional to normal muscle development. They displayed their work in a slideshow presentation with "before" slides, accompanied by captions warning of the dangers of steroids and other illegal substances for building muscle, and "after" slides with statements about good health, diet, and fitness. Proud of the brief slideshow they had created, Elton and Angelo were given special opportunities to share the slides with other students in the cross-age tutoring program. The elementary school's principal was so impressed she made sure the slides were shown to the children during drug awareness events that year.

Ruby was pleased that the reading buddy relationship was a confirmed success for both Elton and Angelo. For Angelo, he gained valuable print experiences around purposeful, meaningful uses of literacy. In addition, he benefited from regular interaction with an older boy who as a role model helped Angelo recognize that reading and writing can be naturally integrated into a boy's male identity. At the same time, for Elton, agency and efficacy as a reader increased, factors that contributed to an overall improvement in his academic performance and his decision to remain in school that year. And in an interview with Ruby at the conclusion of the program, Elton even expressed possible interest in becoming a teacher— something unthinkable before his experiences as a reading buddy.

It has been shown that when boys' preferences for alternatives to traditionally formatted print texts are honored within the classroom, their engagement and achievement increases. Additionally, teachers have explored alternative ways of delivering literacy curricula to boys. Teachers can discover the literate practices male youth engage in with alternative texts beyond the classroom walls and weave boys' interest in and use of these texts into their instructional routines. Youth media, such as music, interactive websites, computer and video games, and graphic novels or comic books can be bridges to academic literacy and learning. As a result, boys are more eager to read and respond to these texts.

BOY TALK

Dane, 15, Looks Into an Ethological Mirror in the Pages of *Incognegro* by Mat Johnson and Warren Pleece

I'm the kind of kid who would rather play basketball than read. It's not that I really don't like to read. I read a lot when I was young. Books just don't seem interesting anymore compared with the other stuff I like to do. But *Incognegro* (Johnson & Pleece, 2009) was different.

This was an amazing book. My history teacher gave it to me. He said he thought I would like it. He was right. We have been learning about how blacks in the south were lynched all the time. They would be taken out of their houses at night. Some were even taken from jail. My teacher told us that some blacks with real light skin who worked for newspapers in the North risked their lives to go South and write articles about lynchings. They called this going "incognegro."

The main character is a real light colored black guy named Zane Pinchback. So am I. My mother is white and my father is from Ethiopia. Some kids with tans look darker than me. My hair is curly but not kinky. Some say I'm not really an African American. Maybe they're right, but I feel like one. My parents are cool about who I hang out with. My friends are all black.

I also like this book because it's a graphic novel. For me, these kinds of books are a lot easier to read. I can read the words and if I'm not sure what's going on or if the dialogue isn't too interesting, I can also look at the illustrations. The illustrations in this book are awesome. They really help you get into the story.

Zane is a reporter for a newspaper in Harlem. He decides to go incognito or as the book calls it "incognegro" to Mississippi before civil rights to investigate the murder of a white woman. His own brother is accused of the murder. Zane uses his light skin to sneak down South. Whites want to lynch Zane's brother. Zane has to do everything he can to find out the truth and save his brother.

I have a lot of respect for blacks who fought for civil rights. They risked their lives. Zane is afraid whites will figure out he's black, but he does what he can for his brother anyway. Reading about Zane and looking at the drawings of him, his brother, the angry whites, and the other people made the book so real.

Could I ever show the kind of courage Zane does or all those people who fought for their rights? I don't know. But I think I am strong enough and proud enough. There's one part of the book where Zane is looking right into your eyes. He is in Mississippi and he has found out who really killed the white woman. When I look into Zane's eyes in that picture, it's like I can see myself. He's scared but confident that he must do the right thing.

CHAPTER 7

Community Partners in Boys' Literacy Growth

I have no idea how my parents or someone else could get me to read because I don't like reading. No one ever read to me before I fell asleep. No one ever bought me a book or some reading material they knew I might be into. And no one ever said, "You can do it, man," or something like that.

—Esteban, ninth grader

For someone who says he does not have a suggestion for how adults can encourage their sons to read, Esteban certainly gets to the heart of the matter, doesn't he? Parents and other adults can take advantage of Esteban's "advice," however, by giving boys everything that Esteban was deprived of and by helping to condition boys to love reading.

Trying to spark a reluctant boy to read can be a full-time, often frustrating enterprise. Male youth often find themselves in a handicapping cycle that begins with peer pressure that urges them to avoid reading because it is not "cool." This disuse leads to a loss of reading skill, which then brings on a disdain for reading because it is associated with incompetence and vulnerability (Smith & Wilhelm, 2004). This disdain causes boys to form a mask of indifference to reading, which leads to a further decline in reading ability. Demanding boys to read only what we think they should be reading may condemn them to relive this cycle throughout adolescence and may actually help create the "hardened" nonreader.

Parents and other adults can help struggling readers reverse cycles of aliteracy through a number of caring and clever approaches. Teachers of adolescents should be advocates of these positive interactions between boys, books, and adults. Teachers also should seek to enlist more men in programs and activities that allow men to be role models of active literacy and honorable masculinity. For example, teachers can encourage members of communities to start father–son reading clubs. One such club called "Books and Balls" works as follows: Sons choose a book for the club to read; then once a month, fathers and sons meet at a local indoor soccer arena to eat pizza and discuss the books before they play soccer (Maughan, 2001). Another book club, which teachers who work with African American boys should be aware of, called "Men of Books" was started by and for African American males (Houser, 2001). The goal of this club is to make the statement that black males are readers, and black male authors have something to say to black men and boys. Men of Books provides a forum for enjoying fiction and exchanging thoughts on social and political problems. Other successful clubs that bring dads and older men into the club's activities include "Boys Books and Blokes," a project run by Kaye Lowe at the University of Canberra, Australia; Greg Hill's "Guys Read" program in Fairbanks, Alaska, USA; and the "He-Man Book Club," led by Peter Fusaro, principal of Flathead High School in Kalispell, Montana, USA.

The bottom line is this: Every concerned adult can inspire teen and preteen boys to read. At school, this includes teachers, aides, counselors, administrators, older students, and other staff members. Demonstrations of the genuine power all school personnel have to influence youth in positive ways come from programs like Armstrong's Pathways to Teaching (Dandy, 1998) at Armstrong Atlantic State University in Savannah, Georgia, USA. The program is designed to take noncertified school district employees and offer them tuition and other support to enable them to take college courses and become fully licensed teachers. Dandy's program identifies workers, such as janitors and lunchroom staff, in minority schools who have promise in helping children develop and retain positive attitudes toward their education. More specifically, the male personnel often become magnets for young boys who are attracted to anyone offering them a positive model of what it means to be a man. The idea for the program came to Dandy as she observed how support staff at schools often acted as nonsanctioned counselors, mentors, supporters, and disciplinarians—roles sorely needed for many inner-city minority youth.

As I have pointed out elsewhere in this book, finding positive male role models for boys is no small matter. Over 25 million children and youth in the United States are currently living without their biological fathers in the home. Adolescent boys of color appear to suffer most. Youth with absent fathers are (a) more likely to be poor and incarcerated, use drugs, and engage in criminal behavior; (b) more likely to experience educational, emotional, health, and behavioral problems; (c) twice as likely to drop out of high school; (d) more likely to be victims of physical and sexual abuse; and (e) twice as likely to be teen parents (Horn & Sylvester, 2002).

The following vignettes give testimony to the fact that almost anyone at home or in neighborhoods and communities can help boys stay the course in reading and learning. In each of the following cases, teachers of these teen and preteen boys played a supportive role for the people who were interested in making a difference in boys' literacy futures. All the strategies and approaches in this chapter are unique yet share some important features: Instead of being pulled kicking and screaming to reading experiences, boys were invited to engage in literacy with few strings attached, with texts that were personally exciting and by adults who were active readers themselves.

It Can Take Two Dads to Make a Reader

A couple of years ago, while I was working on a grant to provide professional development in literacy across the curriculum for schools in the District of Columbia, I met a teacher in one of the project high schools who told me about Andre and the remarkable literacy support he had received at home and then put me in touch with his parents. As I soon discovered, Andre's parents were James and Phillip, a gay couple. They had raised Andre since he was three, first as foster parents then as adoptive parents. At 15, the strapping, bi-racial offspring of an African American father and Russian mother, Andre was already over six-feet tall and a standout on the gridiron and hardwood. His parents, neither big sports fans, had to develop a taste for football and basketball, becoming enthusiastic boosters for Andre's sports teams.

Andre was also an academic standout due, in no small measure, to the reading boosters James and Phillip had been for him throughout his life with them. James put it this way:

> Being gay is not something someone learns. It's in your genes, like skin color and eye color. After all, straight parents raised us. We never thought about which side Andre would fall on—straight or gay—that's just never been important to us. And God knows, he doesn't get his athletic ability from us. But what we always knew we could influence was his attitudes toward learning and reading. And from the day we got him, we've tried to be the best role models for those things...and it's paid off.

When Andre was a very young boy, he began exhibiting interest in catching, throwing, and bouncing balls, so James and Phillip made sure they read to him daily from books on those topics. This is when his imagination for books and stories was ignited. Although Andre was read to from a variety of books, when he was given a choice, he would find books about sports. One of his favorites when he was around 5 years old was *My Football Book* (Gibbons, 2000). He couldn't wait to read this book with his dads and would never grow tired of it, because James and Phillip brought excitement and freshness to each experience with the book and others like it.

Andre learned to read with these books. As a result of the repeated read-alouds by his caring parents, he recognized letters and sounds and many common sight words. Bedtime was always spent reading together, and James and Phillip took the time to read to Andre virtually whenever he requested. What his dads instinctively understood was that if Andre was to become a regular reader he had to have daily print experiences with texts that he enjoyed. They also knew that if they created warm and loving contexts around books, Andre would associate reading with feelings of security and joy, increasing the likelihood that he would return to these book experiences often.

As Andre moved through elementary and middle school, his preference for texts related to sports, particularly football and basketball, only increased. James and Phillip continued to satisfy his tastes, even while they made certain Andre was exposed to books and texts on a wide range of topics. The house was always filled with books and magazines, and Andre was not permitted to have a television or a computer in his room. His dads attribute these conditions to the fact that Andre was and remains an engaged and regular reader.

Andre especially enjoyed reading Gordon Korman's The Monday Night Football Club series books. He devoured every one of the unusual but fun series stories about boys who get together to watch professional football games on TV and discover a jersey that allows them to join in the actual games by magically entering the bodies of their favorite players. Andre also went through a phase when he read nothing but Mike Lupica's sports books, such as *Travel Team* (Lupica, 2005), *Long Shot* (Lupica, 2008a), *Summer Ball* (Lupica, 2008b), and *Two-Minute Drill* (Lupica, 2009).

As Andre entered high school, Deuker's (2008) novel *On the Devil's Court* offered him a character in Joe Faust who, like him, was driven to prove himself on the basketball court. Faust's obsession results in the selling of his soul to the devil to help his team to a perfect winning season. When the wins keep coming and his grades go from C's to A's, Faust is convinced a special force is assisting him. In the end, however, Joe Faust comes to realize that his athletic and academic successes were due to his effort and not to supernatural causes.

James and Phillip also took advantage of further opportunities to boost Andre's reading interests and increase time with print. They created rituals around books and reading, preserving time every day for reading. In the evening during the week after dinner, when homework was finished and the TV was off, the three of them would lounge in the living room with a print source of their choosing and read for 15 to 30 minutes or longer, depending upon other activities and how engaged they were with the reading material. Weekends often included trips to the library and the bookstore, where they would linger with new books and tasty treats from the coffee shop.

All of these efforts by Andre's parents made a significant difference in his literate life. Instead of imposing their interests on Andre or being judgmental about what he read, James and Phillip continued to nurture his reading interests. This wasn't always easy, because Andre preferred books that reinforced a certain male stereotype. Nonetheless, the benefits of an open-minded approach far outweighed the potential undesired effects. And the benefits were many. Andre entered school already a reader, filled with an understanding of the power of print to teach him new things. He took advantage of this skill and will to read and learn and became an academic standout. James and Phillip were very proud of Andre's scholastic accomplishments, but were equally proud of him for his athletic prowess and helped merge his fascination with sports with his love of reading. Phillip said of Andre on this point,

> So here's this hulking young man in our house in our care who is as straight as they come, who had it in him from the start to be a jock. But he's really not a jock at all. He's a very loving and caring boy, too. And thoughtful. I really believe there are some simple lessons to be learned here about things parents can do, straight or gay, to help our sons develop their minds and their bodies in healthy ways.

Buddy Reading: Being Cool, Being a Reader

Think about how atypical the following scene is. Mando, a 15-year-old Hispanic American in a taut, white sleeveless undershirt that exposes his muscular shoulders and arms, and Rickey, a 6-year-old Latino child, sit on the front stoop of Rickey's house...reading a book together. Mando has a crew cut, and his left forearm bears the name of his current or former sweetheart Delia. It is a muggy, hot summer morning in Corpus Christi, Texas, USA, but these boys are being real "cool" sharing Rickey's favorite story, *Where the Wild Things Are* (Sendak, 1988), which has now become a feature motion picture (Jonze & Hanks, 2009). As Mando reads, with Rickey leaning in closely, he points to each word and invites Rickey to read along or say the words on his own. They soon finish the story for the second time, and Mando heads down the street to join his buddies, who are on their way to the park with a basketball. Rickey puts down the book and reaches for the large metal dump truck beside him, zooming it across the porch.

This is Molina, the same neighborhood I have referred to often in this book. Gangs are down the street, crack houses are around the corner, pit bulls pace menacingly behind chicken-wire fences, and some men sleep off drug or alcohol binges or congregate on street corners, throwing dice and drinking from bottles in paper bags. What makes Mando so special? He was in a buddy reading program the previous year. His English teacher, Maria, paired Mando with Rickey to help him learn to read; she also knew that they lived on the same block. Twice a week, Mando practiced his reading skills and thought more seriously about what it takes to be a good reader, while Rickey had the opportunity to see a "big, tough boy" reading, to read along with him, and to talk about stories with him. Mando, who also has three younger sisters, took a shine to this young *vato* (loose translation for *buddy*).

Because Rickey lived so close, Mando continued reading with him a couple of days a week during the summer. Mando knew Rickey's mother and realized she was trying to raise five children on her own while working as a waitress 6 days a week at Rinconcitos, a Mexican restaurant.

Every concerned adult can exploit boys' inner Patriarch by creating situations in which young men can provide reading and learning guidance for boys. Practical knowledge and research evidence lend credence to this learning-by-teaching model. Through years of scientific investigation, for example, Wittrock (1989) has proven that when students generate their own learning, it is more permanent and meaningful. In other words, when students become teachers, as in Mando's case, they generate learning for themselves and others.

In homes where the father is absent, older boys often take on the role of surrogate dad (Dance, 2001). Evidently, mothers who do not have husbands often groom their older sons for parent-like responsibilities to share the chores of raising other children (Silverstein & Rashbaum, 1995). Although child psychologists have voiced caution about mothers who expect their sons to be husband substitutes, one extremely helpful role an adolescent boy can play in a single-parent household is that of a model and encourager of reading and learning.

Stewart, a superintendent and dear friend of mine, died tragically a couple of years ago. His passing was made all the more heartrending because of the two young daughters and adolescent son he left behind. Stewart's widow Traci, who is a local elementary school principal, has strived to avoid pressuring her son, Roger, into the role of surrogate fatherhood. She has, however, continued to hold her family together by preserving a family ritual of nightly reading. Roger's participation in reading to and with his sisters has become more prominent since his father's absence, perhaps because Traci has given him wide latitude with respect to the kinds of things the family reads. According to Traci, Roger usually suggests books and stories for the family to read. For instance, after the four of them saw the movie *Harry Potter and the Half-Blood Prince* (Yates, Heyman, & Barron, 2009), Roger read the book by J.K. Rowling (2006) to his sisters. Afterward, they talked about the similarities and differences between the film and the story.

Teachers can work with concerned individuals outside of the family to help boys find buddies for shared reading opportunities. Taking advantage of the inner Patriarch, coaches, pastors, and recreation counselors can bring older and younger boys together through reading. This is precisely what Daniel, a youth center volunteer, was able to do after talking with a local junior high school teacher who made the suggestion. When the boys who showed up to use the basketball courts were forced indoors because of rain, wind, or chill, Daniel urged the older boys to read with the younger ones. The center has a television, shelves full of board games, and several portable tables. Daniel made certain that there were plenty of paperback books on hand as well. Although there is only one rickety bookcase, usually crammed with books, Daniel stores others in cardboard boxes and milk crates. Daniel explained how he kept such a steady supply of books for a relatively small cost:

> I lose 10 or so books a month, but I consider that to be a good problem.... It usually means kids are taking the books home and reading them. I buy them for almost nothing at garage sales and Goodwill stores. The library has donated discarded books...so most of them are giveaways anyway. Some of the guys will ask me if they can have a book, and I always say it's OK.

Daniel proceeded to describe how he encourages, but never forces, the children to read. He hopes to connect boys who are trying to make good choices with others, both young and old, doing the same. Daniel has watched many such relationships form. For example, 15-year-old Antoine is often seen playing with and mentoring 8-year-old Thomas. Both boys are growing up without their fathers. Their relationship started when they began reading *Trino's Choice* (Gonzalez-Bertrand, 1999) together.

While monitoring the center, Daniel spends as much time as feasible reading. As he terms it, he is a "born-again" reader, and he wants the kids to see him enjoying books. He loved *Trino's Choice* because it takes place in San Antonio, the city of his birth. He was brought to remember many of the same troubles that Trino experiences, such as growing up without an adult male's guidance, living in poverty, being constantly threatened by gangs, and just squeaking by in school. As Daniel said,

> It was easy for me to sell this book because I lived the life, and it was hard getting out. These boys around here, especially the teenagers, all have problems at home and at school. Most don't have dads living with them. They can barely pay their bills. They live in Section 8 housing [federally subsidized] that's crowded, noisy, and not the best place for a young man to feel good about himself.

Antoine and Thomas were hooked by the first chapter and returned to the center nearly every day for a while to read it. Antoine asked Daniel to keep the book with him, so it would be there when they came back. The book eventually disappeared from the center's collection altogether, but no one is complaining—except the other boys who have heard about it and now want to read it. Daniel plans to replace the missing copy because,

> What's special about the story is it's realistic and it shows how a kid...can decide to stay out of trouble and make something of himself. I tell these kids that even if they feel they were born with bad luck, they can give themselves a chance for something better...but it's up to them. Being a good reader is the way I finally made it out, so I know it can really help.

Because he stands up against criminality and turns courageously toward positive influences, Trino offers readers an image of the Warrior archetype.

From Hobbies to Books: Using Toy Soldiers to Engender Reading

As a preteen, Theo still seemed to be interested in little more than playing with his toy soldiers. His parents, Jack and Peggy, had busy careers that subjected them to long days and weekends at work. When Theo's reading scores edged near the minimally acceptable cutoff on the district's standardized test, Peggy and Jack found themselves at school one afternoon, meeting with his teacher Karlene. She recommended some tutoring and agreed to provide it herself a couple of days after school.

Theo came to the reading center in September of the new school year. He was 11 years old and in the sixth grade. Karlene was surprised by Theo's lackluster reading performance. She had come to discover that despite material privilege, a nuclear family, and educated parents, Theo exhibited the signs of a classic nonreader. What further surprised her was his unenthusiastic reaction to her questions about his interests. He reported no hobbies, no involvement with sports, and few regular or predictable activities that he looked forward to after school or on weekends.

Her follow-up chat with Jack and Peggy focused on helping them see the connection between having an interest in something and being motivated to read about that interest. Boys often need help discovering their interests; yet, in households where parents are extremely busy, boys are usually left to their own devices to discover what turns them on. Unfortunately, all too often, default leisure-time activities will be chosen, such as watching television and playing computer games. Karlene, therefore, urged Theo's parents to get more involved in how Theo spent his free time. This would help them find ways of engaging Theo in reading. She advised that the best way to accomplish this might be to capitalize on anything that Theo had already found enjoyable.

Theo's parents cleared their schedules for the next few weekends and dedicated themselves to spending time with Theo both outdoors and indoors. For instance, they went to the zoo for the first time in two or three years, an evening baseball game played by a local minor league squad, and the beach. Some indoor activities included putting puzzles together, playing board games, watching movies, and upon Theo's urging, setting up his arsenal of plastic soldiers and weapons on a mock battlefield. Theo was proud of his replicas of U.S., German, and Japanese soldiers.

Theo's response to these activities convinced Jack and Peggy that they should begin with his only genuine interest—his toy soldiers. While looking at various sets of army men in a hobby shop, Jack and Theo became inspired to build a diorama of a World War II battle. As a boy, Jack was an avid modeler, building everything from airplanes to ships to cars. His boyhood hobby was all but forgotten until he and Theo brainstormed about the diorama project. Their work would require research of World War II, as well as techniques for creating miniature though lifelike displays. Jack found Theo to be as enthusiastic about this family project as anything he had ever done and reasoned it was because they were working as a unit, father and son—a rarity of late.

They began their project by making trips to the local library and various bookstores for appropriate reference material. They checked out *Great Battles of World War II* (MacDonald, 2004) and *D-Day: The Liberation of Europe Begins* (Murray, 2007). These books are histories of various battles for junior high school students, such as the Nazi invasion of Poland, the D-Day invasion, the Battle of the Bulge in Europe, the attack on Pearl Harbor, and fighting in Guam and the Philippines. The books include plenty of black-and-white and color photos of actual battle scenes. For information on creating dioramas and miniature displays, Theo and Jack found two excellent resources at a couple of bookstores: Jerry Scutts's (2000) *World War II Dioramas* and Francois Verlinden's (2003) *Building Military Dioramas* (Vol. VII). These books displayed a variety of war dioramas showing burnt buildings, weathered machines and men, and field hospitals and included detailed descriptions of the techniques for re-creating them.

Theo and Jack set aside time each evening to look through and read the books they had gathered in preparation for creating their own diorama. Theo toiled cheerfully on every detail as the two of them spent the next two months bonding in a way that they had never done before. The project became so all-encompassing that Jack began taking less and less work home; he also limited his weekend work to a couple of hours on Sunday evenings. Activity on the diorama became a kind of curative for the workaholic funk Jack had found himself in. It also gave him and Theo time to renew the critical father–son bond, which had become frayed.

On a large piece of plywood, Jack and Theo crafted a remarkable replica of the Ardennes forest, which was the last-gasp offensive of another German invasion into France, as well as a turning point in the Battle of the Bulge. U.S. and German soldiers were arrayed in opposition among hedgerows, trees, and burnt-out buildings, and they were also in foxholes and behind tanks. Borrowing techniques from the diorama books to create further realism, Theo and Jack had rigged a device that would emit smoke onto the mock battlefield. In addition to this achievement of visual authenticity, Theo could recount each detail of the battle, demonstrating the power of personal interest as a motivator for learning.

As for the payoff on the "literacy ledger," Jack was able to reintroduce Theo to the pleasure of reading by finding out what his interests were, then engaging him with the appropriate literature. Similar to Theo, many boys who have adequate literacy skills will often stop reading when (a) reading at home is not being modeled and (b) school reading has more to do with skills, lessons, and tests than with personal enjoyment and growth. As a result of the diorama project, Theo continued to seek and read books about World War II. Peggy even found a slim but exciting book titled *Heroes Don't Run: A Novel of the Pacific War* (Mazer, 2007) that Theo quickly finished. All of these books now leave him asking for more. According to Karlene, Theo's renewed interest in reading surely contributed to the improvement he demonstrated on the district's standardized reading test the following year.

Even Cowboys Get the Blues: Reading as Adolescent Therapy

South Texas ranchers are a rugged breed. The endless hot, sunny, dry, and windy days leave the boys and men who spend their time working outside as weathered and tough as the land, which is strewn with mesquite, yucca, and prickly pear cacti.

Sonny's 16-year-old son Kip had devoted his young life to cattle ranching. He was the heir apparent to his dad's 700-acre spread and 500 head of mixed Santa Gertrudis, Red Brangus, and Texas Longhorn; that is, until the bottom dropped out for Sonny and hundreds of other small to midsize ranchers. The area was hit by a severe drought, coming on the heels of nearly 10 years of drier-than-average weather. Land for grazing withered, feed and hay prices soared, and water holes evaporated. Sonny could not afford to maintain his herd and pay the mortgage on a new barn. By the end of the summer, with no drought relief in sight, Sonny was forced to sell his entire herd at ridiculously low prices.

Kip was devastated. What hurt most was the realization that it could take years for his father to rebuild a herd that was large enough to make the ranch profitable. Meanwhile, predictions of continuing drought conditions seemed to come daily from meteorologists and agronomists. Kip had no backup plan. He had been squeaking by in school like the other rancher boys who fully expected to continue in the footsteps of their fathers and grandfathers who had been ranchers.

This tale came to me by way of Kip's English teacher, Marc. Kip's father was a lanky man in his mid-50s who, with a Stetson in his grooved hands, called on Marc as he was grading papers in his classroom. Sonny was a sincere and intelligent man who knew Kip was going to need help building his reading and learning skills to complete high school and learn a new trade. He confided in Marc that he did not want Kip to become a rancher because it had become too risky, offering an unpredictable living.

Sonny told Marc he could not remember ever seeing his son reading a book simply for the fun of it, and that he did not spend much time reading his schoolbooks, either. First, Marc told Sonny to do whatever he could in a positive way to induce Kip to read. Marc suggested he begin by finding books about ranching, cattle, and the Wild West and make them available to Kip. Sonny revealed that he himself had become a nonreader given the arduous, time-consuming demands of maintaining a ranch. Because he was now entering a form of semiretirement, however, he would have much more time to read. Marc emphasized how important it was for Sonny to take advantage of his role model status by demonstrating the pleasure of reading. Kip and Sonny would also have more leisure time as ranching chores wound down. Last, Marc reinforced the fact that Kip would not become a competent reader unless he read often. "Reading itself will help build his reading skills," Marc stressed. Their conversation ended with Marc giving Sonny directions to the big discount bookstore, so he could make a stop before heading back to the ranch.

The next morning, Marc found a voice-mail message from Sonny, thanking him for his time and help. He also let Marc know that he had purchased a handful of "really good books" about ranching and cowboys that he was sure would interest Kip. He promised to read them as well.

Sonny was true to his word on all counts. Marc became aware of the full measure of Sonny's commitment to get Kip enthused about reading as he watched Kip evolve into a young man who read and enjoyed books. Kip told Marc about such books as *Bob Sharp's Cattle Country: Rawhide Ranching on Both Sides of the Border* (Sharp, 1985), which is Sharp's memoir of cattle ranching in northern Mexico during the 1920s and 1930s. Sharp, the son of a dentist, dropped out of college in 1922 to work with cattle on the Mexico–Arizona border, eventually becoming the top hand in the ranching empire of Colonel William Green. Kip loved this book and the others that his dad brought home. Sonny was equally engrossed by these books, which described through pictures and text a life similar to the one Sonny and his father had cut out for themselves.

Another favorite book that Kip shared with Marc and talked about unceasingly if given the chance was Dick Hyson's (1998) *The Calling*. As the book's title suggests, the desire to become a rancher is not unlike other occupations of destiny. Frank Dalton is the main character, who is half Comanche, half white. He teaches the young tenderfoot R.C. Roth what the cowboy world is all about. Kip said Hyson's storytelling is straightforward and true to life, based on his own ranch family experiences. Other books with a distinctly Texan flavor include Don Graham's (2004) *Kings of Texas: The 150-Year Saga of an American Ranching Empire*, Kathleen Jo Ryan's (1999) *Deep in the Heart of Texas: Texas Ranchers in Their Own Words*, and Louise O'Connor's (1991) *Cryin' for Daylight: A Ranching Culture in the Texas Coastal Bend*. Ryan's book was especially poignant because actual ranchers disclose, in a one-on-one interview format, glimpses into the lives of people involved in cattle ranching. Kip said that he and his father talked a great deal about a couple of ranchers' stories concerning the challenges of passing the ranch on to the younger generation. One rancher, like Sonny, tells of dissuading his son from taking on the unpredictable lifestyle of cattle ranching even though the son feels it is in his blood.

In the end, Kip seemed to profit handsomely from his new habit of independent reading. The last I heard, Marc told me Kip had graduated from high school and joined the Reserve Officers' Training Corps (ROTC) at a local community college. "He wants to work on radar, or so he says," Marc continued, "and he asked me if there were any interesting books on that topic, too."

Driving Ms. Ritchie: Running Errands to the Bookstore

Next to paying for braces, the most trauma-inducing event for me as a parent was when my daughter Hannah received her driver's license. One positive result was that she could begin taking herself to and from school, work, the movies, sporting events, and dates; however, this is balanced by the downside of gas and repair expenses, higher insurance rates, and a nonstop fear of some unthinkable calamity involving my daughter, her friends, and the family car.

When single mom Karen (also known as Ms. Ritchie) watched her son Ben open his official letter from the Department of Transportation and hold his first operator's license, she said she could only stare in disbelief at this 11th grader who towered over her by nearly 6 inches. She felt totally unprepared for the move from bicycles to go-carts, and now this. Ben immediately requested to "go for a spin" in her car, which was the only one in the family. She relented and was struck by a brainstorm while cruising the neighborhood.

Ben, like most guys his age, was becoming increasingly involved in extracurricular activities, such as work, homework, and track practice, leaving little room for leisure reading. Karen, an elementary school teacher, was particularly sensitive to Ben's growing disaffection with reading. When Ben was in seventh grade, she began noticing what seemed like a complete reversal of his earlier fascination with reading. This coincided with a prodigious growth spurt, Karen's divorce from Ben's father, and a spot on the junior varsity track team as a distance runner. Karen has always been a compulsive reader, finding solace and escape from work and parenting in books, especially murder mysteries. Her estranged ex-husband read the weekend paper—period.

As Ben entered adolescence, Karen found herself and Ben in constant power struggles over how he should spend his free time. She demanded that he read, and she thrust books upon him with the vague hope that they would rekindle his passion for literature. Ben refused to read any of them. Karen said that for at least two years, the only material she ever saw him read was his monthly magazine on running, and then for just the first few days after its arrival. She felt as if she had hit a dead end.

As Ben drove and talked about the kind of car he wanted to buy, Karen hatched a new plot to engage Ben in reading. "Ben, I've got a couple of library books in the backseat that are due. Do you know how to get to the Greenwood Branch?" Karen asked. It was brilliant—Ben could drive her car, but she would send him on frequent errands to the bookstore and library where he would have to pick up, look for, and buy books.

That first time, Ben sat in the car while Karen returned her books and checked out some new ones. On the next trip, she coaxed him inside; he sat thumbing through magazines as she perused the shelves of the mystery-thriller area. The big payoff came when she started asking Ben for rides to the bookstore. The large chain bookstore held some tantalizing incentives, such as the coffee shop, which sold baked goods that Ben found irresistible. The drive was longer, as well, and required negotiating several heavy-traffic avenues, meaning that their trips to the bookstore would often last an hour or longer. In time, Ben fell into a routine that is familiar to many patrons of these new, larger bookstore chains: With a cup of coffee and a biscotti, he would lounge in one of the commodious chairs or sofas and read while Karen browsed. When Ben met Myra, a senior, during one of their trips to the discount bookstore, it quickly became his regular haunt. Myra's devotion to books began to rub off on him, especially because one of his reasons for reading was to be able to talk with Myra.

Ben continued to read even after their relationship faded because, even though he had not noticed, reading had become his new habit. As Karen put it,

> I knew if I could just get him around books again, he'd eventually start taking advantage. When you're in a library or bookstore, there isn't much else you can do with yourself except read...and that's what Ben started to do.

What began as errands to the library and bookstore connected to a young man's driving privileges turned into a young man's rediscovery of reading for fun.

Baseball Saved Us: Learning to Soft-Pedal Reading

Books are a tough sell for boys. That's all there is to it. Reading, as I have mentioned, becomes uncool for males when they are in their preteens and seems to get worse as they move through adolescence (Bauerlein & Stotsky, 2005; Sax, 2007). Why is this pattern so predictable? One compelling explanation is that U.S. culture portrays reading as a female activity. This is reinforced for boys nearly every day in school, where primarily women teach them to read, or at home, where the person who reads to them is almost certainly a woman. Once adolescent boys lose interest in books, these tough sells are even less likely to be successful. Buddy's parents, Charlotte and Louis, found this out the hard way.

Buddy was a precocious boy. Small for his age and possessing a squeaky voice, he was reading well by the time he entered kindergarten at age 5. Charlotte, a bank manager, and Louis, a successful attorney, often had Buddy read in front of friends and guests. To everyone's amazement, Buddy gave near perfect oral renditions of text from popular news magazines. Teachers also showcased his exceptional decoding skills, glowing with undeserved pride—undeserved because Buddy's remarkable reading ability was for him, as it is for most precocious readers, a special gift that transcends instruction and easy explanation.

His reading progress continued until Buddy, quite suddenly, stopped reading at age 9. Buddy had discovered baseball and took to it with fanatical zeal. I know how a young boy's attraction to this game can be so strong that it consumes nearly every minute of his day, because I was also a baseball fanatic during my childhood. Buddy's parents watched helplessly as he eschewed reading for collecting baseball cards, playing catch with others, or just playing with the ball by himself (throwing a ball against the steps or garage, or throwing it in the air), well into the evening. He wore an Astros cap, shirt, and trousers; when he could get away with it, he even slept with his cap on.

Buddy received his lowest reading test scores ever in fifth grade, and his parents felt they could no longer ignore his disaffection with books. They enrolled him in a special summer camp for boys who were "motivationally challenged" about school, reasoning that his obsession with baseball might be knocked out of him by the rigors of scholastic boot camp. Buddy survived two weeks in the Texas Hill Country. After being away from the game he loved so desperately, however, he seemed to become even more obsessive about baseball and responded with greater aversion to any mention of books, school, or plans for his academic future.

At the beginning of Buddy's sixth-grade year, Charlotte responded to one of my advertisements for clinical reading services, which I had distributed throughout the community. Charlotte was disconsolate. I was, unfortunately, all too familiar with her story, which was like countless others I have heard from parents who had taken extreme measures to get their sons to read. I was unable to be encouraging to Charlotte because our clinic's roster was full for the semester. I told her not to despair, but to be patient and, above all, not to do anything that would make the situation more intractable than it already appeared. "Motivating boys to read requires a delicate touch," I told her. "Thrusting books upon Buddy will, in all likelihood, force him to dig in his heels even more."

Within a month, I was on the telephone with Louis. His voice was edged with impatience as he cataloged the ways he had tried to "deal with" Buddy's antipathy toward reading. Louis recalled how, when growing up poor in Puerto Rico, his own father had demanded nothing short of a total commitment to his studies from him. "It paid off for me in the long run because my good grades made it possible for me to get into Baylor Law School. Buddy doesn't stand a chance at college if he keeps up this baseball nonsense." He wanted to know, because I was the "reading expert," what they should do.

Beyond my professional identity, I have also been the father of a preteen, so I have plenty of empathy for parents who cannot understand why their adolescent progeny are not as serious minded about learning and reading as they themselves are. It is as though parents expect their children to be perfect academic soldiers marching in step down the path of scholastic accomplishment that the parents have devised. When children reach the middle grades and begin asserting their selfhood, it is felt most grievously by those so naive as to think conformity is somehow programmed into them. Louis, and Charlotte to a lesser extent, could not understand how Buddy, growing up in a household of privilege and being raised by university graduates and successful professionals, could be anything but a young scholar. Even more harmful, however, was Louis's savaging of Buddy's self-esteem and burgeoning masculine identity. Louis did more harm than good by devaluing Buddy's love of baseball, which is a traditional and healthy diversion for males, and giving him no alternative but to read and study.

Buddy was only behaving like a boy. The insistence that he suspend his devotion to baseball and return to a time when he read often and with uncanny ability was pure folly. This demand is similar to asking a teenager to stop growing, be in bed by 8:00 p.m., and always like what mom and dad like. The way to improve Buddy's situation was to prevent any further deterioration of his relationship with his parents and create a supportive home environment that lovingly and patiently guided him back to reading. The key to this change was in Charlotte and Louis's midst all along, but it would take a few more months of misery before they lifted the blinders and recognized the reparative—baseball.

By the beginning of the second grading period that year, Buddy had developed psychosomatic stomach ailments, such as cramps, gas, sourness, and tightness. These ailments, which had started once or twice a week, became daily complaints. Doctors found nothing and suggested therapists and antianxiety drugs. There was finally a breakthrough just before Christmas.

Louis's brother John, Buddy's favorite uncle, was an executive in an auto parts manufacturing plant based in San Juan, Puerto Rico. He invited Buddy to spend a week with him during the upcoming school holiday. That week, the two of them indulged themselves with baseball. The Puerto Rican, Cuban, and Dominican clubs boast some of the best athletes the major leagues have ever signed, such as Roberto Clemente and Tony Perez from years past, and current stars Sammy Sosa and Pedro Martinez. Buddy and his uncle were at the ballpark every day, enjoying the outstanding play of these clubs. It was just the antidote for a young man beleaguered by demanding parents and psychosomatic distress.

Something else happened on that holiday, however, which initiated Buddy's journey back to reading. John's Christmas presents to his nephew were the following books: *Cal Ripken, Jr.: My Story* (Ripken & Bryan, 1999), *At the Plate with Ken Griffey Junior* (Christopher, 1997), and *What Hearts* (Brooks, 1992). Brooks's book tells a serious story about Asa, who is a boy about Buddy's age. Throughout his parents' divorce, seven moves in three years, and a new life with a gruff "fake" dad, Asa finds solace and courage in the one thing he knows well—baseball. In this way, *What Hearts* evokes the Warrior archetype. The other books that John gave Buddy also provide links to positive male archetypes. The two biographies recount the lives and athletic prowess of Cal Ripken and Ken Griffey, Junior, reminding young readers that in this era of illicit drug use among athletes honorable sports figures are still around. These men have conducted themselves with humility and gratitude both in and out of the ballpark, and each man is a generous contributor to programs for youngsters. Uncle John's gifts were refreshingly absent of demands or threats. They were offered openly, freely, and without parental or authoritative strings. Buddy thanked his uncle and set the books aside. He did not look at them again until his flight home, when he opened the Cal Ripken book and read the inscription: "From one baseball nut to another. Enjoy! Love, Uncle John."

A philosophy professor who graciously mentored me during my stormy sophomore year at college once told me that, sometimes, when people stop trying so hard to get what they want, things will come to them. This insight often needs repeating. Charlotte and Louis had to learn it or they might have created an insuperable emotional rift between themselves and their son. After talking with John and doing some serious self-examination the week that Buddy was away (when the emotional waters were calm), Louis took his first step toward reparation. For Christmas, he bought Buddy a first-baseman's glove.

As he ruminated over his past failures to mold his son into a faithful student and cheerful reader, Louis realized that he had plenty of latent feelings about baseball. He had also loved the game as a youngster. He was a talented baseball player and was ready to play wherever and whenever, but the exigencies of a poverty-stricken life on the outskirts of San Juan had forced him to give up his love for the game. His father worked tirelessly to support Louis, John, and their three sisters, and they were all successful. Buddy's obsession with baseball reminded Louis of a life of dissipation he was destined to live had he not a strong need to survive and the incentive of a better life, so Louis had worked hard, was studious, and above all, had given up that "silly pastime." Louis began to realize, however, that he still enjoyed baseball and decided to reconnect with his son by allowing himself to share his own love of baseball with Buddy.

I am pleased to report that this tale has a happy ending. Buddy started reading again that spring. It began with the sports page from the newspaper. Both he and Louis read stories together about the Astros: their spring training; which players were traded, acquired, and injured; batting averages; pitching records; and so on. The two of them made it to baseball's opening day game. (Louis allowed Buddy to miss school so they could be together on such a memorable occasion.) Buddy soon found himself reading books about baseball. He finally returned to the three books from his uncle and read them with a ferocity that reminded Charlotte and Louis of the "old" Buddy. The next fall, Buddy was allowed to join Little League as long he kept up his grades. The last report I had gotten on him was that he had qualified for the district's special middle school for children who qualify as gifted and talented students, and he was doing fine.

Charlotte called to tell me one last thing as well. She said that Buddy had bought his father a special birthday present—a picture book titled *Baseball Saved Us* (Mochizuki, 1993). This is a splendid book for boys both young and old. It takes place during a time of national embarrassment in the United States, when Japanese Americans were interned in camps during World War II. The main character and narrator is a boy of around 10 or 11, who describes how the inmates band together to create a life of dignity and diversion from the barbed wire, spartan accommodations, and incessant watch of guards wearing dark glasses and carrying automatic rifles. The story culminates in a baseball game played by the adolescent Japanese American boys within the prison grounds. The narrator has the deciding hit and wins the game for his team. As the boy rounds the bases, he notices that the guard who looks the most menacing allows a subtle grin to spread over his face, acknowledging the boy's feat. Buddy wrote on the inside cover, "The title of this book reminded me of us. I hope you like this story as much as I did. Love, Buddy."

Family Book Club: Bargaining With Chores

In my small family of three, it is crucial that we all pitch in. So, theoretically, every third day is my turn to clean up after dinner, and, theoretically, every other third day is my daughter Hannah's turn. As a preteen, she was given to a natural inclination toward shirking anything that smacks of parental-imposed responsibility and constantly tried to negotiate an alternative chore. Despite her complaints, this system worked fairly well but depended on each of us holding our end of the bargain.

Bargaining with after-dinner chores was worth it to single mom Roberta, whose three adolescent sons hated doing dishes more than any other household chore. Ever since they were old enough to help, Roberta has had them clearing the table; wrapping leftovers; and washing, drying, and putting the dishes away. It was becoming more of a struggle every evening, though. The boys fought her and each other over details and technicalities, made excuses, feigned illnesses, and procrastinated—all in an effort to either lessen the chore or get out of doing it entirely. Roberta was no pushover, however, and managed to get them to finish the job most evenings.

Getting the boys to read was another matter altogether. Roberta was not winning this fight. The days when her sons sat on her lap and listened excitedly to stories or fell asleep in her arms to a bedtime story were a faint memory. The boys spurned the idea of leisure-time reading as emphatically as doing dishes. When Rashad, the youngest, was placed in a remedial reading class at the start of junior high, Roberta realized it was time to find ways to get him and his older brothers more involved with reading at home.

Although of modest means, Roberta held the family together on a nurse's income and had been fortunate to have a day shift for the past three years that gave her time in the late afternoons and evenings to be with her sons. She confided her concern about Rashad to a colleague whose son had been in a similar class the year before and had made rapid progress. This prompted Roberta to get in touch with Rashad's reading teacher.

When Lynn, the reading teacher, met Roberta she was immediately struck by her level of commitment to her boys and her dedication to shift their attitudes about reading. During the course of their conversation,

Lynn asked many questions about Rashad's out-of-school interests. It was then that she discovered Rashad's nemesis—doing dishes. After years of working with parents to find ways of linking literacy to home and community interests and activities, it did not take long to hit on the idea of offering the boys a reprieve from doing the dishes if they would agree to replace this activity with reading. Like most new ideas, it remained somewhat ill defined until Roberta could experiment with possible options to see which worked best.

On her first attempt, Roberta had the guys simply read silently from any source they wanted while she did the dishes. This seemed to work for a week or so, but before long, they were finding ways around it by doing homework (which had always been an activity for after their cleanup), complaining about not having anything good to read, or pretending to lose a favorite book, magazine, or newspaper section. Not to be taken advantage of, Roberta used a new strategy in which the boys took turns reading aloud, not unlike a teacher's old reliable, round-robin reading. This, however, could not be sustained for more than a couple of days before boredom set in, resulting in a ridicule match whenever one of them stumbled on a word.

Finally, Roberta decided she needed to be directly involved with the boys' reading and discussions to keep them attentive and involved. Her solution was to let the after-dinner cleanup wait for 30 minutes while she and her sons read together. It worked. The threats of reassigning after-dinner chores if they did not participate in reading dwindled and eventually disappeared as they rediscovered the pleasure of family reading. Before long, Roberta started referring to them as the "Cooper Book Club," and the name stuck.

Roberta found that the reading material that brought out the best reading and discussion was what the boys picked out themselves. Each had his turn, so no one felt left out. Roberta would occasionally introduce something for the boys to consider. Her material was often rejected, although there were significant exceptions. She managed to get articles on health, diet, and nutrition past the Cooper advisory board. The boys also agreed to read articles about God and spirituality, which were some of Roberta's favorites. In turn, Roberta read articles about sports figures, such as Donovan McNabb, Kobe Bryant, and LeBron James, and musical stars, such as Snoop Dog, Jay-Z, and Lil Wayne. They read anything and everything that was mutually agreeable, regardless of the source. For example, a CD's liner notes were often part of the after-dinner discussions, as were sports trading cards. No one would judge these sources as quality literature; however, simply getting her boys back into the habit of reading for enjoyment was most important to Roberta.

Roberta noticed other benefits that came with her boys' reading habits. For example, dinner conversation was usually centered on what the family was currently reading or about to read; thus, as a result of the Cooper Book Club, there was an increase in text-related conversation between the boys and their mother. This is not an insignificant aspect of Roberta's efforts. Schwarzschild (2000) says that despite the seeming banality of family mealtime,

> Quality mealtime conversation between parents and children has been shown to increase children's mental and verbal abilities...develop important skills...such as...taking turns speaking, and listening to the person talking. Meals are one of the best times for children to pick up new words. Kids whose families chat most during mealtimes have larger word inventories. (p. 95)

In addition to increasing languaging about texts, quality mealtime conversation between parents and children has been shown to reinforce family unity (Bowden & Zeisz, 1997; Larson, Wiley, & Branscomb, 2006). Another potential bonus of the dinnertime book club is the way youth begin associating a pleasurable time in their day, in this case eating, with literacy (Sawyer, 1987). In Roberta's sons' minds, the pleasing aromas, tastes, and general atmosphere of mealtime have become connected in a positive way to reading, discussing, and sharing. How different these connections are when compared with the all-too-frequent negative associations many boys have with school-based reading because of stale instruction, unappealing texts, or fear of humiliation in a setting that places their vulnerability on the line virtually every day.

The Cooper Book Club ultimately heightened the boys' awareness of books. In the past, for example, they would walk down the supermarket aisle with books and magazines or past the entrance to a mall bookstore and not notice either. Roberta's sons were now giving these places a second glance. In fact, the family discovered the novel *Hoops* (Myers, 1999) as a result of a mall bookstore's display of Walter Dean Myers's (2000) novel *Monster*, which caught Rashad's eye.

Roberta found *Hoops* to be a perfect match for her sons, who were basketball-playing, Michael Jordan wannabes. Rashad and his brothers could not get enough of this story and were ready to reread it as soon as they had finished. Roberta wisely acquiesced, reasoning that, like the desire to watch a great movie again, a great book deserves to be read more than once.

When Roberta had first come to Lynn about her concerns for Rashad, Lynn, a former student of mine, told Roberta about my reading clinic. Roberta did contact me about nine months before the clinic, but I did not have any openings for new clients. By the time I contacted her to let her know of an opening in the clinic, Roberta, to my delight, graciously turned down my offer for the best of reasons. She explained that she had told Rashad if he did not improve his reading scores, he would be required to go to the university for remediation. He came through, and Roberta credited this in large part to the help he was getting from Lynn and his new reading habit. As Roberta detailed the changes she had noticed in all her sons, such as their willingness and eventual excitement to read, a sense of ease came over me. I looked out my office window at the students walking across campus and wondered if I might see Rashad among them someday, attending the university, though *not* for remediation.

BOY TALK

Mario, 14, Finds Inspiration to Beat the Streets After Reading *We Beat the Street: How a Friendship Pact Led to Success* by Sampson Davis, George Jenkins, Rameck Hunt, and Sharon Draper

Nobody really knows what it's like out here in the projects unless you live it. People who never been here think it's terrible. It's not that bad. Not all the time. I've seen things that are scary, like kids getting beat up, ladies getting their purses ripped out of their hands, people smoking dope, and guns. But there are good people and I try to have fun, too. That doesn't mean when I get older I want to stay here.

I want to do what Sampson, George, and Rameck do in *We Beat the Street: How a Friendship Pack Led to Success* (Davis, Jenkins, Hunt, & Draper, 2006). When these guys were like my age in the ninth grade they made a pact that they would get out of their neighborhood when they grew up. They lived in New Jersey where things were bad. People were poor. There was lots of crime. I don't blame them for wanting to leave. The book is cool because it's told by Sampson, George, and Rameck. You really get to know these guys. It wasn't easy for them, but they helped each other. They went to the same high school and studied together to help get good grades. Then they went to college. All three of them became doctors and Sampson ended up working in a hospital in his old neighborhood. It was the same hospital he had to go to when he was a little boy and he hurt his foot.

Reading about their lives made me feel like me and my friends can do whatever we want to do. You have to have a goal, George Jenkins said. And you have to have friends and adults who can help you. I have two friends, Mel and Shawn. I told them about this book and they want to read it too. We already watch each other's back, but maybe we could do something like Sampson, George, and Rameck did. I have a teacher in my science class who always helps me. I never liked science that much in junior high, but now I like it. He tells us about all these cool jobs you can have as a scientist. He took us on a field trip to the Hayden Planetarium and I got to meet Niel deGrasse Tyson. He's African American and director of the planetarium in DC. He told me to always stay curious about the world and work hard and have passion for something. The three doctors in my book told stories about important people who helped them make good decisions about what to do when they had problems or got in trouble. Some were teachers, parents, older men, preachers, and policemen.

This book was easy to read for me because I liked it. I felt like Sampson, George, and Rameck were talking just to me. The stories about what they did growing up were fun. I don't like people who are all mouth and no action. There are a lot of people like that where I live. When someone who is still in the projects tells you what to do, you don't want to do it because they're still on the streets. But when Sampson, George, and Rameck tell you about how to get out of the projects you can believe them because they did it.

CHAPTER 8

Turning Adolescent Boys Into Engaged Readers: Final Lessons

Since the publication of the first edition of *To Be a Boy, To Be a Reader* in 2002, concern about boys' personal and academic development has, if anything, grown. In addition to the book I recently coauthored with Debby Zambo, *Bright Beginnings for Boys: Engaging Young Boys in Active Literacy* (Zambo & Brozo, 2009), several other books on the topic (many of which are cited throughout this book) have appeared with new offerings showing up annually. The common theme running through them is that educators need to take more seriously the literate behavior and attitudes of young men, develop empathy for and, in some cases, design special language schemes to honor boys' unique male imaginations. Others, however—like Weaver-Hightower (2008) in his *The Politics of Policy in Boys' Education: Getting Boys "Right"*—challenge what they view as an oversimplified or even a blind advocacy for boys; not without its justification. After all, in spite of what we know about boys' academic struggles, we must also acknowledge that males continue to dominate corporate, political, and institutional life in America.

But literacy scholars, psychologists, and journalists are not inventing a cause. They have become sensitized to the issue by countless teachers, parents, and other concerned adults who witness daily the debilitating effects limited reading skill and lack of reading motivation have on teen and preteen male youth. With predictable regularity, I receive in my e-mail inbox missives from teachers and parents who write to express their frustration with the plight of their sons and male students and their hope that I might have ideas to help. This one from "Cassie," a practicum teacher in North Carolina, is typical:

> I had to send this note to you because your work with boys (young men) really struck me hard. What really brought my concerns to the forefront was my visit to the local high school and seeing how these young men were struggling with reading. It really hurt my heart that they could get past elementary and middle school and are only able to read on a 3rd or 4th grade level. Something is seriously wrong here… Someone has to turn these boys around before they get this far again. This cycle cannot continue. I listened as the young men struggle with words that should not

have given them trouble at all. What can I do, as a prospective teacher, to help turn these boys around and get them interested in reading? I struggled with this all night and it was really on my mind this morning. I see the frustrations on the teachers' faces when they have to deal with this and how it contains the class to learning less. I would like to do something to help these young men to want to read, to enjoy reading, and to see that they need reading in everything that they do.

Of course, I've had plenty of my own experiences like Cassie's. In middle and high schools throughout the United States, I've witnessed inordinate numbers of boys struggling to keep up, staring listlessly into space or with their heads on their desks during lessons, or disrupting the flow of instruction to avoid having their vulnerabilities as readers laid bare or simply out of boredom. I want to describe one such scene in which the teacher failed to garner the interest of boys, in spite of her commendable efforts to connect her students to a critical social issue.

A few years ago, I conducted an evaluation of a secondary reading program in a moderately affluent suburban school district near a large city in the southwestern region of the United States. As part of the evaluation process I spent many hours in reading teachers' classrooms documenting such things as the overall literate environment, the instructional strategies and materials, and the level of student engagement. Of particular concern to me was the gender ratio in these classes because students are placed in them based on low scores on the state mandated reading achievement test. I was struck first, though not surprised, by the fact that every single reading teacher in all five junior highs and the two high schools was female. Yet, the ratio of boys to girls in every classroom was approximately two to one, that is, twice as many boys as girls. Indeed, one class had 14 boys and only 1 girl!

Not only were males overrepresented as students in the reading classes, but so, too, were males of color. The district's demographics were rapidly shifting with a growing student population of ethnic minorities, predominantly African American, Hispanic American, and Asian-Indian American.

One lesson I witnessed during a week's worth of observations conducted in Ms. Willis's junior high reading classroom was revelatory. Ms. Willis was an experienced English teacher of 12 years, in her third year as a seventh- and eighth-grade reading teacher. Her classroom was adorned with popular posters of famous entertainment figures urging students to "read"; there were bookshelves and magazine racks; and the room was also decorated with a variety of colorful posters with information about class rules, grammar, and homework.

The lesson for the week involved reading a newspaper article orally, answering the teacher's whole-class questions, then taking a quiz about the material. The article was a lengthy feature piece from the local newspaper about a woman who had been abused herself and who had set up a shelter for other abused women. This is important stuff. Students should be aware of social issues such as domestic violence. Boys, particularly, need to become sensitized to their own sexist attitudes and behaviors and how these might, if they go unchecked, place them at risk of becoming batterers.

But soon into the very first lesson on the material, it became clear to me that the 16 boys in the class of 22 students were just not engaged by this text or the topic. With a history of low performance in and disaffection toward reading, most of these adolescent males were barely able to muster even a modest level of classroom decorum during the reading of this newspaper article. Boys were repeatedly wandering off task, squirming, tapping their pencils, talking, yelling across the room, laughing, and generally finding every way possible to avoid the text. Ms. Willis's comments to the boys throughout the lessons were disciplinary in nature. When she asked a whole-group question, no one volunteered a response, not even the 6 girls in class, though when pressed, they were the ones likely to give an answer.

I read the article Ms. Willis had asked her class to read and found it very moving and powerful. I wanted Ms. Willis's students to read it and find it powerful as well. I'm certain that as Ms. Willis was cutting the piece out of the paper and preparing it to be copied for her students that she desperately wanted them to connect with its message and have it serve as a catalyst for meaningful and critical dialogue. But that did not happen for the boys in her class; she was plainly unsuccessful in gaining their interest and consequently involving them in meaningful learning.

It's possible to envision greater student involvement had Ms. Willis employed more interesting teaching and learning strategies. But how can we ever hope to bring students to a level of critical awareness about an issue such as domestic abuse if we can't get them to read and engage with a text on the topic in the first place? More pointedly, how can we expect boys who are struggling readers and are generally turned off to reading to become engaged in text that does not interest them—in spite of the fact that we know it should interest them? Simon (1987) comments: "We cannot simply wish *our* stories prevail (p.374)." adding further: "Our authoritative voice is not oppressive by the weight of our own experience and knowledge but if it unwittingly subjugates other voices" (p. 374).

To try to understand these other voices in Ms. Willis's reading class, I interviewed several of her students individually. Sitting in the hall, I heard comments like, "We never read anything interesting in here." "She never lets us read what we like." "The stories in our book are boring." One guy looked at me and with cold contempt replied to my general opening query by saying, "I hate this class."

"What would you prefer to read?" I asked. Responses in order of popularity were sports, funny things, anything with lots of action, and scary stuff.

I'm convinced that if we fail to listen to boys like those in Ms. Willis's class and provide them texts and experiences that they enjoy and that engage their imaginations, we may lose them for good. Herbert (2001) describes nearly 5 million Americans in the 16-to-24 age group who are known as "nowhere kids." These are young people who "live their troubled lives beneath the radar of most public-policy planners" (p. 15). Herbert characterizes this hard-to-reach group as follows:

> Most lack basic job skills as well as solid literacy...they are neither working nor looking for jobs. They are not in vocational training. They are not in manufacturing. They are not part of the information age. They are not included in the American conversation. (p. 15)

And most are male. As this book has stated, to presume that reading skill and motivation alone will transform young men in Ms. Willis's class and the hundreds of thousands of others like them into productive and thoughtful citizens capable of reversing the stunting effects of poverty, alcohol and drug abuse, crime, and irresponsible fathering is recklessly naive; however, to ignore the potential of active literacy for ensuring that fewer adolescent males become nowhere kids is equally naive.

For this growing population of disenfranchised boys and for adolescent males from all of society, we must find texts and experiences with those texts that are engaging to boys, and offer models of positive masculinity. Basic literate practices that struggling and reluctant male readers exhibit daily, such as reading motor vehicle and computer manuals, clothing labels, graphic novels, and even gang graffiti (Aronson, 2001; Moje, 2000), may provide teachers and other adults clues to potential bridging and entry point texts. However, adolescent boys will develop higher levels of literacy only through sustained print encounters with increasingly challenging texts that are no less appealing and offered in stimulating learning contexts.

What the future holds for adolescent boys' literate lives depends in no small part on the recognition by teachers and parents that boys' literate health is vitally important to all of society. It is my hope that this recognition will lead to initiatives and practices that are both imaginative and practical and that will take place in classrooms, libraries, and homes. These practices should strive to bring together teachers, parents, and adolescents with good books and a range of other texts of interest. If you gain any new understandings from this new edition of *To Be a Boy, To Be a Reader* about how to help adolescent males find entry points to active literacy, I hope they are these:

- *The material matters.* In fact, in a recent survey to determine what makes middle school students want to read, the students expressed that the most important reason was *interest* in the reading material (Ivey & Broaddus, 2001). Teachers and parents must make the commitment to determine boys' interests and provide them with reading material tied to those interests.

- *Parents and teachers should respect boys' interests.* Applebee (1993) discovered that the core list of required books in most secondary schools in the United States had been unchanged for many years. Today, the situation is not much different (NEA, 2007). This offers at least one clue as to why so many adolescent boys become disaffected readers. Although books such as *Lord of the Flies* (Golding, 1999) and *A Separate Peace* (Knowles, 1990) may have a place in the literature curriculum of secondary schools, other books that reflect the lives and interests of teen and preteen boys should be a part of that curriculum as well. We have known for many years that a large number of adolescents prefer to read nonfiction, yet it is rare to find this genre in middle school and high school classrooms and libraries (Bean, 2000; Sullivan, 2001; Worthy et al., 1999). When boys say they like anything with sports, action, scary stuff, and comics and graphic novels, they mean it. We should honor boys' interests by making texts on these topics available to them.

- *Books with positive male archetypes are important.* I have shown, along with others (cf. Bean & Harper, 2007), how teen and preteen boys can become engaged readers by reading books that portray males in nonstereotypical ways. Quality young adult fiction and nonfiction that honestly depicts boys and men will help dispel myths about masculinity while offering positive images of masculinity for adolescent males to emulate.

- *All adults can model the pleasures and benefits of active literacy.* As illustrated in Chapter 6, teachers who struggle to make a difference in the literate lives of adolescent males are urged to consider how they can work with parents and other community members to support initiatives and practices that engage and keep boys reading. Any effort is worthy that works against the disaffection toward reading that many young men feel.

- *Boys should be viewed as a resource.* It is perhaps the long, well-documented history of boys' overall academic underachievement and their specific challenges with reading and other verbal skills that has helped contribute to an entrenched, popular perception and, indeed, an expectation that many boys simply will not become thoughtful, accomplished readers. To be sure, reversing perceptions of boys as weak readers and addressing the complex problems facing those who have turned off to reading or are striving to improve their reading abilities will challenge educators for years to come. But viewing boys as a resource holds great promise for helping them overcome literacy and learning difficulties (Alvermann, 2003). Teachers who see potential in their male students, take the time to discover ways of teaching and reaching them that are personally meaningful and culturally responsive, and capitalize on the resources they bring to the classroom (Alloway et al., 2002; Moje, 2002). As I have demonstrated, male youth care about many things and have passions, hobbies, aspirations, and experiences rife with opportunities for genuine curricular links. Exploring these links and inviting boys to find connections between their lifeworlds and school-based literacy may be the key to reducing achievement disparities between them and their female peers (Brozo, 2004).

It seems appropriate to conclude by retelling the story of the English teacher who wrote a friend of mine to describe how her male students in a basic English class, who were disinterested, hostile, listless, and uncooperative, were changed when she introduced them to Terry Davis's (1994) *If Rock and Roll Were a Machine.* Davis's book depicts 16-year-old Bert Bowden's decline from a bright, confident, and popular young man to one who is riddled with self-doubt after a teacher humiliates him in class. Bert embodies the Pilgrim archetype when a couple of adult friends show a willingness to help, and he embarks on a quest to regain his confidence.

After reading this novel, the attitudes of the teenage boys in the English teacher's classroom were transformed. Disinterest gave way to enthusiasm, hostility to curiosity, and opposition to participation. The teacher also noted that one young man who had described himself as a nonreader for life and was convinced nothing could change his mind was now the most involved student in her class.

Stories like this epitomize the importance of matching boys' needs and interests with appropriate texts. It also reminds us that sensitivity to boys' needs is the crucial first step, but to make a difference in boys' literate lives, teachers will need resources that identify appropriate texts and successful teaching practices to assist them in their efforts to reach boys. It is my hope that this new edition of *To Be a Boy, To Be a Reader* will continue to be one of those useful resources.

Literature With Positive Male Archetypes

I have presented evidence in this book that boys have consistent preferences for certain types of text. These preferences develop at a very young age for both boys and girls and appear to be related to general patterns of play and social behavior. For example, researchers investigated preschoolers' choices of fairy tales that they would most like to have read to them; they found clear gender differences in children as young as 2 years old (Collins-Standley, Gan, Yu, & Zillmann, 1996). Girls ages 2 to 4 had a strong and growing preference for romantic tales, whereas boys showed a growing preference for adventure and scary tales. The researchers advance the possibility that these gender-specific genre preferences are part of a "behavior-fosters-interest complex" (Collins-Standley et al., 1996, p. 301), whereby constitutional factors are likely influencing gender-specific preferences for particular fairy tales. In other words, very early in their development, boys acquire more pleasure from stories that help consolidate their unfolding sense of self as males.

This appendix contains titles of current young adult literature organized around the 10 male archetypes described in Chapter 2. These books were screened and selected by me and come principally from titles that I discovered during my research for this new edition.

Many books for adolescents, even good books, can go out of print quickly or become "dated" in the eyes of today's youth. So providing a list of titles that is as current as possible is important to users of this resource.

The titles, grouped according to the most salient archetype, are further classified into the following four categories to aid in the selection of books for teen and preteen boys: Adolescent Novels, Informational Books, Easier Reading, and Graphic Novels. This final category was added to reflect the growing number and variety of high-quality comic books and graphic novels. Although only two to three graphic novel titles are provided for each archetype, they may serve as examples for other similar texts users of this book might find on their own.

It is important to note that the male characters and figures in these books almost always exhibit behaviors consistent with more than one archetype. For purposes of simplification, therefore, I have placed each book within a category based on the archetypal qualities that are dominant in the book's main character or historical figure. This means that in some cases two biographies of the same man may be placed under different archetypes. Teachers can use the guidelines articulated in previous chapters as well as their own creative imaginations for helping boys develop a positive sense of masculinity through enjoyable experiences with the following books. Although I have categorized the young adult literature in these ways, teachers who may feel a book fits better in another category should feel free to use it that way.

Pilgrim

Adolescent Novels

Blue Fingers: A Ninja's Tale (Cheryl Aylward Whitesel) New York: Clarion, 2004.
The Brothers Torres (Coert Voorhees) New York: Hyperion, 2009.
The Car (Gary Paulsen) New York: Bantam Doubleday Dell, 1995.
Car Trouble (Jeanne DuPrau) New York: Greenwillow, 2005.
Daniel Half-Human: And the Good Nazi (David Chotjewitz) New York: Simon & Schuster/Atheneum, 2004.
Extremely Loud and Incredibly Close (Jonathan Safran Foer) Orlando, FL: Houghton Mifflin, 2006.
The Fields and the Hills: The Journey, Once Begun (Harald Bakken) New York: Clarion, 1992.
If Rock and Roll Were a Machine (Terry Davis) New York: Laurel-Leaf, 1994.
La Linea (Ann Jaramillo) New York: Square Fish, 2006.
Night of the Howling Dogs (Graham Salisbury) New York: Laurel Leaf, 2007.
One Fat Summer (Robert Lipsyte) New York: HarperCollins, 1991.
Pacific Crossing (Gary Soto) Orlando, FL: Harcourt Brace Jovanovich, 1992.
Parzival: The Quest of the Grail Knight (Katherine Paterson) New York: Puffin, 2000.
Playing Without the Ball (Rich Wallace) New York: Knopf, 2000.
Right Behind You (Gail Giles) Boston: Little, Brown Young Readers, 2008.
Running Wild (Thomas Dygard) New York: Penguin, 1998.
The Snake-Stone (Berlie Doherty) New York: Viking/Penguin, 1998.
Thirteen Reasons Why (Jay Asher) New York: Penguin, 2007.
Touching Spirit Bear (Ben Mikaelsen) New York: HarperCollins, 2001.
Trouble (Gary Schmidt) New York: Clarion, 2008.
The Wednesday Wars (Gary Schmidt) New York: Clarion, 2007.
Whirligig (Paul Fleishman) New York: Henry Holt and Company, 1998.
The Wreckers (Iain Lawrence) New York: Bantam Doubleday Dell, 1999.

Informational Books

Across America on an Emigrant Train (Jim Murphy) New York: Clarion, 1993.
Black Pioneers: An Untold Story (William Loren Katz) New York: Atheneum, 1999.

Born to Run (Christopher McDougall) New York: Knopf, 2009.

Children of the Dust Bowl: The True Story of the School at Weedpatch Camp (Jerry Stanley) New York: Crown Publishers, 1992.

The Circuit: Stories From the Life of a Migrant Child (Francisco Jimenez) Albuquerque, NM: University of New Mexico Press, 1997.

Columbus and the World Around Him (Milton Meltzer) Danbury, CT: Franklin Watts, 1990.

Flying to the Moon: An Astronaut's Story (Michael Collins) Somerville, MA: Sunburst, 1994.

Ghosts of War: The True Story of a 19 Year Old G.I. (Ryan Smithson) New York: Collins, 2009.

Grass Sandals: The Travels of Basho (Dawine Spivak) New York: Atheneum, 1997.

A Hope in the Unseen: An American Odyssey From the Inner City to the Ivy League (Ron Suskind) Louisville, KY: Broadway, 1999.

Of Beetles and Angels: A Boy's Remarkable Journey from a Refugee Camp to Harvard (Mawi Asgedom) Boston: Little, Brown Young Readers, 2002.

Out of Darkness: The Story of Louis Braille (Russell Freedman) New York: Clarion, 1997.

Tea That Burns: A Family Memoir of Chinatown (Bruce Edward Hall) New York: Free Press, 1998.

The Worst Hard Time: The Untold Story of Those Who Survived the Great American Dust Bowl (Timothy Egan) New York: Mariner, 2006.

Easier Reading

Bearskin (Howard Pyle) New York: Books of Wonder, 1997.

Beyond the Sea of Ice: The Voyages of Henry Hudson (Joan Elizabeth Goodman) New York: Mikaya Press, 1999.

Blood on the River: Jamestown 1607 (Elisa Carbone) New York: Viking, 2006.

Children of Bach (Ellis Dillon) New York: Scribner, 1992.

China Boy (Gus Lee) East Rutherford, NJ: Plume, 1994.

Countdown (Ben Mikaelsen) New York: Disney Press, 1997.

Crossing the Wire (Will Hobbs) New York: HarperCollins, 2006.

Crow and Weasel (Tom Pohrt) Somerville, MA: Sunburst, 1998.

Dance of the Sacred Circle (Kristina Rodanas) Boston: Little, Brown, 1994.

Knights of the Hill Country (Tim Tharp) New York: Laurel Leaf, 2008.

The Lightning Thief (Rick Riordan) New York: Miramax, 2005.

The Merchant of Death (D.J. McHale) New York: Aladdin, 2006.

Peak (Roland Smith) Orlando, FL: Harcourt, 2007.

Secret of the Dolphins (Edward Packard) New York: Bantam, 1993.

Stranded at Plimoth Plantation 1626 (Gary Bowen) New York: HarperCollins, 1994.

Taking Sides (Gary Soto) San Diego, CA: Harcourt Brace, 1992.

3 NBs of Julian Drew (James Deem) New York: Avon, 2000.

The True Adventures of Daniel Hall (Diane Stanley) New York: Penguin, 1995.

Under the Sun (Arthur Dorros) New York: Amulet, 2004.

The Watsons Go to Birmingham—1963 (Christopher Paul Curtis) New York: Bantam Doubleday Dell, 1995.

Graphic Novels
The Arrival (Shaun Tan) New York: Arthur A. Levine, 2007.
Laika (Nick Abadzis) New York: First Second, 2007.

Patriarch

Adolescent Novels
California Blue (David Klass) Topeka, KS: Econo-Clad, 1999.
Canyon Winter (Walter Morey) New York: Puffin, 1994.
Cruise Control (Terry Trueman) New York: HarperTeen, 2005.
The Fool's War (Lee Kisling) New York: HarperCollins, 1992.
Gypsy Davey (Chris Lynch) New York: HarperCollins, 1994.
Hoops (Walter Dean Myers) Minneapolis, MN: Econo-Clad, 1999.
London Calling (Edward Bloor) New York: Knopf, 2006.
The Mailbox (Audrey Shafer) New York: Delacorte Press, 2006.
The Maze (Will Hobbs) New York: Avon, 1999.
The Road (Cormac McCarthy) New York: Knopf/Vintage, 2008.
Shadow Boxer (Chris Lynch) New York: HarperTrophy, 1995.
True Friends (Bill Wallace) New York: Holiday House, 1994.
Tyrell (Coe Booth) New York: Scholastic, 2006.
Yellow Flag (Robert Lipsythe) New York: HarperTeen, 2006.

Informational Books
Andrew Carnegie: Steel King and Friend to Libraries (Zachary Kent) Springfield, NJ: Enslow, 1999.
Eagle Blue: A Team, a Tribe, and a High School Basketball Season in Arctic Alaska (Michael D'Orso) New York: Bloomsbury, 2006.
Elegy on the Death of César Chávez (Rudolpho Anaya) Houston, TX: Cinco Puntos, 2000.
The Meaning of It All: Thoughts of a Citizen Scientist (Richard Feynman) Cambridge, MA: Perseus, 1999.
Michael Jordan: Basketball Great (Sean Dolan) Topeka, KS: Econo-Clad, 1999.
Patriarch: George Washington and the New American Nation (Richard Norton Smith) Boston: Houghton Mifflin, 1997.
Steve Young: Complete Quarterback (Terri Morgan & Samuel Thaler) Minneapolis, MN: Lerner, 1995.
This Land Was Made for You and Me: The Life and Songs of Woody Guthrie (Elizabeth Partridge) New York: Penguin/Viking, 2002.
William Bradford: Rock of Plymouth (Kieran Doherty) New York: 21st Century/ Millbrook, 1999.

Easier Reading
The Backyard Tribe (Neil Shulman) New York: St. Martin's, 1994.
The First Part Last (Angela Johnson) New York: Simon Pulse, 2004.

Frederick Douglass: The Last Day of Slavery (William Miller) New York: Lee & Low, 1995.
Gregor the Overlander (Suzanne Collins) New York: Scholastic, 2004.
The Harmony Arms (Ron Koertge) New York: Avon, 1994.
Martin Luther King (Rosemary Bray) New York: Greenwillow, 1995.
Running Loose (Chris Crutcher) New York: Bantam Doubleday Dell, 1986.
Smiles To Go (Jerry Spinelli) New York: HarperCollins, 2008.
Thomas Jefferson: A Picture Book Biography (James Giblin) New York: Scholastic, 1994.
Too Long a Stranger (Janette Oke) Minneapolis, MN: Bethany House, 1999.

Graphic Novels

Gettysburg: The Graphic Novel (C.M. Butzer) New York: HarperCollins, 2008.
Identity Crisis (Brad Meltzer) New York: DC Comics, 2006.
Jimmy Corrigan: The Smartest Kid on Earth (Chris Ware) London: Jonathan Cape, 2004.

Warrior

Adolescent Novels

Against the Storm (Gaye Hicyilmaz) Boston: Little, Brown, 1992.
The Battle of Jericho (Sharon Draper) New York: Simon Pulse, 2003.
Black Duck (Janet Taylor Lisle) New York: Puffin, 2006.
Code Talker (Joseph Bruchac) New York: Dial, 2005.
The Contender (Robert Lipsyte) New York: HarperCollins, 1991.
Dust Devils (Robert Laxalt) Reno, NV: University of Nevada Press, 1997.
Ghost Soldier (Elaine Alphin) New York: Henry Holt and Company, 2001.
Hitler's Canary (Sandi Toksvig) New York: Roaring Brook Press, 2005.
Iron Thunder (Avi) New York: Hyperion, 2007.
Ironman (Chris Crutcher) New York: Greenwillow, 1995.
Jesse (Gary Soto) New York: Scholastic, 1996.
The Last Mission (Harry Mazer) New York: Dell, 1981.
No Man's Land: A Young Soldier's Story (Susan Bartoletti) New York: Scholastic, 1999.
The Proving Ground (Elaine Alphin) New York: Henry Holt and Company, 1993.
Ran Van: The Defender (Diana Wieler) Toronto, ON: Groundwood, 1998.
Reef of Death (Paul Zindel) New York: Disney Press, 1999.
Scorpions (Walter Dean Myers) New York: HarperTrophy, 1990.
Summerland (Michael Chabon) New York: Miramax, 2004.
Sunrise Over Fallujah (Walter Dean Myers) New York: Scholastic Press, 2009.
The Supernaturalist (Eoin Colfer) New York: Miramax, 2004.
Trino's Choice (Diane Gonzales-Bertrand) Houston, TX: Arte Publico, 1999.
The Walls of Pedro Garcia (Kevin McColley) New York: Delacorte, 1993.
When the Mountain Sings (John MacLean) Boston: Houghton Mifflin, 1992.
Wrestling Sturbridge (Rich Wallace) New York: Knopf, 1997.

Informational Books

Behind Enemy Lines: A Young Pilot's Story (H.R. DeMallie) New York:
Sterling, 2007.

A Boy Becomes a Man at Wounded Knee (Ted Wood with Wanbli Numpa Afraid
of Hawk) New York: Walker and Company, 1995.

Colin Powell: A Man of War and Peace (Carl Senna) New York: Walker and
Company, 1992.

Fire in Their Eyes: Wildfires and the People Who Fight Them (Karen Magnuson
Beil) San Diego, CA: Harcourt Brace, 1999.

I Was a Teenage Professional Wrestler (Ted Lewin) New York: Hyperion, 1994.

Jesse Owens (Tom Streissguth) New York: Lerner, 1999.

Jim Thorpe: Twentieth-Century Jock (Robert Lipsyte) New York:
HarperCollins, 1993.

John Paul Jones: The Pirate Patriot (Armstrong Perry) New York: Sterling, 2006.

Kickoff! (Tiki Barber & Ronde Barber) New York: Simon & Shuster, 2007.

The Life and Death of Crazy Horse (Russell Freedman) New York: Holiday
House, 1996.

The Long Road to Gettysburg (Jim Murphy) Boston: Houghton Mifflin, 2000.

Nelson Mandela: Voice of Freedom (Libby Hughes) Lincoln, NE:
iUniverse.com, 2000.

The Race Beat: The Press, the Civil Rights Struggle, and the Awakening of a Nation
(Gene Roberts & Hank Klibanoff) New York: Knopf/Vintage, 2007.

Still Me (Christopher Reeve) New York: Ballantine, 1999.

Troy Aikman: Super Quarterback (Bill Gutman) Brookfield, CT: Millbrook
Press, 1997.

We Beat the Street—How a Friendship Pact Led to Success (Sampson Davis,
George Jenkins, Rameck Hunt, Sharon Draper) New York: Dutton
Children's, 2005.

Wheelchair Warrior: Gangs, Disability, and Basketball (Melvin Juette & Ronald J.
Berger) Philadelphia: Temple University Press, 2008.

Working Fire: The Making of an Accidental Fireman (Zac Unger) New York:
Penguin, 2004.

A Young Patriot: The American Revolution as Experienced by One Boy (Jim
Murphy) New York: Clarion, 1996.

Easier Reading

Backfield Package (Thomas Dygard) New York: Morrow, 1992.

The Brave (Robert Lipsyte) New York: HarperTrophy, 1993.

The Heartbeat of Halftime (Stephen Wunderli) New York: Avon, 1996.

Mandela: From the Life of the South African Statesman (Floyd Cooper) New York:
Philomel, 1996.

On My Honor (Marion Bauer) New York: Dell Yearling, 1987.

The Printer's Apprentice (Stephen Krensky) New York: Bantam Doubleday
Dell, 1995.

Roughnecks (Thomas Cochran) San Diego, CA: Gulliver, 1999.

Toussaint L'Ouverture: The Fight for Haiti's Freedom (Walter Dean Myers) New
York: Simon & Schuster, 1996.

What Hearts (Bruce Brooks) New York: HarperCollins, 1992.
Zach's Lie (Roland Smith) New York: Scholastic, 2001.

Graphic Novels

Fullmetal Alchemist (Hiromu Arakawa) San Francisco: VIZ Media, 2005.
Monster Zoo (Doug Tennapel) Berkeley, CA: Image Comics, 2008.
Stormbreaker: The Graphic Novel (Anthony Horowitz) New York: Philomel, 2006.

Magician

Adolescent Novels

At All Costs (John Gilstrap) New York: Warner, 1999.
The Curious Incident of the Dog in the Night-Time (Mark Haddon) New York: Knopf/Vintage, 2004.
Cyclops (Clive Cussler) New York: Pocket, 1995.
Daniel X (James Patterson) Boston: Little, Brown, 2009.
Discordia: The Eleventh Dimension (Dena Salmon) New York: Hyperion, 2009.
Dither Farm (Sid Hite) Topeka, KS: Econo-Clad, 1999.
Dragonwings (Laurence Yep) New York: HarperTrophy, 1989.
Eragon (Christopher Paolini) New York: Knopf, 2003.
Escape From Exile (Robert Levy) Boston: Houghton Mifflin, 1993.
The Golden Compass (Phillip Pullman) New York: Del Rey, 1999.
The Invention of Hugo Cabret (Brian Selznick) New York: Scholastic, 2007.
Moonfall (Jack McDevitt) New York: HarperCollins, 1999.
Plunking Reggie Jackson (James Bennett) New York: Simon & Schuster, 2001.
The Ruins of Gorlan (John Flanagan) New York: Puffin, 2006.
The Sea of Trolls (Nancy Farmer) New York: Simon Pulse, 2004.
The Shark Callers (Eric Campbell) San Diego, CA: Harcourt Brace, 1995.
Stars (Eric Walters) Topeka, KS: Econo-Clad, 1999.
Striking Out (Will Weaver) New York: HarperCollins, 1993.
The Subtle Knife (Phillip Pullman) New York: Dell Yearling, 1999.
The Thief Lord (Cornelia Funke) New York: Scholastic, 2000.
The Transall Saga (Gary Paulsen) New York: Laurel Leaf, 1999.
The Warrior Heir (Cinda Williams Chima) New York: Hyperion, 2007.

Informational Books

The Abracadabra Kid: A Writer's Life (Sid Fleishman) New York: Morrow, 1998.
Always Inventing: A Photobiography of Alexander Graham Bell (Tom Matthews) Washington, DC: National Geographic Society, 1999.
Bard of Avon: The Story of William Shakespeare (Diane Stanley) Topeka, KS: Econo-Clad, 1999.
Bill Peet: An Autobiography (Bill Peet) Boston: Houghton Mifflin, 1994.
The Casebook of Forensic Detection (Colin Evans) Chichester, England: John Wiley & Sons, 1998.

Gutenberg (Leonard Everett Fisher) New York: Simon & Schuster, 1993.

Harry Houdini (Adam Woog) San Diego, CA: Lucent, 1995.

Matthew Brady: His Life and Photographs (George Sullivan) New York: Cobblehill, 1994.

Odd Boy Out: Young Albert Einstein (Don Brown) Orlando, FL: Houghton Mifflin, 2004.

Outward Dreams: Black Inventors and Their Inventions (James Haskins) New York: Starfire, 1992.

Rocket Boys: A Memoir (Homer Hickam Jr.) New York: Delacorte, 2000.

Rocket Man: The Story of Robert Goddard (Tom Streissguth) Minneapolis, MN: Carolrhoda, 1995.

Tibaldo and the Hole in the Calendar (Abner Shimony) New York: Copernicus, 1997.

Easier Reading

The Adventures of Ali Baba Bernstein (Johanna Hurwitz) New York: Avon, 1995.

Amazing and Death Defying Diary of Eugene Dingman (Paul Zindel) New York: Starfire, 1989.

47 (Walter Mosley) Boston: Little, Brown, 2005.

The Gift-Giver (Joyce Hansen) New York: Clarion, 1989.

Harry Potter and the Chamber of Secrets (J.K. Rowling) New York: Scholastic, 1999.

Harry Potter and the Sorcerer's Stone (J.K. Rowling) New York: Scholastic, 1999.

The Hound of Rowan (Henry Neff) New York: Yearling, 2008.

The Iron Ring (Lloyd Alexander) New York: Penguin, 1999.

Knights of the Kitchen Table (Jon Scieszka) New York: Penguin, 1994.

Leonardo da Vinci (Diane Stanley) New York: Morrow, 1996.

The Librarian Who Measured the Earth (Kathryn Lasky) Boston: Little, Brown, 1994.

Mozart Tonight (Julie Downing) New York: Bradbury Press, 1991.

Mutation (Robin Cook) East Rutherford, NJ: Berkley Publishing Group, 1991.

The Real McCoy: The Life of an African American Inventor (Wendy Towle) New York: Scholastic, 1993.

Repossessed (A.M. Jenkins) New York: HarperTeen, 2007.

Strays (Ron Koertge) New York: Walker, 2008.

The Tempest by William Shakespeare (Ann Keay Beneduce) New York: Philomel, 1996.

The Wonderful Towers of Watts (Patricia Zelver) New York: Tambourine, 1994.

Graphic Novels

Bleach (Tite Kubo) San Francisco: VIZ Media, 2004.

The Dresden Files: Welcome to the Jungle (Jim Butcher) New York: Del Rey/Dabel Brothers, 2008.

The Great Escape: Tunnel to Freedom (Mike Meserole) New York: Sterling, 2008.

King

Adolescent Novels

Artemis Fowl (Eoin Colfer) New York: Miramax, 2003.
The Astonishing Life of Octavian Nothing, Traitor to the Nation, Vol. 1: The Pox Party (M.T. Anderson) Cambridge, MA: Candlewick Press, 2006.
The Astonishing Life of Octavian Nothing, Traitor to the Nation, Vol. II: The Kingdom on the Waves (M.T. Anderson) Cambridge, MA: Candlewick, 2008.
Borderlands (Peter Carter) New York: Farrar, Straus & Giroux, 1993.
Buddha Boy (Kathe Koja) New York: Francis Foster, 2003.
House of the Scorpion (Nancy Farmer) New York: Atheneum, 2002.
Last Days of Summer (Steve Kluger) New York: Morrow/Avon, 1999.
The Lightning Thief (Rick Riordan) New York: Miramax, 2006.
Mister Pip (Lloyd Jones) New York: Dell Publishing/Dial Press, 2008.
Mortal Engines (Philip Reeve) New York: Eos, 2001.
Walker of Time (Helen Hughes Vick) Sacramento, CA: Roberts Rinehart, 1993.
When Heroes Die (Penny Durant) Topeka, KS: Econo-Clad, 1999.

Informational Books

Alexander the Great (John Gunther) New York: Sterling, 2007.
Arthur Ashe: Breaking the Color Barrier (David Wright) Springfield, NJ: Enslow, 1996.
Cesar Chavez (Ruth Franchere & Earl Thollander) New York: HarperCollins, 1970.
The Curse of King Tut (Patricia Netzley) San Diego, CA: Lucent, 2000.
Franklin D. Roosevelt (Karen Bornemann Spies) Springfield, NJ: Enslow, 1999.
Geronimo: Wolf on the Warpath (Ralph Moody) New York: Sterling, 2006.
The Greatest: Muhammad Ali (Walter Dean Myers) New York: Scholastic, 2001.
King of the World: Muhammad Ali and the Rise of an American Hero (David Remnick) Elk Grove, CA: Vintage, 1999.
The Last Lecture (Randy Pausch) New York: Hyperion Press, 2008.
Lincoln: A Photobiography (Russell Freedman) New York: Clarion, 1989.
The Sea King: Sir Francis Drake and His Times (Albert Marrin) New York: Atheneum, 1995.
Ship of Gold in the Deep Blue Sea (Gary Kinder) Elk Grove, CA: Vintage, 1999.
The Tall Mexican: The Life of Hank Aguirre All-Star Pitcher, Businessman, Humanitarian (Robert Copley) Houston, TX: Arte Publico, 2000.
Winston Churchill: Soldier, Statesman, Artist (John Severance) New York: Clarion, 1996.

Easier Reading

The Book of Three (Lloyd Alexander) New York: Dell Yearling, 1999.
The Fire Pony (W.R. Philbrick) Topeka, KS: Econo-Clad, 1999.
Ghost Canoe (Will Hobbs) New York: Avon/Camelot, 1998.
Gregor the Overlander (Suzanne Collins) New York: Scholastic, 2003.

Honest Abe (Edith Kunhardt) New York: Greenwillow, 1993.
Invitation to the Game (Monica Hughes) New York: Aladdin, 1993.
A Little Bit Dead (Chap Reaver) Topeka, KS: Econo-Clad, 1999.
A Picture Book of Sitting Bull (David Adler) New York: Holiday House, 1993.
Promises to Keep: How Jackie Robinson Changed America (Sharon Robinson)
    New York: Scholastic, 2004.
The Sea of Trolls (Nancy Farmer) New York: Atheneum, 2004.

Graphic Novels

Artemis Fowl: The Graphic Novel (Eoin Colfer) New York: Hyperion, 2007.
Northlanders (Brian Wood) New York: Vertigo, 2008.
Unmanned (Y: The Last Man) (Brian Vaughan) New York: Vertigo, 2003.

Wildman

Adolescent Novels

The Absolutely True Diary of a Part-Time Indian (Sherman Alexie) Boston: Little,
    Brown, 2007.
Airman (Eoin Colfer) New York: Hyperion, 2009.
Angels of the Swamp (Dorothy Whittaker) New York: Walker and
    Company, 1992.
Brian's Return (Gary Paulsen) New York: Random House, 1999.
Brian's Winter (Gary Paulsen) New York: Scholastic, 1996.
Crash (Jerry Spinelli) New York: Knopf, 1996.
Danny Ain't (Joe Cottonwood) New York: Scholastic, 1992.
Far North (Will Hobbs) New York: Avon, 1996.
Jason's Gold (Will Hobbs) New York: Morrow, 1999.
The Last Safe Place on Earth (Richard Peck) New York: Laurel Leaf, 1996.
Leepike Ridge (N.D. Wilson) New York: Yearling, 2007.
Lockie Leonard, Human Torpedo (Tim Winton) Boston: Little, Brown, 1991.
Looking for Alaska (John Green) New York: Penguin, 2005.
The Loop (Nicholas Evans) New York: Dell, 1999.
Never Cry Wolf (Farley Mowat) New York: Bantam, 1983.
The River (Gary Paulsen) New York: Dell Yearling, 1993.
Slam! (Walter Dean Myers) New York: Scholastic, 1998.
Touching Spirit Bear (Ben Mikaelsen) New York: HarperTeen, 2005.
Twisted (Laurie Halse Anderson) Boston: Little, Brown, 2007.
We Are All Guilty (Kingsley Amis) New York: Viking, 1991.
Wilderness Peril (Thomas Dygard) New York: Puffin, 1991.

Informational Books

Born Naked (Farley Mowat) Boston: Houghton Mifflin, 1995.
The Climb: Tragic Ambitions on Everest (Anatoli Boukreev & G. Weston DeWalt)
    New York: St. Martin's, 1998.

The Dangerous Book for Boys (Conn Iggulden & Hal Iggulden) New York: HarperCollins, 2006.

Eiger Dreams: Ventures Among Men and Mountains (Jon Krakauer) New York: Lyons Press, 2009.

Gone A-Whaling: The Lure of the Sea and the Hunt for the Great Whale (Jim Murphy) New York: Clarion, 1998.

The Hemingway Cookbook (Craig Boreth) Chicago: Chicago Review Press, 1998.

Ice Story: Shackleton's Lost Expedition (Elizabeth Cody Kimmel) New York: Clarion, 1999.

Into Thin Air: A Personal Account of the Mt. Everest Disaster (Jon Krakauer) Waxhaw, NC: Anchor, 1999.

Jack London: A Biography (Daniel Dyer) New York: Scholastic, 1997.

The Man Who Was Poe (Avi) New York: Avon, 1997.

Pirates (David Spence) South Bend, IN: Consortium, 2001.

The Saga of Lewis and Clark Into the Uncharted West (Thomas Schmidt & Jeremy Schmidt) New York: Dorling Kindersley, 1999.

Shooting Under Fire: The World of the War Photographer (Peter Howe) New York: Artisan, 2002.

The Story of an Aviator (Marmaduke Randolph Calhoun & Clint Twist) Cambridge, MA: Candlewick Press, 2008.

To the Top of the World: Adventures With Arctic Wolves (Jim Brandenberg) New York: Scholastic, 1997.

A Voyage Long and Strange: Rediscovering the New World (Tony Horwitz) New York: Henry Holt, 2008.

Within Reach (Mark Pfetzer) New York: Puffin, 2000.

Easier Reading

Airborn (Kenneth Oppel) New York: HarperCollins, 2004.

Alabama Moon (Watt Key) New York: Square Fish, 2008.

Angel Falls: A South American Journey (Martin Jordan & Tanis Jordan) New York: Kingfisher, 1995.

Antar and the Eagles (William Mayne) Garden City, NY: Doubleday, 1990.

Captain Hawaii (Anthony Dana Arkin) New York: HarperCollins, 1994.

Capturing Nature: The Writings and Art of John James Audubon (Peter Roops & Connie Roops) New York: Walker and Company, 1993.

Climb or Die (Edward Myers) New York: Hyperion, 1996.

Cowboy Charlie (Jeanette Winter) San Diego, CA: Harcourt Brace, 1995.

Hatchet (Gary Paulsen) New York: Scholastic, 1999.

Hugh Glass, Mountain Man: Left for Dead (Robert McClung) New York: Beech Tree, 1993.

I'm Exploding Now (Sid Hite) New York: Hyperion, 2007.

Into the Deep Forest With Henry David Thoreau (Jim Murphy) New York: Clarion, 1995.

The Lemonade War (Jacqueline Davies) New York: Houghton Mifflin, 2007.

Lewis and Clark: Explorers of the American West (Steven Kroll) New York: Holiday House, 1994.

A Picture Book of Davy Crockett (David Adler) New York: Holiday House, 1996.

Prince Henry the Navigator (Leonard Everett Fisher) New York: Macmillan, 1990.
Things Not Seen (Andrew Clements) New York: Puffin, 2006.
Three Good Deeds (Vivian Van Velde) Orlando, FL: Magic Carpet, 2005.
Walden (Robert Sabuda) New York: Philomel, 1990.

Graphic Novels

Nat Turner (Kyle Baker) New York: Abrams, 2008.
The Strongest Man in the World: Louis Cyr (Nicolas Debon) Toronto:
　　Groundwood, 2007.

Healer

Adolescent Novels

All of the Above (Shelley Pearsall) Boston: Little, Brown, 2008.
Blue Skin of the Sea (Graham Salisbury) New York: Laurel Leaf, 1994.
Bottled Up (Jaye Murray) New York: Speak, 2004.
Bud, Not Buddy (Christopher Paul Curtis) New York: Random House, 1999.
Chinese Handcuffs (Chris Crutcher) New York: Dell, 1996.
Drums, Girls, and Dangerous Pie (Jordan Sonnenblick) New York: Scholastic,
　　2006.
Fat Kid Rules the World (K.L. Going) New York: Putnam, 2003.
Holes (Louis Sacher) New York: Random House, 1999.
Just Like Martin (Ossie Davis) New York: Puffin, 1995.
The Juvie Three (Gordon Korman) New York: Hyperion, 2008.
The Kite Runner (Khaled Hosseini) New York: Penguin/Riverhead, 2004.
Midget (Tim Bowler) New York: Aladdin, 2000.
The Moves Make the Man (Bruce Brooks) New York: HarperTrophy, 1996.
Night of Fear (Peg Kehret) Topeka, KS: Econo-Clad, 1999.
Petey (Ben Mikaelson) New York: Hyperion, 2000.
Trigger (Susan Vaught) New York: Bloomsbury USA Children's, 2007.
Twelve Days in August (Liza Ketchum Murrow) New York: Holiday House, 1993.
Twelve Shots: Outstanding Short Stories About Guns (Harry Mazer) New York:
　　Laurel Leaf, 1998.
Unwind (Neal Shusterman) New York: Simon and Schuster, 2007.

Informational Books

Death Be Not Proud (John Gunther) New York: Harper Perennial Modern
　　Classics, 2007.
Gandhi: Great Soul (John Severance) Boston: Houghton Mifflin, 1997.
John Muir: Wilderness Protector (Ginger Wadsworth) Minneapolis, MN:
　　Lerner, 1992.
Life in Prison (Stanley Williams) New York: SeaStar, 2001.
Phineas Gage: A Gruesome But True Story About Brain Science (John
　　Fleischman) Boston: Houghton Mifflin, 2002.

Stella (Peter Wyden) Waxhaw, NC: Anchor, 1993.

Three Cups of Tea: One Man's Mission to Promote Peace...One Child at a Time (Young Readers Edition; Sarah Thomson, Greg Mortenson, David Oliver Relin) New York: Puffin, 2009.

The Wild Muir: Twenty-Two of John Muir's Greatest Adventures (Lee Stetson) Berkeley, CA: Heyday, 2008.

The Wreck of the Henrietta Marie (Michael Cottman) New York: Harmony, 1999.

Easier Reading

Alexander Graham Bell (Leonard Everett Fisher) New York: Atheneum, 1999.

The Chemo Kid (Robert Lipsyte) New York: HarperCollins, 1992.

Dear Benjamin Banneker (Andrea Pinkney) San Diego, CA: Harcourt Brace, 1994.

Flanders Field: The Story of the Poem by John McCrae (Linda Granfield) Garden City, NY: Doubleday, 1995.

Hoot (Carl Hiaasen) New York: Knopf, 2002.

Just Kidding (Tracy Lidwig) Berkeley, CA: Tricycle Press, 2007.

Keeper of the Universe (Louis Lawrence) Boston: Houghton Mifflin, 1993.

Mariposa Blues (Ron Koertge) Madison, WI: Demco Media, 1993.

Raptor Rescue: An Eagle Flies Free (Sylvia Johnson) New York: Dutton, 1995.

Rescue Josh McGuire (Ben Mikaelsen) New York: Hyperion, 1993.

Silent to the Bone (E.L. Konigsburg) New York: Aladdin, 2002.

Sticks (Joan Bauer) New York: Bantam, 1997.

A Sunburned Prayer (Marc Talbert) New York: Aladdin, 1997.

The Time Cavern (Todd Fonseca) Ann Arbor, MI: Borders Personal Publishing, 2008.

Graphic Novels

Barefoot Gen: The Day After (Keiji Nakazawa) New York: Penguin, 2004.

The Nobody (Jeff Lemire) New York: Titan, 2009.

Tales From the Farm (Jeff Lemire) Marietta, GA: Top Shelf Productions, 2007.

Prophet

Adolescent Novels

An Eye for Color (Norman Silver) New York: Dutton, 1993.

A Fisherman of the Island Sea (Ursula LeGuin) San Diego, CA: Harcourt Brace, 2001.

Guardian (Julius Lester) New York: Amistad, 2008.

Last Shot: A Final Four Mystery (John Feinstein) New York: Yearling, 2005.

Maniac Magee (Jerry Spinelli) New York: Harper Trophy, 1990.

New Found Land: Lewis and Clark's Voyage of Discovery (Allan Wolf) Cambridge, MA: Candlewick Press, 2007.

The Postman (David Brin) New York: Bantam, 1990.

Raiders Night (Robert Lipsythe) New York: HarperTeen, 2006.

Scat (Carl Hiaasen) New York: Knopf, 2009.
S'gana the Black Whale (Sue Stauffacher) Anchorage: Alaska Northwest, 1992.
Seventh Son (Orson Scott Card) New York: Tor, 1993.
Slave Day (Rob Thomas) New York: Simon & Schuster, 1997.
What Is the What: The Autobiography of Valentino Achak Deng: A Novel (Dave Eggers) New York: Knopf/Vintage, 2007.

Informational Books

American Shaolin: Flying Kicks, Buddhist Monks, and the Legend of Iron Crotch: An Odyssey in the New China (Matthew Polly) New York: Penguin/Gotham, 2007.
Art Attack: A Short Cultural History of the Avant-Garde (Marc Aronson) New York: Clarion, 1998.
Einstein: Visionary Scientist (John Severance) New York: Clarion, 1999.
Flash! The Associated Press Covers the World (Vincent Alabisco) New York: Abrams, 2000.
I Have a Dream: The Life and Words of Martin Luther King, Jr. (Jim Haskins) Brookfield, CT: Millbrook Press, 1992.
Jacques Cousteau: Champion of the Sea (Catherine Reef) Breckenridge, CO: Twenty-First Century, 1992.
The Last Lecture (Randy Pausch) New York: Hyperion, 2008.
Lawrence of Arabia (Alistair MacLean) New York: Sterling, 2006.
Letters to a Young Brother (Hill Harper) New York: Gotham, 2006.
Malcolm X: By Any Means Necessary (Walter Dean Myers) New York: Scholastic, 1995.
Martin Luther King: The Peaceful Warrior (Edward Clayton & David Hodges) Huntington Beach, CA: Archway, 1996.
Men of Color: Fashion, History, Fundamentals (Lloyd Boston) Wedmore, England: Artisan, 2000.
Now Is Your Time! The African-American Struggle for Freedom (Walter Dean Myers) New York: HarperCollins, 1992.

Easier Reading

Adam Canfield of The Slash (Michael Winerip) Cambridge, MA: Candlewick Press, 2005.
Coming Home: From the Life of Langston Hughes (Floyd Cooper) New York: Philomel, 1994.
Flush (Carl Hiaasen) New York: Knopf Books for Young Readers, 2005.
Gandhi (Leonard Everett Fisher) New York: Simon & Schuster, 1995.
Gulf (Robert Westall) New York: Scholastic, 1996.
Jip: His Story (Katherine Paterson) Scholastic, 1997.
Leagues Apart: The Men and Times of the Negro Baseball League (Lawrence Ritter) New York: Morrow, 1995.
The Missing Manatee (Cynthia DeFelice) New York: Farrar, Straus & Giroux, 2005.
The Moon Is a Harsh Mistress (Robert Heinlein) New York: Tor, 1996.

Operation Redwood (S. Terrell French) New York: Amulet, 2009.
Rudy (James Ellison) New York: Bantam, 1993.
Starry Messenger (Peter Sis) New York: Farrar, Straus & Giroux, 1996.
Stumptown Kid (Carol Gorman and Ron Findley) New York: HarperCollins, 2007.
Swear to Howdy (Wendelin Van Draanen) New York: Yearling, 2005.

Graphic Novels

Che: A Graphic History (Spain Rodriguez) New York: Verso, 2008.
Little Rock Nine (Marshall Poe) New York: Aladdin, 2008.
Malcolm X: A Graphic Biography (Andrew Helfer) New York: Hill and Wang, 2006.

Trickster

Adolescent Novels

Artemis Fowl (Eoin Colfer) New York: Miramax, 2003.
The Brief Wondrous Life of Oscar Wao (Junot Diaz) New York: Penguin/ Riverhead, 2007.
The Good Liar (Gregory Maguire) New York: Clarion, 1999.
In a Dark Wood (Michael Cadnum) New York: Penguin, 1999.
Inca Gold (Clive Cussler) Topeka, KS: Econo-Clad, 1999.
Juggler (John Morressey) Minneapolis, MN: Econo-Clad, 1999.
Oddballs (William Sleator) New York: Puffin, 1995.
Rama: A Legend (Jamake Highwater) Bridgewater, NJ: Replica, 2001.
Slot Machine (Chris Lynch) New York: HarperTrophy, 1986.
Someday This Pain Will be Useful to You (Peter Cameron) New York: Farrar, Straus and Giroux, 2007.
Someone Was Watching (David Patneaude) Topeka, KS: Econo-Clad, 1999.
Stanford Wong Flunk Big Time (Lisa Yee) New York: Scholastic, 2005.
Stone Cold (Pete Hautman) New York: Aladdin, 2000.
There's No Surf in Cleveland (Stephanie Buehler) New York: Clarion, 1993.
The Wednesday Wars (Gary Schmidt) Orlando, FL: Houghton Mifflin, 2007.
A Wizard of Earthsea (Ursula LeGuin) New York: Bantam, 1984.
Zen and the Art of Faking It (Jordan Sonnenblick) New York: Scholastic, 2007.

Informational Books

Born Standing Up: A Comic's Life (Steve Martin) New York: Simon & Schuster/ Scribner, 2008.
Boy: Tales of Childhood (Roald Dahl) New York: Viking, 1988.
Legacy of Ashes: The History of the CIA (Tim Weiner) New York: Knopf/ Anchor, 2008.
Mark Twain: America's Humorist, Dreamer, Prophet (Clinton Cox) New York: Apple Publishing, 1999.

Prince of Humbugs: A Life of P.T. Barnum (Catherine Andronik) New York: Atheneum, 1994.

Easier Reading

The Adventures of Reddy Fox (Thornton Burgess) New York: Dover, 1992.
Anything Can Happen in High School (and It Usually Does) (William McCants) Topeka, KS: Econo-Clad, 1999.
Attaboy, Sam! (Lois Lowry) New York: Dell Yearling, 1993.
Charles Dickens: The Man Who Had Great Expectations (Diane Stanley) New York: Morrow, 1993.
Creepers (Keith Gray) New York: Putnam, 1997.
Darnell Rock Reporting (Walter Dean Myers) New York: Dell Yearling, 1996.
The Fat Man (Maurice Gee) New York: Aladdin, 1999.
Jumper (Steven Gould) New York: Tom Dougherty Associates, 1993.
Maxx Comedy (Gordon Korman) New York: Hyperion, 2007.
Pish Posh, Said Hieronymous Bosch (Nancy Willard) San Diego, CA: Harcourt Brace, 1991.
Punished! (David Lubar) Plain City, OH: Darby Creek, 2005.
Robin Hood (Margaret Early) New York: Abrams, 1996.
The Shakespeare Stealer (Gary Blackwood) New York: Puffin, 2000.
Shredderman: Attack of the Tagger (Wendelin Van Draanen) New York: Knopf, 2004.
Skellig (David Almond) New York: Dell Yearling, 2000.

Graphic Novels

Artemis Fowl: The Graphic Novel (Eoin Colfer) New York: Hyperion, 2007.
Case Closed (Gosho Aoyama) San Francisco: VIZ Media, 2004.
Houdini: The Handcuff King (Jason Lutes, Nick Bertozzi) New York: Hyperion Books for Children, 2007.

Lover

Adolescent Novels

·*Airborn* (Kenneth Oppel) New York: HarperCollins, 2004.
•*Drums, Girls and Dangerous Pie* (Jordan Sonnenblick) New York: Scholastic, 2004.
The Gospel According to Larry (Janet Tashjian) New York: Holt, 2001.
Heart of a Champion (Carl Deuker) New York: Avon, 1994.
Jake, Reinvented (Gordon Korman) New York: Hyperion, 2005.
A Life for a Life (Ernest Hill) New York: Simon & Schuster, 1998.
·*Looking For Alaska* (John Green) New York: Speak, 2006.
My Brother Stealing Second (Jim Naughton) New York: HarperCollins, 1989.
Nowhere to Call Home (Cynthia DeFelice) New York: Farrar, Straus & Giroux, 1999.

The One Who Came Back (Joann Mazzio) Boston: Houghton Mifflin, 1992.

Phoenix Rising (Karen Hesse) New York: Puffin, 1995.

Rats Saw God (Rob Thomas) New York: Aladdin, 1996.

The Schwa Was Here (Neal Shusterman) New York: Puffin, 2006.

A Solitary Blue (Cynthia Voight) New York: Scholastic, 1993.

Staying Fat for Sarah Byrnes (Chris Crutcher) New York: Laurel Leaf, 1995.

Street Love (Walter Dean Myers) New York: Amistad, 2006.

Tiger, Tiger, Burning Bright: A Novel (Ron Koertge) New York: Orchard, 1994.

Under the Blood Red Sun (Graham Salisbury) New York: Dell Yearling, 1995.

Informational Books

Carl Sandburg: A Biography (Milton Meltzer) New York: 21st Century/
Millbrook, 1999.

Face Forward: Young African American Men in a Critical Age (Julian Okwu) San
Francisco, CA: Chronicle, 1997.

In a Sacred Manner I Live (Neil Philip) Boston: Houghton Mifflin, 1997.

Jack and Rochelle: A Holocaust Story of Love and Resistance (Lawrence Sutin,
Rochelle Sutin, & Jack Sutin) St. Paul, MN: Graywolf Press, 1996.

John Lennon: All I Want is the Truth (Elizabeth Partridge) New York: Penguin/
Viking, 2005.

Learning About Dignity From the Life of Martin Luther King, Jr. (Jeanne
Strazzabosco) New York: PowerKids Press, 1997.

Modoc: The True Story of the Greatest Elephant That Ever Lived (Ralph Helfer)
New York: HarperPerennial, 1998.

The Poet Slave of Cuba: A Biography of Juan Francisco Manzano (Margarita
Engle) New York: Henry Holt, 2006.

Ralph Bunche: Winner of the Nobel Peace Prize (Anne Schraff) Springfield, NJ:
Enslow, 1999.

Start Something: You Can Make a Difference (Earl Woods & The Tiger Woods
Foundation) New York: Simon & Shuster, 2006.

Talking Peace: A Vision for the Next Generation (Jimmy Carter) New York:
Penguin, 1993.

Easier Reading

The Barn (Avi) New York: Avon, 1996.

The Cay (Theodore Taylor) New York: Avon, 1991.

A Couple of Kooks and Other Stories About Love (Cynthia Rylant) New York:
Orchard, 1990.

Fast Sam, Cool Clyde, and Stuff (Walter Dean Myers) New York: Viking, 1988.

Flipped (Wendelin Van Draanen) New York: Knopf, 2001.

Freak the Mighty (Rodman Philbrick) New York: Scholastic, 2001.

Harris and Me (Gary Paulsen) New York: Dell Yearling, 1995.

Lives and Legends of the Saints (Carole Armstrong) New York: Simon
& Schuster, 1995.

Phineas L. MacGuire...Erupts! (Francis O'Roark Dowell) New York:
Atheneum, 2007.

The Pool Party (Gary Soto) New York: Dell Yearling, 1995.
Romiette and Julio (Sharon Draper) New York: Simon & Schuster, 2005.
Saint Valentine (Robert Sabuda) New York: Atheneum, 1992.
Shadow Like a Leopard (Myron Levoy) Lincoln, NE: iUniverse.com, 2000.
Shiloh (Phyllis Reynolds Naylor) New York: Aladdin, 2000.
Sleeping Freshmen Never Lie (David Lubar) New York: Dutton, 2005.
Soldier's Heart (Gary Paulsen) New York: Laurel Leaf, 2000.
Teammates (Peter Golenbock) San Diego, CA: Harcourt Brace, 1990.
Walt Whitman (Nancy Loewen) Mankato, MN: Creative Editions, 1993.

Graphic Novels

The Fountain (Darren Aronofsky) New York: Vertigo, 2006.
King: A Comics Biography of Martin Luther King, Jr. (Ho Che Anderson) Seattle, WA: Fantagraphic, 2005.

REFERENCES

Alexander, P.A., Kulikowich, J.M., & Hetton, T.L. (1994). The role of subject matter knowledge and interest in the processing of linear and nonlinear texts. *Review of Educational Research, 64*(2), 210–253.

Alliance for Excellent Education. (2007, October). *The high cost of high school dropouts: What the nation pays for inadequate high schools.* Washington, DC: Author. Retrieved January 21, 2010, from www.all4ed.org/files/archive/publications/HighCost.pdf

Alloway, N., Freebody, P., Gilbert, P., & Muspratt, S. (2002). *Boys, literacy and schooling: Expanding the repertoires of practice.* Sydney, NSW, Australia: Department of Education, Science and Teaching. Retrieved January 21, 2010, from www.dest.gov.au/NR/rdonlyres/835D5DAC-D69C-4716-91EE-CB6E2DCDA934/1564/BoysLiteracy.pdf

Alvermann, D.E. (2003). *Seeing themselves as capable and engaged readers: Adolescents and re/mediated instruction.* Naperville, IL: Learning Point Associates.

Anderson, R.C., Wilson, P.T., & Fielding, L.G. (1988). Growth in reading and how children spend their time outside of school. *Reading Research Quarterly, 23*(3), 285–303. doi:10.1598/RRQ.23.3.2

Anderson, W. (1990). *Green man: The archetype of our oneness with the Earth.* New York: HarperCollins.

Annie E. Casey Foundation. (2008). *Kids Count 2008 data book online.* Retrieved August 5, 2009, from datacenter.kidscount.org/databook/2008/Default.aspx

Applebee, A.N. (1993). *Literature in the secondary school: Studies of curriculum and instruction in the United States.* Urbana, IL: National Council of Teachers of English.

Arnold, P.M. (1995). *Wildmen, warriors, and kings: Masculine spirituality and the Bible.* New York: Crossroad.

Aronson, M. (2001). *Exploding the myths: The truth about teenagers and reading.* Lanham, MD: Scarecrow.

Atwell, N. (1998). *In the middle: New understandings about writing, reading, and learning* (2nd ed.). Boston: Boynton Cook.

Baines, L. (1994). Cool books for tough guys: 50 books out of the mainstream of adolescent literature that will appeal to males who do not enjoy reading. *The ALAN Review, 22*(1), 43–46.

Baker, L., & Wigfield, A. (1999). Dimensions of children's motivation for reading and their relations to reading activity and reading achievement. *Reading Research Quarterly, 34*(4), 452–477. doi:10.1598/RRQ.34.4.4

Bauerlein, M., & Stotsky, S. (2005, January 25). Why Johnny won't read. *The Washington Post,* p. A15.

Baumeister, R.F., Campbell, J.D., Krueger, J.I., & Vohs, K.D. (2003). Does high self-esteem cause better performance, interpersonal success, happiness, or healthier lifestyles? *Psychological Science in the Public Interest, 4*(1), 1–44. doi:10.1111/1529-1006.01431

Bean, T.W. (2000). Reading in the content areas: Social constructivist dimensions. In M.L. Kamil, P.B. Mosenthal, P.D. Pearson, & R. Barr (Eds.), *Handbook of reading research* (Vol. 3, pp. 629–644). Mahwah, NJ: Erlbaum.

Bean, T.W., & Harper, H. (2007). Reading men differently: Alternative portrayals of masculinity in contemporary young adult fiction. *Reading Psychology, 28*(1), 11–30. doi:10.1080/02702710601115406

Birkerts, S. (1994). *The Gutenberg elegies: The fate of reading in an electronic age.* New York: Fawcett.

Birkerts, S. (2007). *Reading life: Books for the ages.* Minneapolis, MN: Graywolf.

Bitz, M. (2004). The comic book project: Forging alternative pathways to literacy. *Journal of Adolescent & Adult Literacy, 47*(7), 574–586.

Blair, H. (2000). Genderlects: Girl talk and boy talk in a middle years classroom. *Language Arts, 77,* 315–323.

Blankenhorn, D. (1995). *Fatherless America: Confronting our most urgent social problem.* New York: Basic.

Bond, T.F. (2001). Giving them free rein: Connections in student-led book groups. *The Reading Teacher, 54*(6), 574–584.

Booth, D. (2002). *Even hockey players read: Boys, literacy and learning.* Markham, ON: Pembroke.

Bowden, B.S., & Zeisz, J.M. (1997, August). *Supper's on: Adolescent adjustment and frequency of family mealtimes.* Paper presented at the 105th Annual Convention of the American Psychological Association, Chicago.

Boyd, F.B. (2000). The cross-aged literacy program: Developing mediational activity to assist ninth-grade African American students who struggle with literacy and schooling. *Reading & Writing Quarterly, 16*(4), 381–398. doi:10.1080/10573560050129222

Bromley, K., & Powell, P. (1999). Interest journals motivate student writers. *The Reading Teacher, 53*(2), 111–112.

Browne, R., & Fletcher, R. (Eds.). (1995). *Boys in schools: Addressing the real issues—behaviours, values and relationships.* Sydney, NSW, Australia: Finch Publishing.

Brozo, W.G. (2002). *To be a boy, to be a reader: Engaging teen and preteen boys in active literacy.* Newark, DE: International Reading Association.

Brozo, W.G. (2004). It's okay to read, even if other kids don't: Learning about and from boys in a middle school book club. *The California Reader, 38*(2), 5–13.

Brozo, W.G. (2005). Adolescents and literacies in a digital world [Book review]. *Journal of Literacy Research, 36*(4), 533–538.

Brozo, W.G. (2006). Bridges to literacy for boys. *Educational Leadership, 64*(1), 71–74.

Brozo, W.G. (2007). Helping boys find entry points to lifelong reading: Book clubs and other strategies for struggling adolescent males. In J. Lewis & G. Moorman (Eds.), *Adolescent literacy instruction: Policies and promising practices* (pp. 304–318). Newark, DE: International Reading Association.

Brozo, W.G., & Brozo, C.L. (2009). From manga to Macbeth: Building bridges to academic text. *International School, 11*(3), 25–26.

Brozo, W.G., & Gaskins, C. (2009). Engaging texts and literacy practices for adolescent boys. In K. Wood & W. Blanton (Eds.), *Literacy instruction for adolescents: Research-based practice* (pp. 170–186). New York: Guilford.

Brozo, W.G., & Hargis, C. (2005). Taking seriously the idea of reform: One high school's efforts to make reading more responsive to all students. In P. Shannon & J. Edmondson (Eds.), *Reading education policy* (pp. 134–148). Newark, DE: International Reading Association.

Brozo, W.G., & Schmelzer, R.V. (1997). Wildmen, warriors, and lovers: Reaching boys through archetypal literature. *Journal of Adolescent & Adult Literacy, 41*(1), 4–11.

Brozo, W.G., Shiel, G., & Topping, K. (2007). Engagement in reading: Lessons learned from three PISA countries. *Journal of Adolescent & Adult Literacy, 51*(4), 304–315. doi:10.1598/JAAL.51.4.2

Brozo, W.G., & Simpson, M.L. (2007). *Content literacy for today's adolescents: Honoring diversity and building competence.* Upper Saddle River, NJ: Merrill/ Prentice Hall.

Brozo, W.G., Walter, P., & Placker, T. (2002). "I know the difference between a real man and a TV man": A critical exploration of violence and masculinity through literature and the media in a junior high school in the 'hood. *Journal of Adolescent & Adult Literacy, 45*(6), 530–538.

Bügel, K., & Buunk, B. (1996). Sex differences in foreign language text comprehension: The role of interests and prior knowledge. *Modern Language Journal, 80*(1), 15–31. doi:10.2307/329055

Bureau of Labor Statistics. (1999). *Unemployment and the newest high school dropouts.* Washington, DC: U.S. Department of Labor.

Bushman, J.H., & Haas, K.P. (2006). *Using young adult literature in the English classroom* (4th ed.). Upper Saddle River, NJ: Prentice Hall.

Canada, G. (1998). *Reaching up for manhood: Transforming the lives of boys in America.* Boston: Beacon.

Canadian Council on Learning. (2009). *Why boys don't like to read: Gender differences in reading achievement.* Retrieved August 12, 2009 from www.ccl-cca.ca/pdfs/LessonsInLearning/02_18_09-E.pdf

Cauthen, N.K., & Fass, S. (2008). *Measuring poverty in the United States.* New York: National Center for Adolescents in Poverty, Columbia University, Mailman School of Public Health.

Cavazos-Kottke, S. (2005). Turned out but turned on: Boys' (dis)engaged reading in and out of school. *Journal of Adolescent & Adult Literacy, 49*(3), 180–184. doi:10.1598/JAAL.49.3.1

Centers for Disease Control and Prevention. (2005, September 2). Mental health in the United States: Prevalence of and diagnosis and medication treatment for Attention Deficit/Hyperactivity Disorder—United States, 2003. *MMWR Weekly, 54*(34), 842–847. Retrieved August 10, 2009, from www.cdc.gov/ mmwr/preview/mmwrhtml/mm5434a2.htm

Chance, R. (2000). SmartGirl.com reading survey: What are the messages for librarians? *Journal of Youth Services in Libraries, 13*(3), 20–23.

Chandler-Olcott, K., & Mahar, D. (2003). Adolescents' anime-inspired fanfictions: An exploration of multiliteracies. *Journal of Adolescent & Adult Literacy, 46*(7), 556–566.

Children's Defense Fund. (2009). *Protect children not guns 2009*. Retrieved August 10, 2009, from http://www.childrensdefense.org/child-research-data-publications/data/protect-children-not-guns-report-2009.html.

Cho, G., Choi, H., & Krashen, S. (2005). Hooked on comic book reading: How comic books made an impossible situation less difficult. *Knowledge Quest, 33*(4), 32–34.

Chun, C.W. (2009). Critical literacies and graphic novels for English-language learners: Teaching *Maus*. *Journal of Adolescent & Adult Literacy, 53*(2), 144–153. doi:10.1598/JAAL.53.2.5

Chung, Y.B., Baskin, M.L., & Case, A. (1999). Career development of black males: Case studies. *Journal of Career Development, 25*(3), 161–171.

Clark, C., & Foster, A. (2005). *Children's and young people's reading habits and preferences: The who, what, why, where and when*. Gainesville, FL: The National Literacy Trust. Retrieved August 10, 2009, from www.literacytrust.org

Coles, M., & Hall, C. (2001). Boys, books and breaking boundaries: Developing literacy in and out of school. In W. Martino & B. Meyenn (Eds.), *What about the boys? Issues of masculinity in schools* (pp. 211–221). Buckingham, England: Open University Press.

Coles, M., & Hall, C. (2002). Gendered reading: Learning from children's reading choices. *Journal of Research in Reading, 25*(1), 96–108. doi:10.1111/1467-9817.00161

Collins, C., Kenway, J., & McLeod, J. (2000). *Factors influencing the educational performance of males and females in school and their initial destinations after leaving school*. Canberra, Australia: Analysis and Equity Branch of the Department of Education, Training and Youth Affairs.

Collins-Standley, T., Gan, S.-L., Yu, H.-J., & Zillmann, D. (1996). Choice of romantic, violent, and scary fairy-tale books by preschool girls and boys. *Child Study Journal, 26*(4), 279–302.

Connell, D., & Gunzelmann, B. (2004, March). The next gender gap: Why are so many boys floundering while so many girls are soaring? *Instructor*, 14–17.

Connell, R.W. (1989). Cool guys, swots and wimps: The interplay of masculinity and education. *Oxford Review of Education, 15*(3), 291–303. doi:10.1080/0305498890150309

Cooper-Mullin, A., & Coye, J.M. (1998). *Once upon a heroine: 450 books for girls to love*. Chicago: NTC/Contemporary Publishing Group.

Cowden, T., Viders, S., & Lafever, C. (2000). *The complete writer's guide to heroes and heroines: Sixteen master archetypes*. Los Angeles: Lone Eagle.

Cutter, M.J. (2000). Philomela speaks: Alice Walker's revisioning of rape archetypes in *The Color Purple*. *MELUS, 25*(3/4), 161–180. doi:10.2307/468241

Daly, P., Salters, J., & Burns, C. (1998). Gender and task interaction: Instant and delayed recall of three story types. *Educational Review, 50*(3), 269–275. doi:10.1080/0013191980500306

Dance, L.J. (2001). Shadows, mentors, and surrogate fathers: Effective schooling as critical pedagogy for inner-city boys. *Sociological Focus, 34*(4), 399–415.

Dandy, E.B. (1998). Increasing the number of minority teachers: Tapping the para-professional pool. *Education and Urban Society, 31*(1), 89–103. doi:10.1177/0013124598031001007

Davis, T.C., Byrd, R.S., Arnold, C.L., Auinger, P., & Bocchini, J.A., Jr. (1999). Low literacy and violence among adolescents in a summer sports program. *The Journal of Adolescent Health, 24*(6), 403–411. doi:10.1016/S1054-139X(98)00148-7

Day, J.C., & Newburger, E.C. (2002). *The big payoff: educational attainment and synthetic estimates of work-life earnings. US Bureau of the Census, Current Population Reports* (pp. 23–210). Washington, DC: U.S. Government Printing Office.

deLaszlo, V.S. (1959). *The basic writings of C.G. Jung.* New York: Modern Library.

Doiron, R. (2003). Boy books, girl books: Should we re-organize our school library collections? *Teacher Librarian, 30*(3), 14–16.

Dreher, M.J. (2003). Motivating struggling readers by tapping the potential of information books. *Reading & Writing Quarterly, 19*(1), 25–38. doi:10.1080/10573560308206

The Education Alliance. (2007). *Gender differences in reading achievement: Policy implications and best practices.* Charleston, WV: Author.

Ellickson, P.L., Martino, S.C., & Collins, R.L. (2004). Marijuana use from adolescence to young adulthood: Multiple developmental trajectories and their associated outcomes. *Health Psychology, 23*(3), 299–307. doi:10.1037/0278-6133.23.3.299

Farrell, A.D., & Meyer, A.L. (1997). The effectiveness of a school-based curriculum for reducing violence among urban sixth-grade students. *American Journal of Public Health, 87*(6), 979–984. doi:10.2105/AJPH.87.6.979

Fashola, O.S. (Ed.). (2005). *Educating African American males: Voices from the field.* Thousand Oaks, CA: Corwin.

Ferrell, W. (2001). *The myth of male power.* New York: Berkley Trade.

Filozof, E.M., Albertin, H.K., Jones, C.R., Steme, S.S., Myers, L., & McDermott, R.J. (1998). Relationship of adolescent self-esteem to selected academic variables. *The Journal of School Health, 68*(2), 68–72. doi:10.1111/j.1746-1561.1998.tb07194.x

Fink, R.P. (1995). Successful dyslexics: A constructivist study of passionate interest reading. *Journal of Adolescent & Adult Literacy, 39*(4), 268–280.

Fisher, D. (2001). Cross age tutoring: Alternatives to the reading resource room for struggling adolescent readers. *Journal of Instructional Psychology, 28*(4), 234–240.

Flynn, J.M., & Rahbar, M.H. (1994). Prevalence of reading failure in boys compared with girls. *Psychology in the Schools, 31*(1), 66–71. doi:10.1002/1520-6807(199401)31:1<66::AID-PITS2310310109>3.0.CO;2-J

Francis, D.R. (2007). Why do women outnumber men in college? Retrieved August 10, 2009, from www.nber.org/digest/jan07/w12139.html

Franzak, J.K. (2006). Zoom: A review of the literature on marginalized adolescent readers, literacy theory, and policy implications. *Review of Educational Research, 76*(2), 209–248. doi:10.3102/00346543076002209

Freeman, C. (2004). *Trends in educational equity of girls and women.* Washington, DC: U.S. Department of Education, National Center for Education Statistics. Retrieved August 10, 2009, from nces.ed.gov/pubsearch/pubsinfo.asp?pubid=2005016

Gambell, T., & Hunter, D. (1999). Surveying gender differences in Canadian school literacy. *Journal of Curriculum Studies, 32*(6), 689–719.

Garbarino, J. (1999). *Lost boys: Why our sons turn violent and how we can save them.* New York: Free Press.

Garry, J., & El-Shamy, H. (2005). *Archetypes and motifs in folklore and literature: A handbook.* Armonk, NY: M.E. Sharpe.

Gathercole, S.E., & Alloway, T.P. (2008). *Working memory and learning: A practical guide for teachers.* Thousand Oaks, CA: Sage.

Geraci, P.M. (2003). Promoting positive reading discourse and self-exploration through a multi-cultural book club. *Journal of Correctional Education, 54*(2), 54–59.

Gilmore, D. (1990). *Manhood in the making: Cultural concepts of masculinity.* New Haven, CT: Yale University Press.

Goodman, J. (with Kuzmic, J., & Wu, X.). (1992). *Elementary schooling for critical democracy.* Albany: State University of New York Press.

Gorman, M. (2003). *Getting graphic! Using graphic novels to promote literacy with preteens and teens.* Worthington, OH: Linworth.

Green, T. (2000). Responding and sharing: Techniques for energizing classroom discussions. *The Clearing House, 73*(6), 331–334.

Greene, J.P., & Winters, M.A. (2006). *Leaving boys behind: Public high school graduation rates.* Retrieved August 10, 2009, from www.manhattaninstitute .org/html/cr_48.htm#05

Greenspan, S. (with Lewis, N.B.). (2000). *Building healthy minds: The six experiences that create intelligence and emotional growth in babies and young children.* Cambridge, MA: Perseus.

Grigg, W.S., Daane, M.C., Ying, J., & Campbell, J.R; (2003). *The nation's report card: Reading 2002* (NCES 2003–521). U.S. Department of Education, National Center for Education Statistics. Washington, DC: U.S. Government Printing Office.

Grigg, W., Donahue, P.L., & Dion, G. (2007). *The nation's report card: 12th-grade reading and mathematics, 2005* (NCES 2007–468). U.S. Department of Education, National Center for Education Statistics. Washington, DC: U.S. Government Printing Office.

Grim, J.A. (1984). *The shaman: Patterns of Siberian and Ojibway healing.* Norman: University of Oklahoma Press.

Gunzelmann, B., & Connell, J. (2006). The new gender gap: Social, psychological, neuro-biological, and educational perspectives. *Educational Horizons, 84*(2), 94–101.

Guthrie, J. (Ed.). (2008). *Engaging adolescents in reading.* Thousand Oaks, CA: Corwin.

Guthrie, J., Alao, S., & Rinehart, J. (1997). Engagement in reading for young adolescents. *Journal of Adolescent & Adult Literacy, 40*(6), 438–446.

Guthrie, J., & Wigfield, A. (2000). Engagement and motivation in reading. In M.L. Kamil, P.B. Mosenthal, P.D. Pearson, & R. Barr (Eds.), *Handbook of reading research* (Vol. 3, pp. 403–422). Mahwah, NJ: Erlbaum.

Guthrie, J.T., Hoa, L.W., Wigfield, A., Tonks, S.M., & Perencevich, K.C. (2006). From spark to fire: Can situational reading interest lead to long-term reading motivation? *Reading Research and Instruction, 45*(2), 91–117.

Hall, C., & Coles, M. (1997). Gendered readings: Helping boys develop as critical readers. *Gender and Education, 9*(1), 61–68. doi:10.1080/09540259721457

Hallfors, D., Verea, J.L., Iritani, B., Cho, H., Khatapoush, S., & Saxe, L. (2009). Truancy, grade point average, and sexual activity: A meta-analysis of risk indicators for youth substance use. *Journal of School Health, 72*(5), 205–211. doi:10.1111/j.1746–1561.2002.tb06548.X

Hamre, B.K., & Pianta, R.C. (2006). Student-teacher relationships. In G.G. Bear & K.M. Minke (Eds.), *Children's needs III: Development, prevention, and intervention* (pp. 59–72). Washington, DC: National Association of School Psychologists.

Hatfield, C. (2005). *Alternative comics: An emerging literature.* Jackson: University Press of Mississippi.

Hawkins, M.R. (2004). Researching English language and literacy development in schools. *Educational Researcher, 33*(3), 14–25. doi:10.3102/0013189X033003014

Hechinger, J. (2008, August 8). Problem: Boys don't like to read. Solution: Books that are really gross. Retrieved August 11, 2009, from online.wsj.com/article_email/SB121814900158422243-lMyQjAxMDI4MTE4MTExNDE5Wj.html

Herbert, B. (2001, September 3). In America: On the way to nowhere. *The New York Times*, p. A15.

Herbert, B. (2007, March 5). Education, education, education. *The New York Times.* Retrieved August 5, 2009, from donkeyod.wordpress.com/2007/03/05/education-education-education/

Herz, S., & Gallo, D. (2005). *From Hinton to Hamlet: Building bridges between young adult literature and the classics* (2nd ed.). Westport, CT: Greenwood.

Hewlett, S.A., & West, C. (1998). *The war against parents: What we can do for America's beleaguered moms and dads.* New York: Houghton Mifflin.

Hinchman, K.A., Alvermann, D.E., Boyd, F.B., Brozo, W.G., & Vacca, R.T. (2003). Supporting older students' in- and out-of-school literacies. *Journal of Adolescent & Adult Literacy, 47*(4), 304–310.

Hoffman, L. (1999, September). What boys like. *Lingua Franca, 9*, 11–13.

Hofstetter, C.R., Sticht, T.G., & Hofstetter, C.H. (1999). Knowledge, literacy, and power. *Communication Research, 26*(1), 58–80. doi:10.1177/009365099026001004

Horn, W.F., & Sylvester, T. (2002). *Father facts* (4th ed.). Germantown, MD: National Fatherhood Initiative.

Horton, R. (2005). Boys are people too: Boys and reading, truth, and misconceptions. *Teacher Librarian, 33*(2), 30–32.

Houser, P. (2001). Let's hear it for the boys. *Black Issues Book Review, 3*(3), 72–73.

Hughes-Hassell, S., & Rodge, P. (2007). The leisure reading habits of urban adolescents. *Journal of Adolescent & Adult Literacy, 51*(1), 22–33. doi:10.1598/JAAL.51.1.3

Hull, G., & Schultz, K. (2002). *School's out! Bridging out-of-school literacies with class-room practice.* New York: Teachers College Press.

Hunsader, P.D. (2002). Why boys fail—And what we can do about it. *Principal, 82*(2), 52–54.

Ivey, G. (1998). Discovering readers in the middle level school: A few helpful clues. *NASSP Bulletin, 82*(600), 48–56. doi:10.1177/019263659808260009

Ivey, G., & Broaddus, K. (2001). "Just plain reading": A survey of what makes students want to read in middle school classrooms. *Reading Research Quarterly, 36*(4), 350–377. doi:10.1598/RRQ.36.4.2

Jacobs, D. (2007). More than words: Comics as a means of teaching multiple literacies. *English Journal, 96*(3), 19–25.

Jacobson, J., Thrope, L., Fisher, D., Lapp, D., Frey, N., & Flood, J. (2001). Cross-age tutoring: A literacy improvement approach for struggling adolescent readers. *Journal of Adolescent & Adult Literacy, 44*(6), 528–537.

Jaeger, L., & Demetriadis, S.N. (2002). Book club on a budget. *School Library Journal, 48*(3), 47.

Johnson, D.M., Peer, G.G., Baldwin, R.S. (1984). Protagonist preferences among juvenile and adolescent readers. *The Journal of Educational Research, 77*(3), 147–150.

Johnson, R. (1989). *He: Understanding masculine psychology.* New York: Warner.

Jones, P., & Fiorelli, D.C. (2003). Overcoming the obstacle course: Teenage boys and reading. *Teacher Librarian, 30*(3), 9–13.

Jordan, E. (1995). Fighting boys and fantasy play: The construction of masculinity in the early years of school. *Gender and Education, 7*(1), 69–86. doi:10.1080/713668458

Jung, C.G. (1955). *Modern man in search of a soul.* London: Harvest.

Jung, C.G. (1968). *Man and his symbols.* New York: Dell.

Katz, H., & Sokal, L. (2003). Masculine literacy: One size does not fit all. *Reading Manitoba, 24*(1), 4–8.

Keddie, A., & Mills, M. (2008). *Teaching boys: Developing classroom practices that work.* Sydney, NSW, Australia: Allen & Unwin.

Kehler, M.D., Davison, K.G., & Frank, B. (2005). Contradictions and tensions in the practice of masculinities in school: Interrogating embodiment and "good buddy" talk. *Journal of Curriculum Theorizing, 21*(4), 59–72.

Kipnis, A. (1994). Men, movies, and monsters: Heroic masculinity as a crucible of male violence. *Psychological Perspectives, 29*(1), 38–51.

Kirst, M.W. (2003, August). *College preparation and grade 12 NAEP.* Paper prepared for the National Commission on NAEP 12th Grade Assessment and Reporting, Washington, DC.

Kleinfeld, J. (1999, Winter). Student performance: Males versus females. *The Public Interest, 134*, 3–20.

Knabb, M. (2003). Rapping to review: A novel strategy to engage students and summarize course material. *Advances in Physiology Education, 27*(1–4), 157–159.

Knapp, B.L. (1984). *A Jungian approach to literature.* Carbondale: Southern Illinois University Press.

Knapp, B.L. (2003). *French fairy tales: A Jungian approach.* Albany: State University of New York Press.

Knobel, M. (1998). *Everyday literacies: Students, discourse, and social practice.* New York: Peter Lang.

Knobloch, S., Callison, C., Chen, L., Fritzsche, A., & Zillmann, D. (2005). Children's sex-stereotyped self-socialization through selective exposure to entertainment: Cross-cultural experiments in Germany, China, and the

United States. *The Journal of Communication, 55*(1), 122–138. doi:10.1111/j.1460-2466.2005.tb02662.x

Kong, A., & Fitch, E. (2003). Using Book Club to engage culturally and linguistically diverse learners in reading, writing, and talking about books. *The Reading Teacher, 56*(4), 352–362.

Kragler, S., & Nolley, C. (1996). Student choices: Book selection strategies of fourth graders. *Reading Horizons, 36*(4), 354–365.

Krashen, S.D. (2003). *Explorations in language acquisition and use: The Taipei lectures.* Portsmouth, NH: Heinemann.

Langerman, D. (1990). Books and boys: Gender preferences and book selection. *School Library Journal, 36*(3), 132–136.

Langker, S. (1995). Boys' team also does well. In R. Browne & R. Fletcher (Eds.), *Boys in schools: Addressing the real issues—behaviour, values and relationships* (pp. 190–200). Sydney, NSW, Australia: Finch Publishing.

Larimer, R.E., & Schleicher, L. (Eds.). (1999). *New ways in using authentic materials in the classroom.* Washington, DC: TESOL.

Larson, R.W., Wiley, A.R., & Branscomb, K.R. (2006). *Family mealtime as a context of development and socialization: New directions for child and adolescent development.* San Francisco: Jossey-Bass.

Lenters, K. (2007). From storybooks to games, comics, bands, and chapter books: A young boy's appropriation of literacy practices. *Canadian Journal of Education, 30*(1), 113–136.

Libsch, M.K., & Breslow, M. (1996). Trends in non-assigned reading by high school seniors. *NASSP Bulletin, 80*(584), 111–116. doi:10.1177/019263659608058417

Lietz, P. (2006). A meta-analysis of gender differences in reading achievement at the secondary school level. *Studies in Educational Evaluation, 32*(4), 317–344. doi:10.1016/j.stueduc.2006.10.002

MacArthur, C., Graham, S., & Fitzgerald, J. (Eds.). (2005). *Handbook of writing research.* New York: Guilford.

Margolis, H., & McCabe, P.P. (2004). Self-efficacy: A key to improving the motivation of struggling learners. *The Clearing House, 77*(6), 241–249. doi:10.3200/TCHS.77.6.241-249

Martin, A.J. (2003). Boys and motivation. *Australian Educational Researcher, 30*(3), 43–65.

Martin, C., Martin, M., & O'Brien, D. (1984). Spawning ideas for writing in the content areas. *Reading World, 24*(1), 11–15.

Martin, R. (2003). Connecting with boys at lunch: A success story. *Teacher Librarian, 30*(3), 27–28.

Maughan, S. (2001, May 7). You go, guys. *Publishers Weekly, 248,* 41–42.

McCarthey, S.J., & Moje, E.B. (2002). Identity matters. *Reading Research Quarterly, 37*(2), 228–238. doi:10.1598/RRQ.37.2.6

McClure, A. (2008). *Making it better for boys in schools, families, and communities.* London: Network Continuum.

McDaniel, M.A., Waddill, P.J., Finstad, K., & Bourq, T. (2000). The effects of text-based interest on attention and recall. *Journal of Educational Psychology, 92*(3), 492–502. doi:10.1037/0022-0663.92.3.492

McFall, J. (2004, August/September). Boys and books. *Reading Today, 22*(1), 20–21.

McGuire, M. (1997). Taking a storypath into history. *Educational Leadership,* *54*(6), 70–74.

Mead, M. (1969). *Male and female: A study of the sexes in a changing world.* New York: Dell.

Mead, S. (2006). *The truth suggests otherwise: The truth about boys and girls.* Washington, DC: Education Sector.

Moje, E.B. (2000). Reinventing adolescent literacy for new times: Perennial and millennial issues. *Journal of Adolescent & Adult Literacy, 43*(1), 4–11.

Moje, E.B. (2002). Re-framing adolescent literacy research for new times: Studying youth as a resource. *Reading Research and Instruction, 41*(3), 211–228.

Moje, E.B. (2006). Motivating texts, motivating contexts, motivating adolescents: An examination of the role of motivation in adolescent literacy practices and development. *Perspectives, 32*(3), 10–14.

Mok, J., & Cheung, S. (2004). *Book reading culture of youth in Hong Kong.* Hong Kong: The Hong Kong Federation of Youth Groups.

Mokhtari, K., Reichard, C.A., & Gardner, A. (2009). The impact of internet and television use on the reading habits and practices of college students. *Journal of Adolescent & Adult Literacy, 52*(7), 609–619. doi:10.1598/JAAL.52.7.6

Moore, R., & Gillette, D. (1992). *The king within: Accessing the king in the male psyche.* New York: Morrow.

Morrell, E., & Duncan-Andrade, J.M.R. (2002). Promoting academic literacy with urban youth through engaging hip-hop culture. *English Journal, 91*(6), 88–92. doi:10.2307/821822

Mortenson, T. (2008, June 6). Where the boys were. *The Chronicle of Higher Education, 54*(39), A30.

Mui, Y.Q. (2004, December 13). Schools turn to comics as trial balloon: Novel Md. program uses genre to encourage reluctant readers. *The Washington Post,* p. B01.

Mullis, I.V.S., Campbell, J.R., & Farstrup, A.E. (1993). *NAEP 1992: Reading report card for the nation and the states.* Washington, DC: U.S. Department of Education.

Mullis, I.V.S., Martin, M.O., Gonzalez, E.J., & Kennedy, A.M. (2003). *PIRLS 2001 international report: IEA's study of reading literacy achievement in primary schools.* Chestnut Hill, MA: International Study Center, Boston College.

Murphy, P., & Elwood, J. (1998). Gendered experiences, choices and achievement—exploring the links. *International Journal of Inclusive Education, 2*(2), 95–118. doi:10.1080/1360311980020202

Nagourney, E. (2007, July 31). Consequences: Reading skills are tied to a longer, healthier life. *The New York Times.* Retrieved January 22, 2010, from www.nytimes.com/2007/07/31/health/31cons.html?_r=1

National Center for Education Statistics. (2000). *Trends in educational equity of girls and women* (NCES 2000-030). Washington, DC: U.S. Department of Education.

National Center for Education Statistics. (2007). *The nation's report card: Reading 2007.* Retrieved August 12, 2009, from nationsreportcard.gov/reading_2007/

National Center for Education Statistics. (2008). *Trends in NAEP: Long-term trend assessment average reading scale scores and score gaps for students age 17, by* gender: 1971–2008. Retrieved June 8, 2009, from nationsreportcard.gov/ltt_2008/ltt0008.asp?tab_id=tab3&subtab_id=Tab_1#chart

National Endowment for the Arts. (2007). *To read or not to read: A question of national consequence*. Washington, DC: Author.

National Literacy Trust. (2001). *What research suggests schools can do to improve boys' performance*. London: Author.

Neckerman, K.M. (2004). *Social inequality*. New York: Russell Sage Foundation.

Newkirk, T. (2002). *Misreading masculinity: Boys, literacy, and popular culture*. Portsmouth, NH: Heinemann.

Newman, M. (2005). Rap as literacy: A genre analysis of hip-hop ciphers. *Interdisciplinary Journal for the Study of Discourse, 25*(3), 399–436. doi:10.1515/text.2005.25.3.399

Nicolle, R. (1989). Boys and the five-year void. *School Library Journal, 35*(3), 130–135.

Nichols, S. (1980). *Jung and tarot: An archetypal journey*. York Beach, ME: Samuel Weiser.

Nippold, M.A., Duthie, J.K., & Larsen, J. (2005). Literacy and leisure activity: Free-time preferences of older children and young adolescents. *Language, Speech, and Hearing Services in Schools, 36*(2), 93–102. doi:10.1044/0161-1461 (2005/009)

Noguera, P.A. (2008). *The trouble with Black boys: And other reflections on race, equity, and the future of public education*. New York: Jossey-Bass.

Norton, B., & Vanderheyden, K. (2004). Comic book culture and second language learners. In B. Norton & K. Toohey (Eds.), *Critical pedagogies and language learning* (pp. 201–221). New York: Cambridge University Press.

O'Brien, D. (2001). "At-risk" adolescents: Redefining competence through the multiliteracies of intermediality, visual arts, and representation. *Reading Online, 4*(11). Retrieved June 17, 2009, from www.readingonline.org/newliteracies/lit_ Index.asp?HREF=/newliteracies/obrien/index.html

Office of Juvenile Justice and Delinquency Prevention. (2006). *Juvenile offenders and victims: 2006 national report*. Washington, DC: U.S. Department of Justice. Retrieved August 10, 2009, from ojjdp.ncjrs.org/ojstatbb/nr2006/index.html

Ollmann, H.E. (1993). Choosing literature wisely: Students speak out. *Journal of Reading, 36*(8), 648–653.

Organisation for Economic Co-operation and Development. (2001). *Learning for tomorrow's world: First results from PISA 2003*. Paris: Author.

Pailliotet, A.W. (2003). Integrating media and popular-culture literacy with content reading. In R.C. Richards & M.C. McKenna (Eds.), *Integrating multiple literacies in K–8 classrooms: Case commentaries and practical applications* (pp. 172–189). Mahwah, NJ: Erlbaum.

Parke, R., & Brott, A. (1999). *Throwaway dads: The myth and barriers that keep men from being the fathers they want to be*. Boston: Houghton Mifflin.

Pearson, C., & Seivert, S. (1995). *Magic at work: Camelot, creative leadership, and everyday miracles*. Garden City, NY: Doubleday.

Perie, M., Grigg, W., & Donahue, P. (2005). *The nation's report card: Reading 2005* (NCES 2006–451). U.S. Department of Education, National Center for Education Statistics. Washington, DC: U.S. Government Printing Office.

Peter, K., & Horn, L. (2005). *Gender differences in participation and completion of undergraduate education and how they have changed over time*. Washington, DC: National Center for Education Statistics. Retrieved August 10, 2009, from nces.ed.gov/pubsearch/pubsinfo.asp?pubid=2005169

Petrosky, A.R. (1982). From story to essay: Reading and writing. *College Composition and Communication, 33*(1), 19–36. doi:10.2307/357842

Public Safety Performance. (2007). *Public safety, public spending: Forecasting America's prison population 2007–2011*. Retrieved August 12, 2009, from www.pewtrusts.org/uploadedFiles/wwwpewtrustsorg/Reports/State-based_policy/PSPP_prison_projections_0207.pdf

Radin, P. (1969). *The trickster: A study in American Indian mythology*. Westport, CT: Greenwood.

Raphael, T.E., Florio-Ruane, S., & George, M. (2001). Book club plus: a conceptual framework to organize literacy instruction. *Language Arts, 79*(1), 159–169.

Register, C.A., Williams, D.R., & Grimes, P.W. (2001). Adolescent drug use and educational attainment. *Education Economics, 9*(1), 1–18. doi:10.1080/09645290124529

Rousseau, J.J. (1979). *Emile, or on education*. New York: Basic.

Samuels, B.G. (1989). Young adults' choices: Why do students "really like" particular books. *Journal of Reading, 32*(8), 714–719.

Sanderson, G. (1995). Being "cool" and a reader. In R. Browne & R. Fletcher (Eds.), *Boys in schools: Addressing the real issues—behaviour, values and relationships* (pp. 152–167). Sydney, NSW, Australia: Finch Publishing.

Sanford, K. (2005). Gendered literacy experiences: The effects of expectation and opportunity for boys' and girls' learning. *Journal of Adolescent & Adult Literacy, 49*(4), 302–315. doi:10.1598/JAAL.49.4.4

Sawyer, W. (1987). Literature and literacy: A review of research. *Language Arts, 64*(1), 33–39.

Sax, L. (2007). *Boys adrift: The five factors driving the growing epidemic of unmotivated boys and underachieving young men*. New York: Basic.

Schaum, M. (2000). "Erasing angel": The Lucifer-trickster figure in Flannery O'Connor's short fiction. *The Southern Literary Journal, 33*(1), 1–26. doi:10.1353/slj.2000.0013

Schwarz, G.E. (2002). Graphic novels for multiple literacies. *Journal of Adolescent & Adult Literacy, 46*(3), 262–265.

Schwarzschild, M. (2000). Alienated youth: Help from families and schools. *Professional Psychology, Research and Practice, 31*(1), 95–96. doi:10.1037/0735-7028.31.1.95

Scieszka, J. (2003). Guys and reading. *Teacher Librarian, 30*(3), 17–18.

Silverstein, O., & Rashbaum, B. (1995). *The courage to raise good men*. New York: Penguin.

Simon, R.I. (1987). Empowerment as a pedagogy of possibility. *Language Arts, 64*(4), 370–382.

Simpson, A. (1996). Fictions and facts: An investigation of the reading practices of girls and boys. *English Education, 28*(4), 268–279.

Skaliotis, M. (2002, October). Key figures on cultural participation in the European Union. Paper presented at the International Symposium on Culture Statistics, Montreal, QC.

Slade, M., & Trent, F. (2000). What the boys are saying: Examining the views of boys about declining rates of achievement and retention. *International Education Journal, 1*(3), 201–229.

Sloan, G.D. (1991). *The child as critic: Teaching literature in elementary and middle schools* (3rd ed.). New York: Teachers College Press.

Smith, M.W., & Wilhelm, J.D. (2002). *"Reading don't fix no Chevys": Literacy in the lives of young men.* Portsmouth, NH: Heinemann.

Smith, M.W., & Wilhelm, J.D. (2004). "I just like being good at it": The importance of competence in the literate lives of young men. *Journal of Adolescent & Adult Literacy, 47*(6), 454–461.

Smith, M.W., & Wilhelm, J.D. (2005). Asking the right questions: Literate lives of boys. *The Reading Teacher, 58*(8), 788–789.

Smith, S.L., & Cook, C.A. (2008). *Gender stereotypes: An analysis of popular films and TV.* Los Angeles: University of Southern California, Annenberg School for Communication & Journalism. Retrieved December 28, 2009, from www.thegeenadavisinstitute.org/downloads/GDIGM_Main_Findings.pdf

Sokal, L., Katz, H., Adkins, M., Grills, T., Stewart, C., & Priddle, G. (2005a). Boys will be "boys": Variability in boys' experiences in literacy. *The Alberta Journal of Education Research, 51*(3) 216–230.

Sokal, L., Katz, H., Adkins, M., Grills, T., Stewart, C., & Priddle, G. (2005b). Factors affecting inner-city boys' reading: Are male teachers the answer? *Canadian Journal of Urban Research, 14*(1), 107–130.

Sommers, C.H. (2000). *The war against boys: How misguided feminism is harming our young men.* New York: Simon & Schuster.

St. Jarre, K.R. (2008). Don't blame the boys: We're giving them girly books. *English Journal, 97*(3), 15–16.

Strauss, V. (2005, March 15). Educators differ on why boys lag in reading: Gap stokes debate over teaching approaches, curricula. *The Washington Post,* p. A12.

Strommen, L.T., & Mates, B.F. (2004). Learning to love reading: Interviews with older children and teens. *Journal of Adolescent & Adult Literacy, 48*(3), 188–200. doi:10.1598/JAAL.48.3.1

Sturtevant, E.G., Boyd, F.B., Brozo, W.G., Hinchman, K.A., Moore, D.W., & Alvermann, D.E. (2006). *Principled practices for adolescent literacy: A framework for instruction and policy.* Mahwah, NJ: Erlbaum.

Sullivan, E. (2001). Some teens prefer the real thing: The case for young adult nonfiction. *English Journal, 90*(3), 43–47. doi:10.2307/821307

Sullivan, M. (2004). Why Johnny won't read: Schools often dismiss what boys like. No wonder they're not wild about reading. *School Library Journal, 50*(8), 36–39.

Sullivan, M. (2009). *Connecting boys with books 2: Closing the reading gap.* New York: American Library Association.

Sum, A., Khatiwada, I., McLaughlin, J., & Tobar, P. (2007). *The educational attainment of the nation's young black men and their recent labor market experiences: What can be done to improve their future labor market and educational prospects?* Boston: Center for Labor Market Studies, Northeastern University.

Tatum, A.W. (2005). *Teaching reading to black adolescent males*. Portland, ME: Stenhouse.

Tatum, A.W. (2006). Engaging African American males in reading. *Educational Leadership, 63*(5), 44–49.

Taylor, B.M., Frye, B.J., & Maruyama, G.M. (1990). Time spent reading and reading growth. *American Educational Research Journal, 27*(2), 351–362.

Taylor, D.L. (2004). "Not just boring stories": Reconsidering the gender gap for boys. *Journal of Adolescent & Adult Literacy, 48*(4), 290–298. doi:10.1598/JAAL.48.4.2

Time Line of Worldwide School Shootings. (2009). Retrieved August 10, 2009, from www.infoplease.com/ipa/A0777958.html

Turner, J.C. (1995). The influence of classroom contexts on young children's motivation for literacy. *Reading Research Quarterly, 30*(3), 410–441. doi:10.2307/747624

Turner, J., & Paris, S. (1995). How literacy tasks influence children's motivation for literacy. *The Reading Teacher, 48*(8), 662–673.

Tyre, P. (2008). *The trouble with boys: A surprising report card on our sons, their problems at school, and what parents & educators must do*. New York: Crown.

Unrau, N., & Schlackman, J. (2006). Motivation and its relationship with reading achievement in an urban middle school. *The Journal of Educational Research, 100*(2), 81–101. doi:10.3200/JOER.100.2.81-101

U.S. Census Bureau. (2008). *Characteristics of teenagers 15 to 19 years old*. Retrieved August 10, 2009, from factfinder.census.gov/servlet/STTable?_bm=y&-geo_id=01000US&-qr_name=ACS_2008_1YR_G00_S0902&-ds_name=ACS_2008_1YR_G00_&-_lang=en&-_caller=geoselect&-redoLog=false&-format=</eref>

U.S. Chamber of Commerce, Center for Workforce Preparation. (2004). *A chamber guide to improving workplace literacy: Higher skills, bottom-line results*. Washington, DC: Author. Retrieved January 21, 2010, from www.uschamber.com/icw/publications/reports/training.htm

Vacca, J.S. (2008). Crime can be prevented if schools teach juvenile offenders to read. *Children and Youth Services Review, 30*(9), 1055–1062. doi:10.1016/j.childyouth.2008.01.013

Weaver-Hightower, M.B. (2008). *The politics of policy in boys' education: Getting boys "right."* New York: Palgrave Macmillan.

Weber, M.J. (1993). Immersed in an educational crisis: Alternative programs for African-American males. *Stanford Law Review, 45*(4), 1099–1131. doi:10.2307/1229205

Weeks, L. (2001, May 14). Aliteracy: Read all about it, or maybe not: Millions of Americans who can read choose not to: Can we do without the written word? *The Washington Post*, p. C1.

Weiner, S. (2002). Beyond superheroes: Comics get serious. *Library Journal, 127*(2), 55–58.

Weston, J.L. (1997). *From ritual to romance*. New York: Dover.

White, B., & Johnson, T.S. (2001). We really do mean it: Implementing language arts standard #3 with opinionnaires. *The Clearing House, 74*(3), 119–123.

White, C. (2002). Reclaiming incarcerated youth through education. *Corrections Today, 64*(2), 174–188.

White, R. (2005). Comics in the classroom. Retrieved August 30, 2009, from www.learnnc.org/lp/pages/631

Whitmire, R. (2006, January 23). Boys and books. Boy trouble. *New Republic, 234*(2), 15–18.

Willeford, W. (1969). *The fool and his scepter: A study in clowns and jesters and their audience.* Evanston, IL: Northwestern University Press.

William, C. (2001). Does it really matter? Young people and popular music. *Popular Music, 20*(2), 223–242.

Williams, B.T. (2004). Boys may be boys, but do they have to read and write that way? *Journal of Adolescent & Adult Literacy, 47*(6), 510–515.

Wittrock, M.C. (1989). Generative processes of comprehension. *Educational Psychologist, 24*(4), 345–376. doi:10.1207/s15326985ep2404_2

Worthy, J., Moorman, M., & Turner, M. (1999). What Johnny likes to read is hard to find in school. *Reading Research Quarterly, 34*(1), 12–27. doi:10.1598/RRQ.34.1.2

Wrobleski, L. (2004, January). Interest journals: From "I don't know what to write about" to chat rooms on paper. *New England Reading Association Journal, 40*(1), 52.

Young, J.P., & Brozo, W.G. (2001). Boys will be boys, or will they? Literacy and masculinities. *Reading Research Quarterly, 36*(3), 316–325. doi:10.1598/RRQ.36.3.4

Younger, M., & Warrington, M. (with Gray, J., Rudduck, J., McLellan, R., Bearne, E., Kershner, R., & Bricheno, P.). (2005). *Raising boys' achievement.* National Literacy Trust. Retrieved August 12, 2009, from www.dcsf.gov.uk/research/data/uploadfiles/RR636.pdf

Zambo, D., & Brozo, W.G. (2009). *Bright beginnings for boys: Engaging young boys in active literacy.* Newark, DE: International Reading Association.

Zirkel, S. (2002). Is there a place for me? Role models and academic identity among white students and students of color. *Teachers College Record, 104*(2), 357–376. doi:10.1111/1467-9620.00166

LITERATURE AND MEDIA CITED

Alexie, S. (2007). *The absolutely true diary of a part-time Indian.* Boston: Little, Brown.

Anaya, R. (1999). *My land sings: Stories from the Rio Grande.* Ill. A. Cordova. New York: Morrow Junior.

Asimov, I. (1994). *Isaac Asimov's great space mysteries.* New York: Modern Publishing.

Bader, B., & Harrison, N. (2007). *Who was Martin Luther King, Jr.?* New York: Penguin Group.

Becker, E. (1992). *America's Vietnam War: A narrative history.* Boston: Houghton Mifflin.

Biesty, S. (1993). *Cross-sections: Man-of-war.* New York: Dorling Kindersley.

Bloor, E. (2008). *London calling.* New York: Knopf Books for Young Readers.

Brooks, B. (1992). *What hearts.* New York: HarperCollins.

Campbell, G. (2009). *The boys' book of survival: How to survive anything, anywhere.* New York: Scholastic.

Childress, A. (1973). *A hero ain't nothin' but a sandwich.* New York: Coward, McCann & Geoghegan.

Christopher, M. (1997). *At the plate with Ken Griffey Junior.* Boston: Little, Brown.

Clayton, E., & Hodges, D. (1996). *Martin Luther King: The peaceful warrior.* Huntington Park, CA: Archway.

Copley, R.E. (2000). *The tall Mexican: The life of Hank Aguirre all-star pitcher, businessman, humanitarian.* Houston, TX: Arte Publico.

Crutcher, C. (1995). *Ironman.* New York: Greenwillow.

Curtis, C.P. (1995). *The Watsons go to Birmingham—1963.* New York: Bantam Doubleday Dell.

Dahl, R. (1988). *Boy: Tales of childhood.* New York: Viking.

Dahl, R. (1998). *Willy Wonka and the chocolate factory.* Ill. Q. Blake. New York: Puffin.

Dahl, R. (2000). *James and the giant peach.* Ill. L. Smith. New York: Penguin.

Davis, S., Jenkins, G., Hunt, R., & Draper, S. (2006). *We beat the street: How a friendship pact led to success.* New York: Puffin.

Davis, T. (1994). *If rock and roll were a machine.* New York: Laurel-Leaf.

Deuker, C. (2008). *On the devil's court.* Boston: Little, Brown.

Doyle, A.C. (1930). *The complete Sherlock Holmes.* Garden City, NY: Doubleday.

Edwards, E. (2008). *Meet Derek Jeter: Baseball's superstar shortstop.* New York: PowerKids Press.

Equiano, O., & Cameron, A. (2000). *The kidnapped prince: The life of Olaudah Equiano.* New York: Random House.

Frazier, C. (1997). *Cold mountain.* New York: Atlantic Monthly Press.

Gibbons, G. (2000). *My football book.* New York: HarperCollins.

Golding, W. (1999). *Lord of the flies.* London: Penguin.

Gonzalez-Bertrand, D. (1999). *Trino's choice.* Houston, TX: Arte Publico.

Graham, D. (2004). *Kings of Texas: The 150-year saga of an American ranching empire.* New York: Wiley.

Grylls, B. (2007). *Born survivor: Survival techniques from the most dangerous places on Earth.* London: Channel 4.

Guterson, D. (1995). *Snow falling on cedars.* Elk Grove, CA: Vintage.

Hemingway, E. (1981). *The Nick Adams stories.* New York: Macmillan.

Hemingway, E. (1995). The short happy life of Francis Macomber. In *The short stories: The first forty-nine stories with a brief introduction from the author* (pp. 51–76). New York: Simon & Schuster.

Hickam, H.H., Jr. (2000). *Rocket boys: A memoir.* New York: Delacorte.

Hobbs, W. (1989). *Bearstone.* New York: Avon.

Hobbs, W. (1996). *Far north.* New York: Avon.

Hobbs, W. (1998). *Ghost canoe.* New York: HarperCollins.

Hobbs, W. (2002). *Wild Man Island.* New York: HarperCollins.

Hort, L., & Brown, L. (2006). *Nelson Mandela.* New York: DK Children.

Hyson, D. (1998). *The calling.* Boulder: University Press of Colorado.

Irving, J. (1997). *The imaginary girlfriend: A memoir.* New York: Acacia Press.

James, L., & Bisinger, B. (2009). *Shooting stars.* New York: Penguin.

Jeffrey, L. (1997). *Simon Wiesenthal: Tracking down Nazi criminals*. Springfield, NJ: Enslow.

Jendricks, N. (2006). *Dunks, doubles, doping: How steroids are killing American athletics*. Guilford, CT: Globe Pequot.

Johnson, M., & Pleece, W. (2009). *Incognegro*. London: Titan.

Jonze, S., & Hanks, T. (Directors). (2009). *Where the wild things are*. [Motion Picture]. United States: Universal Studios.

Jordan, M., & Vancil, M. (2006). *Driven from within*. New York: Atria.

King, M.L., Jr. (1963). Letter from Birmingham Jail. In *Why we can't wait* (pp. 23–33). New York: Harper & Row.

Kipling, R. (1999). The man who would be king. In *The man who would be king and other stories* (pp. 1–174). New York: Oxford University Press.

Knowles, J. (1990). *A separate peace*. New York: Holt, Rinehart and Winston.

Krakauer, J. (1996). *Into the wild*. Garden City, NY: Doubleday.

Kreidler, M. (2007). *Four days to glory: Wrestling with the soul of the American Heartland*. New York: HarperCollins.

Lee, H. (1960). *To kill a mockingbird*. New York: Warner.

LeGuin, U. (1997). *Lathe of heaven*. New York: Avon.

Lipsyte, R. (1992). *The chemo kid*. New York: HarperCollins.

Littlefield, B. (1993). *Champions: Stories of ten remarkable athletes*. Boston: Little, Brown.

Lupica, M. (2005). *Travel team*. New York: Philomel.

Lupica, M. (2008a). *Long shot*. New York: Philomel.

Lupica, M. (2008b). *Summer ball*. New York: Philomel.

Lupica, M. (2009). *Two-minute drill*. New York: Philomel.

MacDonald, J. (2004). *Great battles of World War II*. Edison, NJ: Chartwell.

Macy, S. (1995). *A whole new ball game: The story of the all-American girls professional baseball league*. New York: Puffin.

Massinger, P. (1910). A new way to pay old debts. In C. Eliot (Ed.), *Elizabethan drama in two volumes* (pp. 859–943). New York: P.F. Collier & Son.

Matthews, R. (1999). *Explorer*. Minneapolis, MN: Econo-Clad.

Mazer, H. (2007). *Heroes don't run: A novel of the Pacific war*. New York: Simon & Schuster.

Meader, S.W. (1934). *Lumberjack*. New York: Harcourt, Brace & World.

Meader, S.W. (1939). *Boy with a pack*. New York: Harcourt, Brace & World.

Meader, S.W. (1950). *Whaler 'round the horn*. New York: Harcourt, Brace & World.

Meader, S.W. (1963). *The muddy road to glory*. New York: Harcourt, Brace & World.

Mochizuki, K. (1993). *Baseball saved us*. New York: Lee & Low.

Morey, W. (1993). *Death walk*. Portland, OR: Blue Heron Publishing.

Morressy, J. (1999). *Juggler*. Minneapolis, MN: Econo-Clad.

Murray, D. (2007). *D-Day: The liberation of Europe begins*. New York: Rosen Central.

Myers, W.D. (1990). *Scorpions*. New York: HarperTrophy.

Myers, W.D. (1999). *Hoops*. Minneapolis, MN: Econo-Clad.

Myers, W.D. (2000). *Monster*. New York: HarperCollins.

O'Connor, L. (1991). *Cryin' for daylight: A ranching culture in the Texas Coastal Bend*. Victoria, TX: Wexford Publishing.

Pastan, A., & Levi, P. (2004). *Martin Luther King, Jr*. New York: DK.

Paulsen, G. (1990). *The crossing*. New York: Laurel-Leaf.

Pausch, R., & Zaslow, R. (2008). *The last lecture*. New York: Hyperion.

Penn, S. (Director & Producer), Linson, A., & Pohlad, W. (Producers). (2007). *Into the wild*. [Motion Picture]. United States: Square One.

Reis, R. (2008). *The dust bowl*. New York: Chelsea House.

Ripken, C., & Bryan, M. (1999). *Cal Ripken, Jr.: My story*. New York: Dial.

Roberts, J. (2005). *Roberto Clemente: Baseball player*. New York: Ferguson.

Roberts, J. (2009). *Breaking the slump: How great players survived their darkest moments in golf—And what you can learn from them*. New York: Harper.

Robertson, J.I. (1992). *Civil War! America becomes one nation*. New York: Knopf.

Rosen, M. (2002). *ChaseR: A novel in emails*. Cambridge, MA: Candlewick.

Rowling, J.K. (2006). *Harry Potter and the half-blood prince*. New York: Scholastic.

Ryan, K.J. (1999). *Deep in the heart of Texas: Texas ranchers in their own words*. Berkeley, CA: Ten Speed Press.

Sacco, J. (2001). *Palestine*. Seattle, WA: Fantagraphics.

Schmidt, G. (2008). *Trouble*. New York: Clarion.

Schraff, A.E. (2008). *Jackie Robinson*. Costa Mesa, CA: Saddleback Educational.

Schultz, R. (1992). *Looking inside the brain*. Santa Fe, NM: John Muir.

Scutts, J. (2000). *World War II dioramas*. New York: Compendium.

Seidman, D. (2004). *Cesar Chavez: Labor leader*. New York: Franklin Watts.

Selznick, B. (2007). *The invention of Hugo Cabret*. New York: Scholastic.

Sendak, M. (1988). *Where the wild things are*. New York: HarperCollins.

Shakespeare, W. (1994). In B.A. Mowat & P. Werstine (Eds.), *The tempest*. New York: Washington Square Press.

Shakespeare, W. (1998). In H. Baker (Ed.), *Twelfth night*. New York: Signet.

Shakespeare, W., Appignanesi, R., & Leong, S. (2007). *Romeo and Juliet*. New York: Abrams Books for Young Readers.

Shan, D. (2002). *Cirque du freak: A living nightmare*. Boston: Little, Brown.

Sharp, R. (1985). *Bob Sharp's cattle country: Rawhide ranching on both sides of the border*. Tucson: University of Arizona Press.

Shields, B., & Sullivan, K. (2009). *WWE encyclopedia*. New York: BradyGames.

Shusterman, N. (2009). *Unwind*. New York: Simon & Schuster.

Spiegelman, A. (1986). *Maus I: A survivor's tale*. New York: Pantheon.

Spinelli, G. (1990). *Maniac Magee*. New York: HarperTrophy.

Stanley, J. (1992). *Children of the Dust Bowl: The true story of the school at Weedpatch Camp*. New York: Crown.

Stevenson, R.L. (1994). *Dr. Jekyll and Mr. Hyde*. New York: Signet.

Stout, G. (2003). *Matt Christopher: On the court with Shaquille O'Neal*. Boston: Little, Brown.

Stout, G. (2004). *Matt Christopher: On the court with Yao Ming*. Boston: Little, Brown.

Strasser, T. (2002). *Give a boy a gun*. New York: Simon Pulse.

Sullivan, G. (1991). *Sluggers: Twenty-seven of baseball's greatest*. New York: Atheneum.

Sutin, L., Sutin, R., & Sutin, J. (1996). *Jack and Rochelle: A Holocaust story of love and resistance*. St. Paul, MN: Graywolf Press.

Swan, R. (2009). *Antarctica 2041: My quest to save the Earth's last wilderness*. New York: Broadway.

Taylor, T. (2007). *The bomb*. Orlando, FL: Harcourt.

Verlinden, F. (2003). *Building military dioramas* (Vol. VII). Chicago: Verlinden Productions.

Whitman, W. (1993). *Leaves of grass*. New York: Modern Library.

Winton, T. (1991). *Lockie Leonard, human torpedo*. Boston: Little, Brown.

Winton, T. (1999). *Lockie Leonard, scumbuster*. New York: Margaret K. McElderry.

Wood, T. (with Numpa, W.). (1995). *A boy becomes a man at Wounded Knee*. New York: Walker and Company.

Woods, E., & The Tiger Woods Foundation. (2006). *Start something: You can make a difference*. New York: Simon & Schuster.

Wunderli, S. (1996). *The heartbeat of halftime*. New York: Avon.

Yakin, B. (Director) & Bruckheimer, J. (Producer). (2000). *Remember the titans*. [Motion Picture]. United States: Walt Disney Pictures.

Yates, D. (Director), Heyman, D., & Barron, D. (Producers). (2009). *Harry Potter and the half-blood prince*. [Motion Picture]. United States: Warner Brothers.

INDEX

Note. Page numbers followed by *f* indicate figures.

Hemingway, E., 100
Herbert, B., 4, 12, 97, 186
Herz, S., 18
Hetton, T.L., 18
Hewlett, S.A., 24, 29
Heyman, D., 166
Hickam, H.H., Jr., 57
Hill, G., 161
Hinchman, K.A., 139
Hoa, L.W., 17
Hobbs, W., 60
Hodges, D., 68
Hoffman, L., 94
Hofstetter, C.H., 3
Hofstetter, C.R., 3–4, 12
Horn, L., 12
Horn, W.F., 161
Horner, D., 132–133
Hort, L., 34
Horton, R., 14
Houser, P., 161
Hughes-Hassell, S., 94, 139
Hull, G., 139
Hunsader, P.D., 3
Hunt, R., 181
Hunter, D., 13, 94
Hyson, D., 171

I

illiteracy, 1
informational books, 18, 20, 69
  on Healer archetype, 203
  on King archetype, 199–200
  on Lover archetype, 207
  on Magician archetype, 198
  on Patriarch archetype, 194–195
  on Pilgrim archetype, 193
  on Prophet archetype, 204
  on Trickster archetype, 206
  on Warrior archetype, 196
  on Wildman archetype, 201
initiation rites, 25, 30, 39
interests
  and book clubs, 150–151, 153
  discovering, 78–90
  grouping for, 83–84
  ignoring, consequences of, 184–186

importance of, 187
inventories on, 87–90, 87f–88f
journals on, 85–87
and reading partnerships, 167–169
introductions, companion, 84–85, 131
intuition, 35
inventories, interest, 87–90, 87f–88f
Iritani, B., 3
Irving, J., 89
Ivey, G., 85, 187

J

Jacobs, D., 139
Jacobson, J., 155
Jaeger, L., 149
James, L., 85
Jeffrey, L., 55
Jendricks, N., 157
Jenkins, G., 181
Johnson, D., 55
Johnson, D.M., 18
Johnson, M., 158
Johnson, R., 15, 25
Johnson, S., 78
Johnson, T.S., 65
Jones, P., 18
Jonze, S., 164
Jordan, E., 33
Jordan, M., 85
journals, 80–81
  end-of-book entries, 128–129
  Healing Project, 65–67
  interest, 85–87
  precautions with, 85
  response, 19
Jung, C.G., 15, 24–26

K

Kafka, F., 102
Katz, H., 15
Keddie, A., 2
Kehler, M.D., 15
Kennedy, A.M., 3
Kenway, J., 13
Khatapoush, S., 3
Khatiwada, I., 11

masculinity
  and reading, 13, 19–20, 92, 173–174
  stereotypes of, 7, 9, 24, 29
Massinger, P., 132
Mates, B.F., 17
Matthews, R., 95
Maughan, S., 161
Mazer, H., 169
McCabe, P.P., 18
McCandless, C., 37
McCarthey, S.J., 13
McClure, A., 2
McDaniel, M.A., 140
McFall, J., 18
McGuire, M., 49
McLaughlin, J., 11
McLeod, J., 13
Mead, M., 28
Mead, S., 13
Meader, S.W., 13
media
  analysis of, 118–119, 126–128
  and masculine stereotypes, 29,
    109–110, 110f
  youth and, 142–148
  See also digital media
mediasphere, 138
Méliès, G., 36
men. See masculinity; positive male
    archetypes; role models
Men of Books, 161
mentors. See role models
Meyer, A.L., 133
Mills, M., 2
mixed-gender classrooms
  and Real Men unit, 103, 105
  and support for boys' literacy, 8–9
  and text selection, 92–93
Mochizuki, K., 177
mock trial, 63–64
modeling
  reading, 168, 170–171, 187–188
  See also role models
Moje, E.B., 13, 18, 186, 188
Mok, J., 17
Mokhtari, K., 17
Moore, R., 15, 25, 44
Morey, W., 151

Morrell, E., 142
Morressy, J., 70
Mortenson, T., 12
motivation
  alternative texts and, 139–140
  challenges with, 11, 13, 17, 78–79,
    184–185
  delicacy with, 173–178
  developing, 15–20
  guidelines for, 18
  positive male archetypes and, 14–15
  practices for, 137
  Rousseau on, 82
Mui, Y.Q., 139
Mullis, I.V.S., 3, 93
Murphy, P., 13
Murray, D., 168
music, 142–145
Muspratt, S., 13
My Bag strategy
  grouping with, 83–84
  in Real Men unit, 111–112
  successes with, 79–83
Myers, W.D., 51, 102, 116–117, 180

N

Nagourney, E., 17, 97
National Center for Education
    Statistics, 3, 12
National Endowment for the Arts, 17,
    187
National Literacy Trust, 138
Native American students, and
    engaged reading, 76–77
Neckerman, K.M., 12
Newburger, E.C., 11
Newkirk, T., 2
Newman, M., 142
Nichols, S., 34
Nicolle, R., 94
Nippold, M.A., 17
Noguera, P.A., 2–3, 97
Nolley, C., 91
nonassigned reading
  and competence, 94
  decline in, 17
  making connections for, 80–82